GARDEN DESIGN
made easy

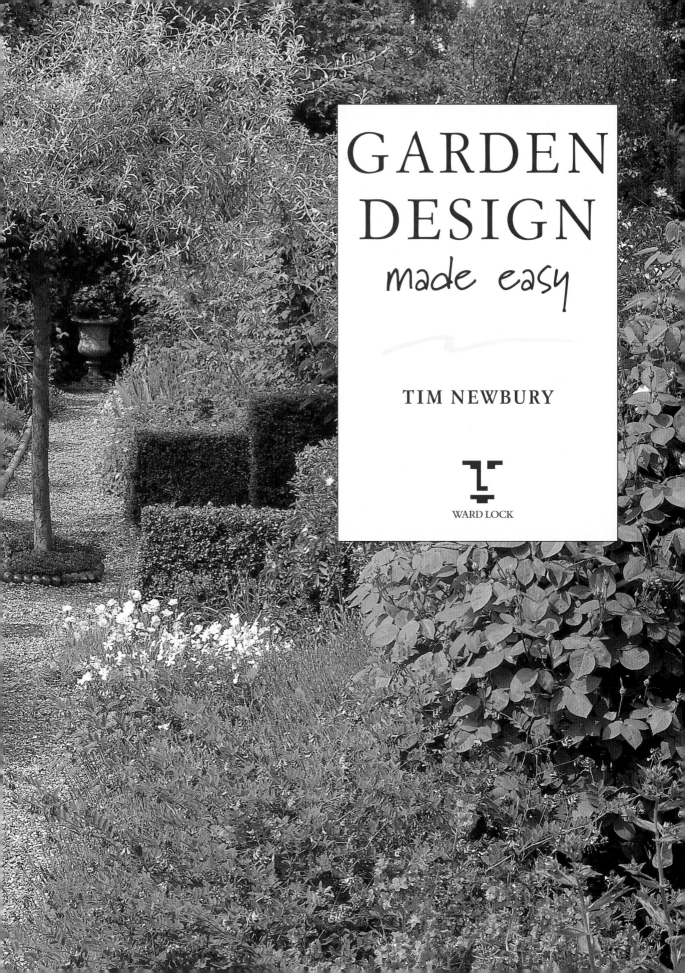

GARDEN DESIGN
made easy

TIM NEWBURY

WARD LOCK

A WARD LOCK BOOK

First published in the UK 1998
by Ward Lock
Wellington House
125 Strand
London WC2R 0BB

A Cassell Imprint

Distributed in the United States
by Sterling Publishing Co., Inc.
387 Park Avenue South, New York, NY 10016-8810

Distributed in Canada
by Cavendish Books Inc.
Unit 5, 801 West 1st Street
North Vancouver, B.C. Canada V7P 1PH

A British Library Cataloguing in Publication Data block for
this book may be obtained from the British Library

ISBN 0-7063-7585-8

Designed by Yvonne Dedman
Illustrations by Wendy Bramall and Kevin Maddison

Printed and bound in Italy
by New Interlitho Italia

Contents

The potentially over-symmetrical paved area has been softened by the foliage that is allowed to fall over the hard edges. The underlying formality of the arrangement is, however, subtly reinforced by the planting, especially the pots of marguerites (*Argyranthemum frutescens*, syn. *Chrysanthemum frutescens*).

Preface

Garden design has become increasingly popular over the years, and there are many books on the subject. But how many of these books actually provide readers with the necessary information to change the look of their gardens with minimum effort and maximum effect? *Garden Design Made Easy* takes the reader through the whole design process in a simple, easy-to-follow way, avoiding confusing jargon and complex diagrams.

Where do you start? Do you want a completely new look or just a few changes? The book opens with suggestions on how to draw up lists of what you want and what you need, and these are followed by advice on assessing your site and preparing a budget.

Next, the book shows you how to create a design that will meet your requirements. Starting with basic shapes, such as formal straight lines or informal curves, *Garden Design Made Easy* shows you how to build up a design by introducing the garden features of your choice, adding the details and, finally, describing how to plant your garden. There is also a 'problem solver' checklist that offers solutions for gardeners who have difficult sites.

Garden Design Made Easy also includes a range of off-the-peg designs for every type and shape of garden imaginable, and there are also ideas that will enable you instantly to transform the look of your garden.

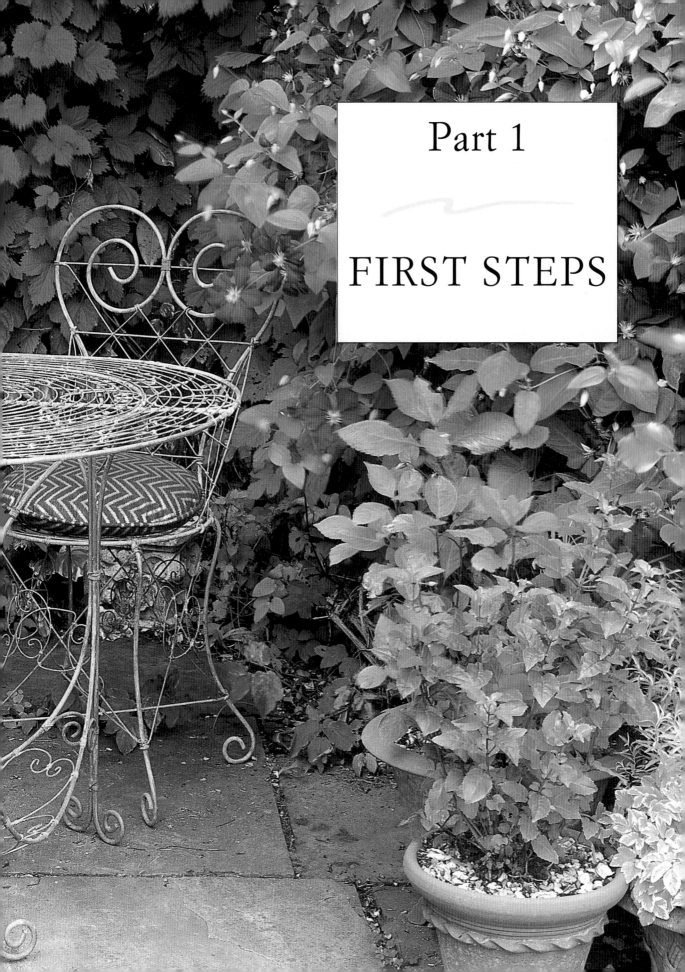

Part 1

FIRST STEPS

What do you want from your garden?

In an ideal world you could make your dream garden as large or as small as you wished and incorporate everything that money could buy, including, of course, a team of full-time gardeners to look after it for you – equipped with the most up-to-date equipment for the purpose!

Most of us recognize that this perfect and idyllic situation is far removed from the realities of everyday life, so it is, therefore, all the more important for us to use what limited space, funds and time we have available in the best possible way to achieve our own ideal garden.

Finding a starting point to begin the process of designing – or in some cases re-designing – a garden is sometimes almost as difficult as carrying out the work itself. Probably the best way to begin is to sit down with paper and pencil and make a list of all the aspects of a garden that give you the greatest pleasure – or would do so if you had them – and that you would, in an ideal world, like to include in your own design. One person might derive immense satisfaction, for example, from having an immaculately manicured, bowling-green-like lawn, which would form the centrepiece of the garden. Another

The old-fashioned flags of the paved area are echoed by the cottage garden feel provided by reliable perennials such as catmint (*Nepeta* spp.), *Geranium psilostemon* and *Diascia cordata*.

might be interested in fish or pond life and would like a garden in which a large pond or water feature would be the focal point. In most cases, however, it is probably more likely that you will want to include a selection of different features that you feel will give you the greatest pleasure. As a starting point for your garden design, make a list of those features that you would regard as desirable and that might be called your 'wants'.

The following checklist will help you to choose those features that you would like to include on your list.

- ✴ Patio, terrace or other sitting area in the sun.
- ✴ Patio, terrace or other sitting area in the shade.
- ✴ Hard-wearing lawn for active recreation.
- ✴ Bowling-green-type lawn for passive recreation or for its appearance.
- ✴ Vegetable garden, fruit garden or both.
- ✴ Greenhouse and coldframes.
- ✴ Water feature (with or without fish), such as pond, stream, waterfall or bubble fountain.
- ✴ Children's play area and equipment, such as swing, sandpit, slide or climbing frame.
- ✴ Arch, pergola or arbour.
- ✴ Summerhouse or gazebo.
- ✴ Raised bed for alpines or herbs.
- ✴ Rockery or scree garden.
- ✴ Bog garden (with or without a water feature).

* Specialist beds or borders for plants such as roses, chrysanthemums or summer bedding.
* Containers for annual bedding or winter shrubs.
* Ornaments, such as statues, sculpture, bird bath, bird table or sundial.
* Garden lighting and irrigation.
* Barbecue, either built in or space for a mobile one.
* Garden furniture.

This is a fairly comprehensive list, and in reality you might find that you need to select only a few of the items for your own garden, depending on your circumstances. The following example illustrates the items a 'wants' list for a typical family garden might include:

* Generously sized patio or other paved area, preferably in the sun and conveniently sited near the house.
* Hard-wearing, relatively large lawn for football, riding bikes and general recreation.
* Separate play area or at least enough space for a swing, slide or other play equipment (this could take up part of the lawn).
* Small vegetable and fruit garden.
* Simple, easy-care areas of mixed perimeter planting, including plants for year-round interest and, a few varieties for cutting or drying.
* Small rockery, probably in sun adjacent to the patio.
* Space for a mobile barbecue.

A different example of a 'wants' list, possibly for a couple with more free time and more disposable income to spend on the garden, might, however, look like this:

* Patio in the sun, and possibly a small alternative sitting area in cool shade at the opposite end of the garden.
* Fine-leaved lawn for putting or croquet or just for looking at.
* Cordon and espalier fruit trees, trained against the boundary walls and fences.
* Large pond for keeping koi and other fish, possibly with a specialist filtration system.
* Pergola to grow climbing roses and other flowering climbers.
* Formal herb garden, possibly built around an old statue or sundial.
* Generous mixed planting in borders and beds.
* Area for growing plants for use purely for cutting and drying.
* Selection of pots and containers to be planted for summer and winter colour.
* Custom-made barbecue area, maybe with additional seating or a raised bed around it.

The small, carefully tended lawn is of greater value for the way in which its shape enhances the appearance of the garden than for the scope it offers for play or relaxation. The seat acts as a focal point, drawing the eye to the false acacia (*Robinia pseudoacacia* 'Frisia') and the screen of willows (*Salix babylonica*) at the far end of the garden.

Having these lovely features in your garden is all very well, but at the same time as considering the desirable aspects, you should also be asking yourself questions such as 'Where do I store the bikes and coal?' 'Is there somewhere to hang out the washing – preferably in the sun, of course?' and 'What's going to happen to the grass clippings after I've mown the lawn.' All of these questions, and more, might be loosely termed as the 'nuts and bolts' or working parts of a garden, and they need to be given as much consideration in your design thoughts as the purely decorative aspects if your garden is going to be practical as well as attractive. At this point, having put together your list of 'wants', you will need to make a second list of the other basic, but necessary, garden features that come under the general heading of essentials or 'needs'.

Right: A rock garden is likely to be a permanent feature, if only because of the size of the rocks and boulders that are required. However, carefully sited on thoroughly prepared ground, a rock garden provides opportunities to grow alpines as well as dwarf and low-growing varieties of species for which there might otherwise not be space.

Left: If space allows, vegetable gardens can be made into features in their own right, especially if purple-leaved varieties and flowering herbs are included to extend the colour scheme of the remainder of the garden.

The following list will help to remind you of what these essential features are:

* Shed or other form of storage facility for garden equipment, furniture, bikes, toys and so on.
* Space (perhaps a carport) for parking an additional vehicle, caravan or boat.
* Space and facilities for pets, such as a dog run or rabbit hutch.
* Paths and adequate paving to allow clean, dry access and movement around the garden in all weathers.
* Fuel store or space for coal, logs or oil tank, and screening to hide an oil or gas tank if necessary.
* Area for storing rubbish bins, such as a concealed bin store with a door.
* Bin or space for composting grass clippings, garden and kitchen waste.
* Water butt for saving rainwater, positioned by the house or next to the shed or greenhouse.
* Space for clothes drying.
* Convenient outside access to water and a safe electricity supply.

At this stage in the process you may well have two lists, one of 'wants' and one of 'needs', each as long as the other and a feeling that everything on these lists is not going to fit into the space

Containers bring flexibility to the garden. Tender plants can be moved under cover in winter, and late-summer gaps in a border can be filled with strategically positioned pot-grown plants. Terracotta pots, overflowing with brilliant geraniums, bring a warm, Mediterranean atmosphere to an otherwise cool green corner.

available – and you may well be right! The question, then, is what can be done about it. Clearly, the solution is to delete some of the features from your lists, so that what is left should fit comfortably into the area of your garden. Deciding on what to omit is not always easy, however, and to help you make this decision, your lists should be written strictly in order of priority, starting with the most important feature and finishing with the least. This way, you can begin to delete the least important items, beginning at the bottom of your lists, in the knowledge that what remains is almost certainly going to provide the basis for a satisfactory garden design.

While you are drawing up your lists of 'needs' and 'wants', it is also worth considering whether your circumstances are likely to change in the short or the long term in ways that might affect your lists. If this is the case, you might want, or indeed need, to take account of these changes in your design. Carrying out such an exercise at this early stage probably will not take long, but the benefits to be gained by avoiding costly or time-consuming errors that result from bad forward planning are great. Although not everyone's circumstances are identical, there are several factors

that will, either together or separately, apply at some point to the majority of gardeners. There will be additions to the family – children and pets – the money available for garden projects may vary over time, and, of course, increasing age may affect how you use the garden.

A typical example of changing use or circumstance is when there are children in the family. While they are small, you might like to build a special area for them to play in, which might, for example, be used as a sandpit. At the same time, you may find the idea of a pond for your own pleasure is rather appealing. It may not be possible to have both these features at the same time, first, because you have to consider how safe a pond might be with small children around, and, second, because there might not be sufficient room for both. A solution would be to build the play area in such a way that it could easily be converted into a pond later on, when the children had grown out of it. With this in mind, you should make the initial structure strong enough to take the weight of water that it will need to support when it is converted into a pond. A brick construction will allow you to put in a flexible pond liner and the edges of this could be secured by adding another course of bricks on top.

Alternatively, the redundant sandpit could be converted into a raised bed by filling it with suitable topsoil, which would make it ideal for use as a herb garden or an alpine scree bed. This could

Generous areas of paving and lawn are essential when children are small. Later on, however, there is less need for such large areas, and here, by simply removing a slab and adding a pergola, a seat and some pots and ornaments, a plain patio corner has been transformed.

act as an interim measure until such time as a pond was viable, or indeed it might even become a permanent feature if you became sufficiently attached to it, in which case you might need to make sufficient provision for a pond elsewhere in your long-term plan as a contingency plan for such a situation!

The conversion of a sandpit to a pond

Brick wall surround
Slabs laid on sand
23cm ←(9in)→
Ground level
Sand
23cm (9in)
Drainage layer of stones/broken bricks
Concrete foundation

Brick on edge laid on top of liner to secure
Pond liner tucked over existing upstand
Mortar joint
Water
33cm (13in)

Compacted sand to bind hardcore and protect liner – minimum thickness 2.5cm (1in)

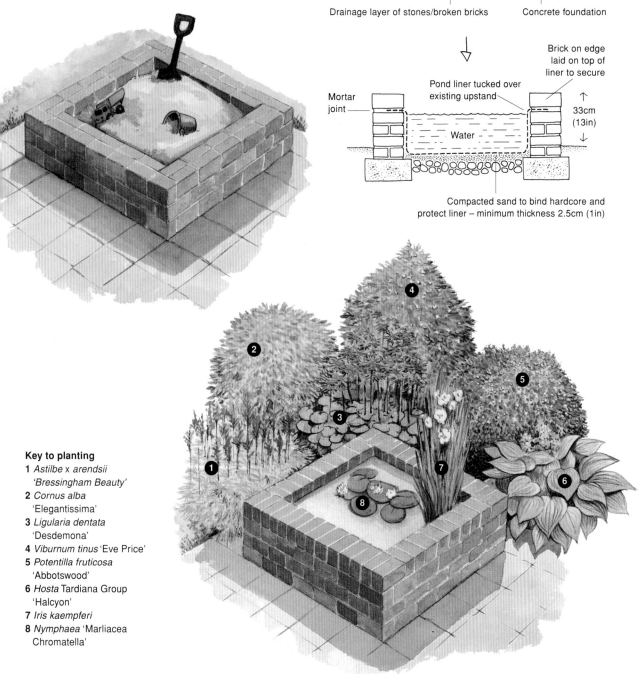

Key to planting
1 *Astilbe* x *arendsii* 'Bressingham Beauty'
2 *Cornus alba* 'Elegantissima'
3 *Ligularia dentata* 'Desdemona'
4 *Viburnum tinus* 'Eve Price'
5 *Potentilla fruticosa* 'Abbotswood'
6 *Hosta* Tardiana Group 'Halcyon'
7 *Iris kaempferi*
8 *Nymphaea* 'Marliacea Chromatella'

Assessing your garden

Every garden, whether it is new or old, will possess a number of physical qualities or attributes that can have a direct bearing on how it will be designed or re-designed. The principal factors to consider are:

✱ The aspect of the garden – that is, the way it faces (north, south, east or west).
✱ The type of soil present – light or heavy, dry or wet, acid, neutral or alkaline.
✱ The topography of the plot – undulating, level, sloping, either from end to end or side to side, or both!
✱ Whether the garden is exposed to wind, lies in a frost pocket or is in a sheltered situation.
✱ How good or bad is the drainage.

In addition to these factors, an established garden may also contain mature trees and shrubs, existing areas of paving, water features or garden buildings. You will have to include these items in your own garden design process, because if there is an existing patio, for example, you will need to determine, first, whether it is the appropriate size and is in the right place for your own purposes and, second, whether the materials from which it is made are attractive and in good condition.

If the answer to both of these questions is 'yes', you may find that this existing feature becomes the starting point for your design. Then, any paths and, if necessary, additional areas of paving

that you need can be built in the same material and style as the existing patio. A word of warning: before embarking on this route, make sure that you can still obtain paving slabs or bricks that are the same pattern and colour.

In much the same way, a mature, shapely tree, which deserves to be retained if at all possible, may influence your design. A garden pond or similar water feature, for example, would need to be positioned away from the main area of shade and the effect of falling leaves from such a tree.

In both these examples you will see how an existing feature can and should be approached in a positive, constructive way to see what can be achieved by retaining or modifying it. Obviously, this will not happen in every garden, and there will be occasions when existing features, such as a rotten pergola or arch, cannot be retained and must be removed.

Aspect

The direction in which a garden, or part of a garden, faces will affect not only the plants that can be grown there successfully but also the location of other garden features that may rely on sun or shade to be effective. For example, as a general rule, patios are best placed where they are in sun for either all or most of the day. On the other hand, if you want to establish a bog garden or a

Above: Redesigning an established garden will often mean incorporating in the new design a mature tree or fine shrub, such as this beautiful double *Paeonia suffruticosa* 'Reine Elizabeth', which may no longer be readily available or which would take many years to achieve its full potential.

Right: Sitting areas should be positioned to take advantage of the available shade during the hottest part of the day. If you intend to eat outdoors regularly, proximity to the kitchen and whether you will be overlooked by neighbours will also influence your decision.

A secluded, shady arbour can be very inviting on a sunny day. Paving a large area with bricks or setts can be expensive, but an arbour such as this would look just as appealing next to a lawn.

Microclimates in town gardens

The great mass of bricks, concrete, tarmacadam and other such impermeable materials that constitutes a built-up area can act like a giant storage heater, soaking up the sun's heat during the day and slowly releasing it at night. As a result, the average temperatures in towns and cities are usually slightly higher than those found further out in the suburbs, which, in turn, may be still higher than those in the open countryside. In summer this can often make town gardens hot and uncomfortable, and it is,

therefore, worth making provision in your design for the inclusion of some form of shade-providing structure or a cool sitting area out of the sun. In winter, however, the artificially higher temperature, even though it is only one or two degrees more, is often sufficient to provide enough frost protection for a range of tender or choice plants that would be less likely to thrive in a more exposed garden, and added to this advantage is the extended growing season that all your plants will experience.

collection of shade-loving hostas, astilbes and primulas, the ideal location would be out of the fierce midday sun, perhaps in the cool shade of a north-facing wall or fence, where these would thrive in the conditions to be found there. You will, therefore, need to find out which parts of your garden are shady and which are sunny, and the only simple way to do this is by observation, preferably over as long a period as possible. The main areas of sun and shade will quickly become apparent, but you might find that a few small areas that are apparently shady in autumn and winter are much sunnier in spring and summer.

Soil

The type of soil in your garden will have a direct bearing on the plants that can be successfully grown in it. The texture can vary from very sandy and light to having a high proportion of clay, which makes it sticky when wet and hard when dry. You should also determine whether it is acid or alkaline in nature, which is basically a measure of how much or how little lime is present. In most situations, the best approach is always to try to select plants that will suit the existing soil rather than to try and change the soil conditions to suit a particular type of plant, although virtually all garden soils will benefit from the addition of organic matter, whether this takes the form of well-rotted manure, composted garden waste or leaf mould.

Climate

Gardens that are exposed to strong winds can often be uncomfortable places for plants as well as for people. Apart from not growing as rapidly as they might in a sheltered spot, plants can also be badly damaged by wind, particularly if it is cold and dry. Observation will allow you quickly

to determine the main direction of the prevailing wind and to identify which, if any, parts of your garden are sheltered from it. The decision you will then have to make is whether to position a feature – such as an arbour – in an area that is already protected or, if this is not the ideal spot, whether you will have to create adequate additional shelter around it.

Providing shelter in a large garden

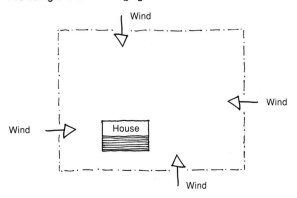

Properties in large or exposed gardens need some form of shelter

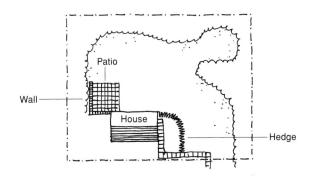

Create two or three small, sheltered spots so that at least one will always be protected, regardless of wind direction

Slopes and changes in level

Few gardens are perfectly level. The slope may be almost imperceptible, perhaps only a few centimetres (inches) from end to end, or so severe

Terraces and steps are generally the most successful way of dealing with sloping gardens. This low-maintenance solution to the problem has been brightened by the pots of colourful annuals and bedding plants.

that it is difficult to walk up and down the garden in comfort. However, most gardens offer an opportunity to introduce changes of level in the form of terraces and steps, which can be included just for their appearance or because they are absolutely necessary. The extent to which you will need or want to change a slope will depend, too, on how the garden will be used. Where you need large, relatively flat areas – for a patio and lawn, for example – the slope might need to be modified quite severely. On the other hand, you may need to adjust the slope only enough to allow plants to establish satisfactorily without the soil eroding.

Drainage

Good drainage is essential in a garden, not only for practical reasons – no one wants to have permanent puddles outside the backdoor – but also for the benefit of plants, including lawns, which will suffer in the long term if the soil is waterlogged because the drainage is inadequate. Areas in a garden that remain under water for a long time after rain or that are permanently boggy, even in summer, are almost certainly badly drained, and you will need to locate and plot the extent of such areas, before deciding how

A permanently damp area can be turned into a bog garden, where it is possible to grow a range of more interesting and unusual varieties than will thrive in an ordinary bed or border. Most hostas and irises flourish in such conditions, as do candelabra primulas (*Primula bulleyana* and *P. pulverulenta*) and moneywort (*Lysimachia nummularia*).

Making the most of existing features

Wherever possible, look at your garden with a view to turning existing features or prevailing conditions to your advantage by seeing if they can make a positive contribution to the design. The following are just a few examples of ways in which this type of approach can pay off.

Sloping garden

* Steps and low retaining walls can be used to provide interesting changes of level, allowing the use of lots of trailing or climbing plants to cascade over.
* Create a rockery or a scree garden on a sunny bank.
* A stream or waterfall can run into a pond lower down a natural slope.

Heavy soil or wet area

* A bog garden is ideal for moisture-loving ornamental plants.
* A natural pond and wet area is the perfect habitat for wild plants and other forms of pond life.

Hot, dry spot in full sun

* A paved area for sunbathing could be built next to a refreshing pool or fountain.
* Slightly tender or unusual plants will grow against a sunny wall or fence, sheltered from the cold wind.
* A pergola or other structure will create shade beneath.

Cold, north facing-corner

* A sitting area or shady arbour will provide escape from the heat of the sun in summer.
* A bed or border can be created for plants that do not like direct sunlight or excessive heat – for example, astilbes, rodgersias and hostas.
* Use the space as a garden utility area for a shed or compost heap.

best to tackle them. Some poor drainage may be caused by localized compaction of the soil – a common problem around newly built houses – and thorough, deep digging can often cure it. Impermeable clay subsoil or a naturally high water table may be another reason for poor drainage, and you can check this out by digging trial holes in various parts of the garden where you suspect there is a problem to see what the subsoil is like and also to find out if there is permanent groundwater. Poor drainage throughout the garden may mean that you will need to install a system of field drains, which will have to be connected to a suitable outlet such as a ditch or soakaway. A small area of wet ground, however, could more easily be turned into a bog garden or a natural pond.

As already mentioned, taking time to observe your garden over a period before you even lift a fork or spade will repay the effort in the long run by helping you to make decisions that, if made hurriedly, might result in a serious waste of your time, effort and money. As part of your observations, you should consider taking photographs at the various stages, starting with the garden as it was at the beginning, and ending up with the finished result. They are not only useful as a record but can be helpful in assisting the design process. A good example of this would be if you want to screen an offending view. Take a photograph of the object, lay a piece of tracing paper over it and sketch on this a variety of ideas such as trellis, fencing, tall shrubs or trees to see which might be the most effective solution. You can try this method with any views of your garden, both looking within it or outside it.

Budgeting and planning

Unfortunately, we do not live in an ideal world, and for most of us the cost of building, developing and maintaining our gardens will be an important factor to consider at the outset and will almost certainly influence the overall garden design to a greater or lesser degree.

For example, if your budget is limited, the cost of buying natural stone for areas of paving may be prohibitive, even before it is laid. There is, however, an increasing range of good quality imitation stone slabs made from concrete, and these are available for half or even a third of the price of the real thing. Similarly, planting a large specimen tree would give an instant feeling of maturity to your garden, but for the same price you might be able to buy four, five or even more smaller ones.

Every time you make a decision involving expenditure, therefore, you need to ask yourself if the benefits that you will gain from it are worth the cost – that is, are you getting value for your money? Is the knowledge that your patio is built with real stone and not an almost identical reproduction equivalent worth spending twice the amount?

Apart from the consideration of value, you also need to ask yourself the following questions:

✻ How much can I afford to spend on my garden now?

✻ How much will I be able to afford to spend later on?
✻ Can I afford to maintain my garden once it is completed in order to keep it in good condition?

Your personal financial circumstances may be such that you cannot afford to pay for the garden to be built in one go, but by phasing the work over a convenient, longer period – two, three or even more years, say – the cost can be spread out to suit your budget, and there are few, if any, gardens in which this phased approach is not successful.

If you do decide to phase the work, it is still preferable, and will help you to avoid wasted time, effort and money, if the garden is designed as an entity from the outset. This approach is far better than dividing your garden into two or three equal sections and designing each section as and when you can afford to work on it. If you treat your garden as a whole, you will know that, no matter how long it takes to build, your garden will eventually be a single design, rather than a piecemeal collection of features that do not necessarily work together.

Preparing a plan that covers several years will also allow you to organize the building work so that you do not find, say, that access to your back garden is suddenly severely restricted because you decided to build a high brick wall and narrow gate at the side of the house first, or that you have laid a beautiful lawn, only to discover that the builders have to trample across it for a week to erect a summerhouse on the far side of it.

From a practical point of view then, and to help your garden project proceed smoothly, you should:

* Make sure that there is always adequate access for the next phase of the proposed work.
* Make sure that there are facilities for the disposal of spoil – surplus topsoil, old hardcore and so on – at all stages of the project and also that there is somewhere to store any materials that are brought onto the site, particularly bulky items like sand and bricks.
* Organize the work in such a way that completed areas will not be damaged or disturbed by work involved in the later stages of the project.
* Decide how you want to maintain any unfinished parts of your garden until they are completed – and remember that this might not be for a year or more.

Keep these four guidelines in mind as you begin to draw up a timetable for your own garden. Following (on page 28) is a fairly typical schedule for a garden development, and you should use it as a checklist to help you to draw up a plan that is in line with your budget and the time you have available. Not all of these stages will apply to every garden – just move on to the next point that seems to apply to your own situation. In addition, of course, the scale of each operation will vary considerably – not every garden is large enough to accommodate a mechanical excavator to dig out wall foundations, for example.

Large country gardens

Traditional country gardens that belong to an old or period house can sometimes be much larger than average, dating from a time when more space was available. Their characteristics, as determined by their size, location and the use of locally available building materials, can be in marked contrast to a smaller, more modern development in the town or countryside. Such properties can often be more isolated, and their gardens may, therefore, be far more exposed and vulnerable to the extremes of weather, particularly the wind. In such a garden, therefore, your priority must be to establish adequate shelter in the form of man-made structures, such as fences or walls, or by planting hedges and shelter belts, particularly of native trees and shrubs that are to be found in the surrounding countryside and will help to blend the garden into it.

Such a garden may, however, command impressive views of its surrounding countryside, and these may form a major feature in your design. You may, therefore, have to reach a compromise between retaining the best views while providing adequate shelter. Only observation over a long period will enable you to make this choice. In a garden of this size and type, it may be easier – and more economical – to try and create just two or three small selected areas that are protected from the wind. These should be planned in such a way that, regardless of the wind direction, there will always be at least one of them that is in shelter.

A large garden offers opportunities for a variety of features. A wide border, for example, can be planted to provide form and foliage interest throughout the year. The eye is drawn past the sheltered seat – shunned by even the cat – to the golden leaves of the false acacia (*Robinia pseudoacacia* 'Frisia') and the evergreen *Choisya ternata* 'Sundance'.

Schedule of work
for garden development

* Cut down long grass and weeds, and gather up and dispose of any general rubbish.
* Cut down and grub out the roots of any unwanted shrubs and trees and dispose of them.
* Break out unwanted paths and areas of paving. Store some of this material for use as hardcore and dispose of the remainder.
* Dig over and prepare an appropriately sized area of soil for heeling in any plants that have to be moved but that you wish to keep for replanting later on. Make sure that this nursery bed is not positioned where it will be in the way.
* Lift the plants that are to be retained and heel them in, preferably when they are dormant (between late autumn and early spring). Keep them well watered and fed while they are actively growing.
* While access is good, use a mechanical digger to excavate foundations for walls, bases for paving and garden buildings, and holes for ponds. In addition, dig out in advance large holes for specimen trees if access is likely to be limited later on.
* Remove from site any surplus subsoil resulting from these excavations.
* Retain and stockpile any good quality topsoil that can be used for making up ground levels, adding to raised beds and for backfilling behind retaining walls. Dispose of surplus soil.
* Lay sections of plastic pipe to act as conduits beneath paving and paths to allow for water pipes, electric cables and irrigation supply lines, which will be fed through later on.
* Lay areas of paving, build walls and construct any other features involving the use of brick, concrete and stone.
* Insert vine eyes into walls as they are built if

wires for climbers will be required later.
* Build wooden or wrought iron structures – summerhouses, fences, pergolas and trellis, either as free-standing features or fixed to walls. Where appropriate, the posts for some of these can be concreted in as part of the paving work.
* Fit wires to walls and fences to support climbers.
* Construct ponds and other types of water feature, place rockery stones if not already in position and backfill with stockpiled topsoil to make up the levels behind and between rocks.
* Eradicate weeds from all planting and lawn areas, and from the topsoil stockpile – this can be carried out at the same time as other preliminary work is progressing and should be repeated as necessary.
* Dig over and prepare all planting and lawn areas as they become available.
* Install armoured electric cable, irrigation feeds and mains water pipes to reach the relevant parts of the garden, passing them through previously laid conduits under paving and paths.
* Install submersible pond pump, pond filter if required and supply hose. Test the system for leaks before burying the pipework.
* Plant any specimen trees and large shrubs if not already in place.
* Lift and replant any heeled-in stock in its final position while it is still dormant.
* Plant climbers and remaining smaller shrubs, perennials and other plants.
* Complete the irrigation and garden lighting systems. Test all systems.
* Sow grass seed or turf lawn.
* Drain pond, clean out any soil or debris, refill and add aquatic plants.
* Hoe out any weed seedlings from all planting areas and apply a mulch.

Carefully positioned features, such as a pergola, can be used to create the illusion that a garden is larger than it actually is. The stepping-stones lead to a small raised area planted with woodland species.

The order of work on this list is not intended to be followed to the letter. It will, however, give you an idea of how to landscape your garden either all in one go, or in several smaller, more easily managed stages. Providing that you remember the basic needs for good access, adequate storage, disposal of surplus waste and materials and protection of finished work, the order in which you carry out the project can often be rescheduled to suit your individual circumstances and requirements.

29

Timing

Anyone who has access to unlimited funds and labour can have their perfect garden virtually overnight, regardless of the size, situation or style. Realistically, though, most of us will have to wait longer, which is not necessarily a bad thing, because it gives us time to watch our gardens develop and the plants mature – and for many people this is half the pleasure of gardening.

Building a garden can take a considerable time, however, and, as with all practical construction projects, there are right and wrong ways of carrying out certain tasks. In all garden projects, the work will depend on the time of year and the weather. It may be tempting to dive straight in and make a start on your garden – especially if it is a new, bare plot or a badly neglected older one – but it is worth taking a note of a few basic principles which, if followed, should help you to avoid making expensive or irritating mistakes that may not come to light until it is too late for you to do anything about them without additional cost and disruption. Your existing garden is most likely to be one, or possibly a combination, of the following broad types:

* A completely bare plot, probably associated with a newly built house.
* An established but neglected, and possibly over-mature, garden in poor condition.
* An established garden that has been well looked after and is in good overall condition.

Each of these three garden types will present a set of challenges to the gardener, some of which are common to all gardens, while others may be peculiar to just one particular type. The following lists summarize the main characteristics of each garden type, and you should bear these in mind as you prepare your new design, remembering which category your garden falls into. These factors may influence both the way that you tackle the garden and, more importantly, the amount of time, effort and money that may be required to achieve a satisfactory result.

The bare plot

* Soil compacted by builder's machinery and general site traffic.
* Builder's rubbish buried in the garden at varying depths.
* Perennial weed roots in the topsoil, either brought in by the builder or present in the original soil.
* Annual weed seeds in the original topsoil or in the soil brought in by the builder.
* Local areas of soil contamination caused by spillages of diesel, paint or other building materials. Topsoil is generally lacking in structure because of poor handling and compaction, and it may also lack organic matter.
* Poor drainage, which might be over the whole garden or in just one or two isolated spots.

The established but neglected garden

* Between late autumn and early spring, dormant perennial plants and bulbs may not be apparent, so you cannot assess what is present.
* Sick or damaged plants, possibly harbouring a variety of pests and diseases.
* Neglected and old plants, badly overgrown or mis-shaped and requiring careful pruning or complete removal.
* Soil probably impoverished because of dense planting and lack of feeding.
* Perennial weed infestation among ornamental plants.
* Damage or wear and tear to structures and features, such as fences, trellis and garden buildings.

Whenever possible, hard landscaping should be completed before beds and borders are planted. When building work is spread over a number of years, make sure that you can obtain sufficient supplies of bricks, setts, or flags to complete the design so that, for example, you can use the same materials for a patio and a paved area away from the house and maintain the continuity of the design.

The established but cared-for garden

* Dormant perennial plants and bulbs may not be apparent.
* The dilemma of having to remove good quality, possibly expensive features, such as a pond or arbour, that unfortunately do not fit in with your own design ideas.
* The dilemma of having to remove well-cared for, healthy specimens of trees, shrubs or other mature plants that do not fit in with your plans or that you dislike.

As part of the development of your garden, therefore, you should ascertain which of the above characteristics apply to your site and decide not only on the best course of action to take to tackle each one but also on the most appropriate time to undertake the work. The rest of this chapter gives you some general guidance on the ideal times for carrying out both preliminary ground clearance and basic soil preparation, as well as the more creative tasks of planting and hard landscaping.

Annual weeds

The task of removing annual weeds can be carried out at almost any time by hoeing or forking. Dry, sunny and windy weather will quickly shrivel up the chopped-off weeds. If you are using a herbicide, the application is usually made at some time from spring to autumn, depending on the individual product and the manufacturer's recommended treatment. Contact herbicides applied in the winter have limited or no effect.

Small gardens

Even if your garden is small, there are ways in which you can make the most of the available space. Planting climbers and wall shrubs against the vertical surfaces will provide plenty of foliage and flowers as well as height, yet take up little valuable space on the ground. Such plants require little more than a pocket of soil let into the paving at the base of each one. Another way of conserving space is to tier your plants by underplanting one or two small, lightly foliaged or fastigiate trees with medium sized deciduous shrubs. Beneath these you could plant shade-tolerant ground-cover perennials and spring- and autumn-flowering bulbs to provide a wide range of colour and seasonal interest within a small area. Where even conventional planting is not possible because of lack of room, planting in containers is a particularly valuable way of growing plants in a small garden. Apart from the intrinsic beauty and attraction of the plants and pots themselves, you can move them around as the mood takes you, and if you need extra temporary space – for a family barbecue, for example – all you have to do is to gather up your pots and tuck them in a corner out of the way.

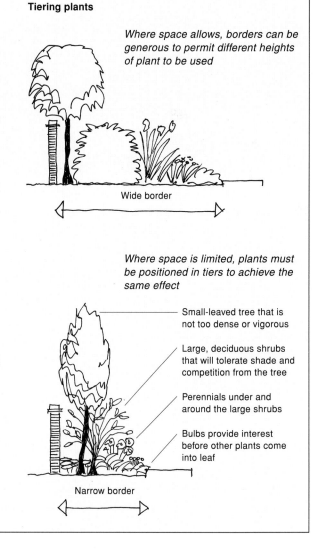

Tiering plants

Where space allows, borders can be generous to permit different heights of plant to be used

Wide border

Where space is limited, plants must be positioned in tiers to achieve the same effect

Small-leaved tree that is not too dense or vigorous

Large, deciduous shrubs that will tolerate shade and competition from the tree

Perennials under and around the large shrubs

Bulbs provide interest before other plants come into leaf

Narrow border

Perennial weeds

Dig or fork out the weeds at any time when the soil is easily workable. Take care to lift the entire weed, because pieces of root left in the soil will probably grow into plants again. Treatment with herbicides is usually most effective between spring and autumn, again according to the product, but some large and established weeds may need two treatments, probably several weeks apart, so do not delay the first treatment until it is too late in the year to apply a second one and follow the manufacturer's instructions on the packet or container.

Planting

In theory, container-grown plants can be planted at almost any time of the year, provided that the soil is neither waterlogged nor frozen. They may also be planted successfully in the height of summer, but will require regular and frequent watering, probably until autumn and even later in some areas. Bare-root or 'open-ground' plants – that is, those dug straight out of the ground – are best planted in the period between late autumn and early spring when they are dormant and can be safely moved. Avoid planting them in waterlogged or frozen ground.

Soil preparation

Both spring and autumn are good times for digging and preparing soil once it has been cleared of weeds, because there is sufficient moisture present to make the ground soft, but not so much that it is waterlogged or sticky. Summer digging is also possible, but in hot, dry weather heavy, clay soils may become so hard that it is almost impossible to get a fork or spade into the ground. Lighter, sandy soils are freer draining, and the

period for digging them can be extended to almost any time, as long as ground conditions are not extreme.

Paving, concreting and brickwork

Generally speaking, all these tasks can be carried out at almost any time of the year, but there are a number of provisos. One is that when the temperature is at or near freezing, mortar and concrete can be damaged or weakened, and in winter such work may need to be protected at night from extremely low temperatures or even temporarily suspended if daytime temperatures are equally low. In addition, in hot, dry conditions, particularly in midsummer, it will be necessary to prevent work involving concrete or cement mortars from drying out too fast, before it has cured properly, by covering it with damp sacking or polythene sheeting.

Grass seeding and turfing

The traditional times for seeding are in early autumn or mid- to late spring. Seed sown in late autumn may germinate successfully but there will not always be sufficient time for the grass to become established before winter, and it may suffer damage from low temperatures. Sowing too early in spring is also not to be recommended because the soil temperature may not yet be high enough for good grass seed germination although it may be high enough for weed seeds, which could quickly take over and smother the grass seedlings when they eventually emerge.

Turfing can be carried out at almost any time from early autumn to late spring, although it is usually best to avoid the midwinter period, when the ground may be waterlogged or frozen and there is no likelihood of root growth. Early autumn may have the advantage over spring, because the soil temperatures are relatively high and there is sufficient moisture to allow a good degree of establishment before winter, resulting in better and earlier growth in spring.

Summer seeding and turfing are also possible but generally require much greater effort – largely in the extra watering that is required – and very high temperatures may actually prevent grass seed from germinating.

Pruning

Most pruning, particularly of heavy limbs of trees, is best carried out when the particular tree or shrub is dormant, which is generally during the period from late autumn to early spring. However, some light pruning can be carried out in midsummer when pruning cuts heal more easily, and for some plants – such as fruit trees – this is beneficial. There are also many spring-flowering shrubs, such as weigela, that should be pruned as soon as they have flowered, even though they are not dormant, and, of course, hedges are a classic example of pruning while in full growth.

Timescale for impatient gardeners

What if you are a gardener who wants to see some quick results and are tempted to take short cuts or to skimp on the basic preparation outlined above to save time and effort and possibly money? In the short term there may not appear to be any obvious problems. Over a longer period, however, you might find that plants begin to look unhealthy because of badly drained or inadequately prepared soil; perennial weeds may start to appear among your shrubs because pieces of root were left behind at weeding time; your patio might start to break-up or subside in places because you did not put down enough hardcore

in the first instance. Basically, any short cuts that you take, particularly in the vital preparation stages of both hard and soft landscaping, will almost always catch you out eventually.

'Impatient' gardeners can usually be divided into two types: those who want to make a start on planting immediately they take on a new garden, so that no valuable growing time is lost; and those who are quite happy to wait for all the landscaping work to be carried out but who then want to see what is effectively an 'instant' garden at the end of this time, without having to wait many years for it to achieve maturity.

If you fall into the first category and want to begin planting straightaway, what can you do to satisfy your needs until the basic construction work is complete? Short-term interest can always be provided by growing a selection of rapidly maturing plants – particularly summer and winter bedding annuals – in pots and containers. If you place these in various key positions as temporary focal points, they will provide highlights and draw attention away from incomplete or unsightly areas of the garden. You can also make temporary screens – from canes and netting, for example – on which you can grow annual climbers, such as sweetpeas and nasturtiums, or possibly faster growing, longer lived climbers, such as varieties of clematis, honeysuckle or golden hop, which you can eventually replant in permanent positions elsewhere in the garden. These screens can be used not only to hide unfinished work in the garden but also as temporary boundaries. If beds and borders are not ready, so that you do not lose any growing time, permanent plants for the garden such as trees, shrubs, perennials and climbers can be grown on in temporary nursery rows, such as in the area that will eventually house your vegetable garden. They can ultimately be moved into their permanent positions as and when the space becomes

Annuals, such as sweetpea (*Lathyrus odoratus*), can be grown in containers to provide temporary colour and fragrance in courtyards or on patios until more permanent plants become established.

The advantages of this instant approach are that you will get an immediate effect in terms of over-all height and scale, and a quick covering of the ground, which will suppress any weeds and conceal bare soil. The implications of this second method that you need to consider are:

* The cost, which could easily be double or treble that of using modestly sized plants at normal spacing.
* The possible effects on the shape and the flowering potential of shrubs and perennials that are planted closer together than usual.
* The extra, longer term management that may be required in the form of pruning, shaping and thinning resulting from the higher density planting.

One final point about the completed, but immature, garden is worth noting. Although in the long term your small trees and shrubs will eventually grow to fill their allotted space, in the first couple of years after planting there may well be large areas of bare soil visible among them. While it is tempting to fill these gaps with short-lived annual bedding, there is a serious danger that in the space of just a few weeks these annuals will completely overshadow your small, permanent plants, particularly choice and relatively slow-growing varieties, and will compete with them for the available moisture, nutrients and light. If you are not careful, you may well end up in a situation whereby the more annuals you plant, the greater the competition for the permanent plants, which will then grow even more slowly and take even longer to fill the space. So the following year you plant even more annuals because the soil is still not covered, and so on. What you should do is to interplant sparingly with annuals if you must, but do not let them encroach in any way on the perennial plants and, if necessary, remove them if they do.

available. This method does, of course, mean that they can be moved only while they are dormant, in the autumn or winter. A more flexible approach is to grow them in containers and pots, since they can be planted out at virtually any time when it is convenient to do so, although they may require more attention, particularly in terms of watering, in the meantime.

For the second kind of impatient gardener who is looking for instant maturity without waiting for plants to develop, the answer is, first, to plant the garden with specimen plants, in particular those varieties of trees and shrubs that are slower growing and would therefore take longer to mature. Second, the smaller, infill plants, such as small-growing shrubs, perennials and grasses, can be planted at a much higher density than normal.

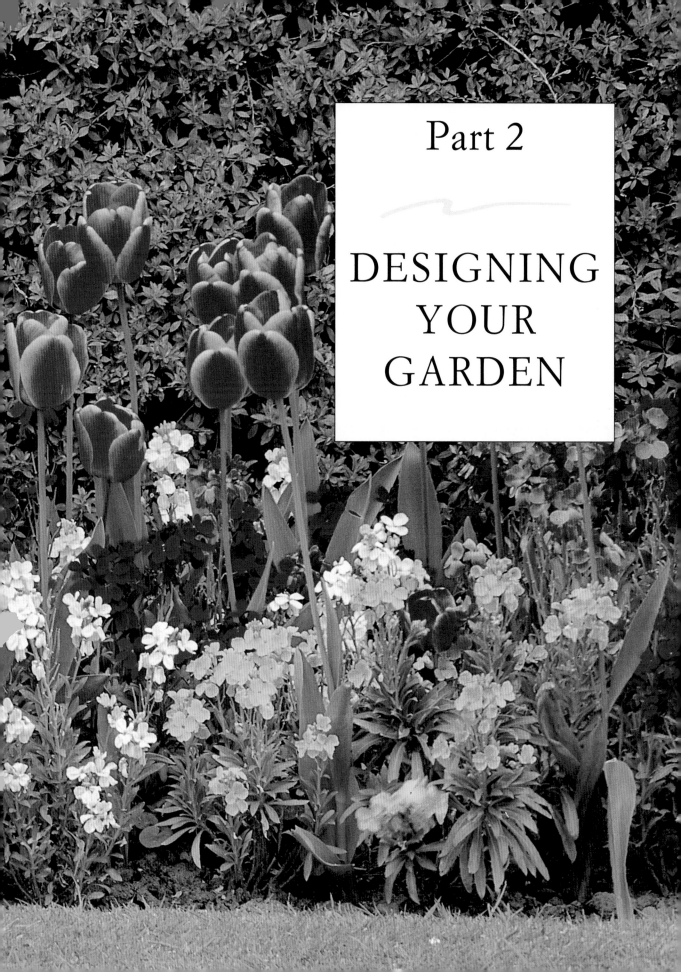

Part 2

DESIGNING YOUR GARDEN

The design

If you have followed the suggestions and instructions outlined in Part 1 you should have sufficient information about the following factors, which are relevant to all garden designs, regardless of the size of garden:

* The overall purpose of the garden – that is, how you want to use it.
* The individual features and ideas that you would like or need to include.
* The existing physical conditions in the garden that will, to varying degrees, affect how you use it and what you put in it.
* The existing features that you will either retain, change to suit your own purposes or remove altogether.
* The cost of building your garden and whether this is to be spent in one initial outlay or spread over several years.
* How and in what order you propose to carry out the necessary work.
* When you are likely to begin the work and how long it will take, bearing in mind those tasks that can be done only at a certain time of year.

By the end of the process, you should have a list of what you want to accomplish and the constraints – physical, time and financial – that, when put together, will result in the best possible garden design to meet your needs.

These factors in themselves do not necessarily make a good garden design, however, any more than a list of ingredients on its own makes a good cake. A successful garden design must not only make sure that the garden works for you from a practical point of view and that everything is in the best place for its purpose, but it must also make the garden look good, too, so that all the elements – whether they are living plants or man-made features – harmonize with each other and create an attractive overall effect.

To achieve this you will need to consider a number of less tangible aspects of garden design, which cannot be measured or quantified in the same way as, say, the size of the patio or how much you can afford to spend on a greenhouse, but without which the resulting garden could end up as a random collection of individual features rather than a unified composition.

Probably one of the most effective ways to 'pull' the elements of a design together is to have a theme to your garden, which you could introduce in one of three simple ways:

* The use of one material throughout the garden.
* The use of a colour scheme.
* The repetition of shapes.

The first of these methods, the use throughout the garden of one particular material that you especially like, is most easily achieved with the hard landscaping. You might, for example, decide on an old red paving brick, which you could use for the patio, the path up the garden and around the edge of the pond.

A colour theme can be introduced in one of two ways. The first is to have a limited combination of complementary colours running through your planting scheme – concentrating on shades of blue and yellow, and whites and silver, for

example. The alternative is to link the various hard landscape materials in the same way.

The third method of incorporating a theme is to repeat a distinctive shape, which need not be limited to patterns on the ground, such as circular lawns and patios. It could also be visible in the vertical plane, in trellises, walls and garden buildings, or even the plants themselves – you could carefully train a holly tree into a sphere, for example.

In addition to providing a theme, shape can also affect your garden design in other ways. and there are two in particular that you will probably find most useful to remember. One is that free-flowing, irregular curves and amorphous, undefined shapes will help to create an air of informality, which is ideal if you want to create an old-fashioned or cottage-style garden. The other is that the use of straight lines and right-angled shapes, such as squares and rectangles, in an organized and symmetrical layout will result in a garden that will tend to be formal and rigid.

Here there are two themes that can be carried through into the rest of the garden. First, the circular theme, illustrated by the paved area, raised pool, archway and even the planted container. Second, the brick in the boundary wall, which is used around the paved area, for the path and to build the pool

Key to planting
1 *Elaeagnus pungens* 'Maculata'
2 *Ceanothus impressus*
3 *Cordyline* purple (in pot)
4 *Lavandula* 'Loddon Pink'
5 *Rosa* 'Schoolgirl'
6 *Hemerocallis* 'Catherine Woodbery' (pink)
7 *Rosa* 'Schoolgirl'
8 *Juniperus squamata* 'Blue Star'
9 *Achillea* 'Moonshine'
10 *Hydrangea macrophylla* 'Blue Wave'
11 *Geranium sanguineum*
12 *Viburnum tinus*

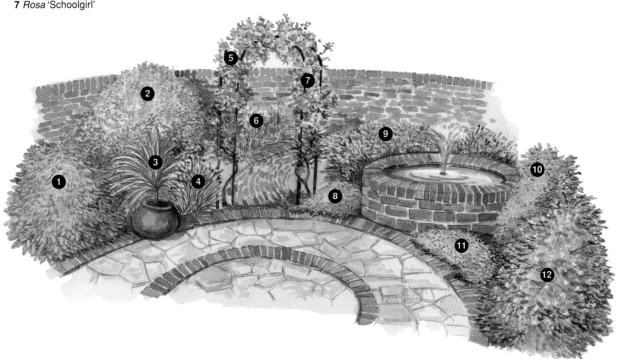

Straight and curved lines create quite different effects

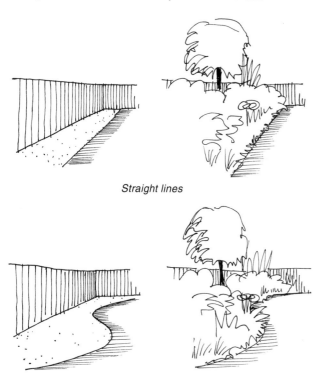

Straight lines

Curved lines

You can influence the effects produced in a garden by adjusting the relative proportions of some of the elements. For example, a tiny, circular lawn surrounded by deep borders densely planted with large shrubs and trees, might create a space that feels enclosed, cosy and private. On the other hand, a much larger circular lawn, enclosed by narrow borders containing small shrubs and perennials will probably seem open and spacious in comparison.

Apart from its use as a visual theme, colour can also be employed to develop a particular mood or atmosphere within a garden. Bright reds and oranges will produce an eye-catching, vibrant effect, full of warmth, while the use of paler blues, yellow and white will tend to have the opposite effect, being cooler and more relaxed. These basic characteristics of colour are useful

Warm colours – reds, yellows and oranges – have the effect of bringing the planting forwards. Heleniums, crocosmias, cannas, achillea, solidago and kniphofias will provide colour from spring into late summer.

Left: Cool colours – blues, mauves and creamy-yellows – tend to recede and can help to make a garden look larger. The silvery leaves of cotton lavender (*Santolina chamaecyparissus*) and *Stachys byzantina* are the perfect foil for *Anaphalis triplinervis*.

Below: Colour in the border does not depend on flowers. Plants with silver or glaucous-blue foliage will lighten borders and provide not only a variety of textures and forms but also a delicate contrast with more robustly coloured flowers. Try reliably hardy plants such as *Stachys byzantina*, cotton lavender (*Santolina chamaecyparissus*) and *Brachyglottis greyii* (syn. *B.* 'Sunshine', *Senecio greyii*).

and can be used to help create a mood within your garden that suits you.

The value of colour in a garden should not be underestimated, and while the technical and finer points of colour – whether it is in the form of light or pigment – may be beyond the scope of this book, several more fundamental aspects are not and will help you achieve your aims.

In simple terms, colour can be broken down into a spectrum, as you see in a rainbow, of red, orange, yellow, green, blue and violet. Reds, oranges and yellows, as already noted, are colours that produce a warm sensation, while greens, blues and violets tend to produce the opposite effect and can seem cooler. In addition, the warmer colours are often exciting and visually stimulating, so that a garden that is composed chiefly of these will be quite a lively affair. On the other hand, colours from the cool end of the spectrum are more likely to introduce a calm, quiet effect into a garden when they are used together. By applying this one fundamental rule you have a means to control the mood or atmosphere of your garden or just a part of it. This does not mean, of course, that the warm and cool colours cannot, or should not, be mixed, and in fact doing so provides you with the means of adjusting the relative warmth or coolness of your garden to suit your own preferences.

A second, equally useful, property of colour in the garden is that warm colours give the distinct impression of being near to you, while cool colours usually appear to be more distant. You have only to look at a distant view of the fields and hills in the broader landscape to realize that objects that look yellow, orange and red in the foreground gradually appear to turn to blues and purples in the distance. This phenomenon can be put to use in a garden design for different purposes. For example, it is possible to make a short garden appear longer than it is by concentrating, as far as possible, all your warm colours at the front of the garden and the cool colours at the back; if you wished you could make a long garden seem shorter by reversing this process.

Some colours – grey, silver and white – are fairly neutral in this respect and don't really fit into either the warm or cool categories. This is a distinct advantage because it means that they can be used in all manner of colour combinations, and they can be excellent foils or backgrounds against which other colours can be set to be seen to best effect. You may, of course, like many gardeners, wish to strike a middle ground approach and want to use a whole range of colours because to do otherwise might mean that you would have to omit some of your favourite plants. In this particular instance, you can use white-flowered and grey- or silver-foliaged plants mixed in with the other colours to act as a buffer and prevent any jarring contrasts that might destroy the effect you are trying to achieve.

Occasionally you may come across a garden that has been designed using just a single colour – blue, yellow or white – as its theme, with all other colours, apart from green, of course, excluded as far as possible. Often, though, you will find that these 'gardens' are part of a much larger garden and as such they are somewhat specialized and are not necessarily either in view or use all the time, as would be the case in a small suburban or town garden. While the effect of such a monochrome garden design can be striking, for an everyday garden it may be of limited value, and you should think carefully about such a design before going ahead with one.

You should also remember that these particular properties of colour do not apply only to plants – although the range of colours covered by them is obviously huge – but also to other materials in your garden. If you are aiming to create a rather quiet, tranquil part of your garden using blue, silver and mauve plants, it might be counter-productive to include in your design a sitting area built from bright red brick.

Elements of
the garden

All gardens are made up of a number of individual elements or parts. Some gardens, particularly large or elaborate ones, can contain a range of these elements, while small or simple gardens may contain only a few. In either case, your garden is going to be most effective if its component elements are not only carefully chosen with reference to your overall design, but are also designed and constructed in such a way that they will last as long as possible. The purpose of this chapter, then, is not only to suggest examples of each of these elements – pergolas, water features, patios and so on – but also to describe how they can be created. There is also advice on how you can get the best out of them in a garden setting.

Walls

Probably the most common use of a wall in a garden is as a boundary between the garden and the land or property that surrounds it. As well as being strong and durable, a well-built wall is also capable of providing a good degree of security and privacy in and around a garden.

Traditionally, brick and natural stone are the most commonly used materials for building walls, although concrete in its various precast forms, such as blocks and bricks, is becoming increasingly popular, largely because of its relatively modest cost in comparison to natural stone but

also because the quality of colours and textures and the general appearance of such products is increasingly improving. However, size for size, most walls, regardless of the chosen material, are relatively expensive to construct compared with other forms of vertical barrier or screen, such as fences and hedges, and this is a factor that you need to consider in the preliminary stages of planning your garden. At this early planning stage, too, you should find out if there are any legal or planning restrictions on building garden walls in your neighbourhood that might determine the height of wall you are allowed to build or limit your choice of materials.

In choosing a style for the wall and a suitable material, you should allow yourself to be influenced by the design or theme of the rest of the garden. If you have decided on an overall colour theme, for example, you will probably want to select a brick that will match or complement this colour, and you might then want to use the same brick in other parts of the garden, such as for an edging to a pond or for the patio, to maintain the theme and style throughout your garden. If your garden is in a recognizably modern style, a brick that is uniform, square-edged and smooth in texture and colour would be a suitable choice, while an old-fashioned, cottage-style garden is more likely to be enhanced by the use of rustic bricks, which might have been

Choosing a style of brick wall

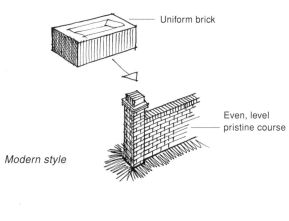

Uniform brick

Even, level
pristine course

Modern style

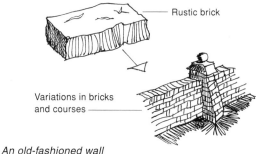

Rustic brick

Variations in bricks
and courses

An old-fashioned wall

As well as screening the garden, walls provide shelter. In addition, they offer the perfect opportunity to introduce height into the garden. When you are planting against a wall, remember that the rootball should be planted away from the too-dry area at the base of the wall.

reclaimed from an old wall and which exhibit a wide variation of colour, shape and even size.

Deciding whether to build a wall yourself or to obtain professional help must also figure prominently in your planning and budgeting. The final decision will probably depend partly on the level of your own skill and ability, partly on the extra cost that employing a builder would involve, and partly on the size and complexity of the wall itself. Simple, low walls – up to, say, 60–75cm (24–30in) high – may be within the scope of someone who has a reasonable practical knowledge and understanding of bricklaying and other associated construction techniques, such as concreting. However, more complicated designs, retaining walls or walls above this height are

Most gardeners will need professional help to build a long or complicated wall

Where space permits, walls within gardens can be curved to emphasize informality and to disguise straight lines

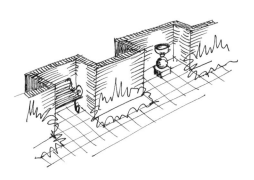

Walls can be dog-legged to create bays for seats, statues and other features or for special plants. Such walls are stronger than the equivalent plain wall

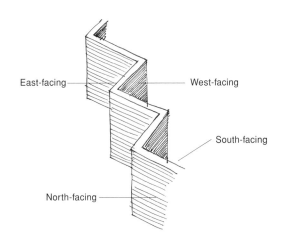

East-facing — West-facing

South-facing

North-facing

Zigzag walls take up more space within a garden, but they create a variety of aspects for different types of planting

probably best left to the professionals, because any error on your part may not only prove to be expensive but may be potentially dangerous. If you are in any doubt, seek professional help.

Regardless of their size, all walls must have solid, level foundations below the ground to provide the strong, stable bases on which they can be built. All other things being equal, the greater the height of the wall, the more substantial the foundation will need to be. The amount of soil to be excavated for such a foundation trench can sometimes prove to be quite considerable, and large volumes are likely to prove both expensive and difficult to dispose of, especially if the soil or subsoil has to be dug out and removed by hand. It might, therefore, be worth finding out if the material that arises from the foundation trench can be used to advantage elsewhere in the garden, particularly if it is good quality topsoil, which can sometimes be in short supply. If you are able to do this, you will avoid the trouble or expense of either having to cart it away or pay someone else to do so for you.

Both mortars for laying bricks and concrete for foundations contain lime in the form of cement, and if the lime is allowed to contaminate garden soil, it can raise its pH value (the measure of its alkalinity or acidity) to a level that is detrimental to certain types of plant, most notably lime-haters such as rhododendrons and camellias. It is important, therefore, to make sure that any mortar or concrete that is spilled onto areas for planting is cleared up at the end of each day and disposed of either by carting it away or by stockpiling it, where it can do no harm, for use later on as hardcore for, say, the base of a patio.

In places where the vertical face of a wall comes into contact with the ground – immediately behind a low retaining wall or in a raised bed, for example – moisture may penetrate the bricks, stones or concrete blocks and cause unsightly staining or even damage. Bricks are particularly susceptible to damage when they get frozen in winter. Two relatively simple techniques can be used to avoid these potential problems. The most obvious one is to use a brick or stone that you know is hard and non-absorbent and through which moisture cannot pass. The other technique is to create a waterproof barrier between the internal face of the wall and the ground or soil behind it. You can achieve this either by applying a generous covering of proprietary waterproofing liquid to the inside face of the wall or by separating it from the ground behind by inserting an impermeable sheet, such as heavy polythene or PVC, between the two. As a further precaution, you should make 'weep holes', which are created simply by omitting the mortar from vertical joints at regular intervals of maybe 1 to 2 metres (1 or 2 yards) along the lowest course of the wall in order to allow excess water to pass through and drain away.

Patios and paving

Wherever there is likely to be regular or heavy pedestrian traffic in your garden, you will need to consider using some form of hard paving in order to prevent these areas from being eventually turned into mud baths or dust bowls. What you choose in the way of materials to pave such an area will depend, first, on its intended purpose and, second, on the way in which this area will fit into your overall garden design in terms of its colour, texture and shape. For example, a general-purpose patio really needs to be made out of concrete or stone flags, bricks or timber in the form of decking, all of which, when laid correctly, should be both level and smooth enough for you to be able to set out chairs, tables and other garden furniture, be sufficiently durable and hard-wearing to take a fair amount of wear

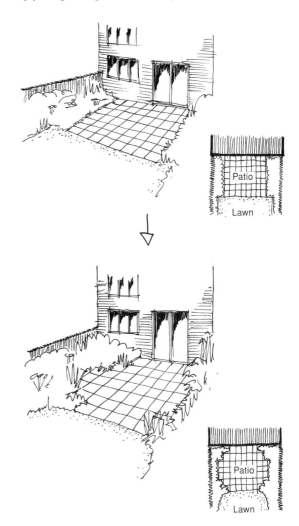

Even a plain paved area can be made more appealing by simply reorganizing the overall shape

and tear and, of course, be comfortable and safe to walk on. On the other hand, a little path meandering around a rockery or through a shrub border might be needed more for cosmetic reasons than practical ones, and there is no reason, therefore, why it could not be easily made from pebbles, stone chippings or ornamental chipped bark, all of which would not be appropriate for a much more heavily or intensively used area.

Patios and other similar areas need to be carefully located for sitting out, with the object of

Quite simple modifications can have maximum effect

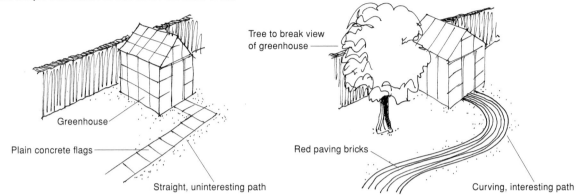

Tree to break view of greenhouse

Greenhouse

Plain concrete flags

Straight, uninteresting path

Red paving bricks

Curving, interesting path

making sure that they are sited not only to be in the sun for as long as possible but also so that they are in a convenient and practical place. In the case of a typical patio, this will usually mean placing it next to the house and, more often than

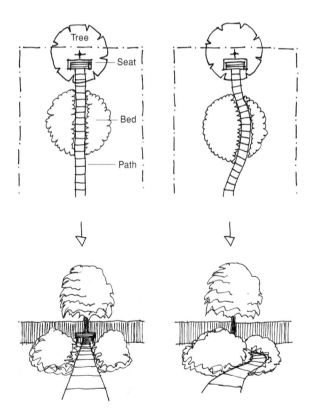

Even minor alterations to the shape or alignment of a path can result in significant changes in the appearance of a garden without altering its purpose

not, this will be immediately outside the back-door or french windows or both. Not everyone enjoys lots of hot sun, however, and you should not rule out the possibility of creating an alternative sitting area, even if it is quite small, in a part of the garden that may get little or no sun in order to provide a certain amount of shade and coolness.

Paths can be broadly divided into two types. First, there are those whose sole function is to get you directly from A to B and whose appearance has no bearing or effect on the rest of the garden. Then there are those paths that not only have to provide access around the garden between different points but that must also fit into the overall appearance and design of the garden as a whole. You will at some stage in the planning of your garden have to decide, therefore, into which of these categories your paths, and indeed your other paved areas, fall in order to help you decide on their style and materials.

Any paved areas that you are likely to use on a regular basis, such as a patio, for example, or paths leading to the front or backdoor of your house, must be adequately constructed in order to avoid settlement and deterioration of the finished surface in the long term, which may not only look unsightly but could also be dangerous. This usually entails removing up to 20cm (8in) or

A straight path, such as this York stone example, can be made more interesting by using randomly placed slabs and by selecting plants that, positioned close to the edge, will grow forwards and obscure the hard edge. Height can be provided by plants such as *Lavatera* 'Barnsley' and a carefully pruned wisteria, while bright summer bedding plants add interest at ground level.

If it is to be of practical value as an area for sitting and eating, a patio must be not only flat and smooth but also sufficiently spacious to accommodate a table and several chairs.

49

more of soil and adding a layer of hardcore, crushed stone or lean concrete – that is, concrete made with only about 50 per cent of the normal amount of cement and water to make a stiff mix – to 15cm (6in) thick in the bottom of the excavation. On top of this layer you should lay your chosen paving material, either onto a wet bed of cement-sand mortar or, in some cases, just sand. Paving for lightly or infrequently used areas can be of a lighter construction, and you can often lay larger units, such as concrete or stone flags directly onto a cement–sand mortar bed, or sometimes just sand, provided that the natural ground beneath these areas is hard and is unlikely to move or settle in the long term.

There are many types of paving slabs available, and inevitably you will find that the cheapest ones are usually the plain, grey concrete variety, with coloured and textured concrete varieties gradually increasing in cost, depending on their quality and type of finish. Natural stone is the most expensive and in some cases is up to ten times the cost of the cheapest concrete examples. Do bear in mind if you are buying the cheapest concrete slabs and even some types of smooth natural stone that they can become dangerously slippery when wet. It might even be worth buying them on a rainy day so that you can test them before committing yourself.

Certain types of brick also make good paving material, and these are available made from both concrete and more traditional natural clay. Concrete paving bricks or blocks – pavers, as they are usually known – tend to be available in only a fairly limited range of colours, but they are reasonably economical when compared with specially made clay paving bricks, which can be up to two or three times more expensive. Some types of ordinary house brick, especially those that are very hard and well-burned, are also suitable for paving purposes – but you should always avoid using soft, crumbly or poor quality bricks, which will eventually break up with frost. If you are in doubt, check with the manufacturer or supplier as to the suitability of your chosen brick for its intended purpose.

Steps and changes of level

Although many gardens, at first glance, appear to be level, in reality very few are, and this fact can often be used to advantage when you are developing a garden design. Even a small change of level, which may require only a shallow step, can have a profound impact and can often add much-needed interest to what would otherwise be a flat vista.

Gentle slope down

Step up

The introduction of a change in level on the gentlest of slopes can have a dramatic effect, especially if it is emphasized by an arch or by the placing of a fastigiate conifer on each side of the step

Weathered brick is one of the most sympathetic materials for hard surfaces, and its inclusion throughout the garden – for retaining walls and steps, for example – will provide a unifying element in a design. As with all garden steps, treads should not be so narrow nor risers so steep that they are awkward, and therefore, dangerous, to use.

At the other extreme, there are gardens where the natural slope of the ground may seem almost excessive, and unless you can modify this steep gradient in some way, the garden cannot be readily used for some or any of its intended purposes. If your garden slopes steeply the solution is to create relatively flat spaces – for lawns and patios, for example – by terracing the garden, using one or more low retaining walls and filling in behind these with soil to create broad stepped areas, each large enough for its particular purpose.

Terracing a slope

A completely impractical, steep slope

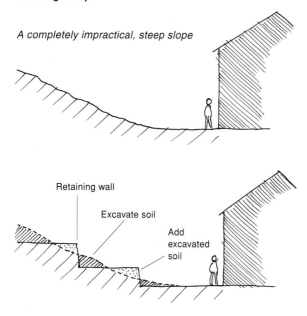

Terracing creates level, usable areas

Whether you have just a minor change of level or a whole series of terraces, you will obviously want to get from one level to another, and to do this you will need to connect them with either steps or a ramp. Ramps are in some ways more desirable than steps because they are generally easier to negotiate, particularly for people with mobility problems or if you need to move grass-cutting equipment or a wheelbarrow, for example, around the garden. The maximum gradient of a ramp that still permits comfortable access, should ideally be not more than about 1 in 12 – gradients steeper than this are generally more difficult to negotiate and are not recommended. For this reason, ramps can take up much more ground space than steps of an equivalent height. Steps, on the other hand, will enable you to move from one level to another over a much shorter distance and therefore need less room, but they can clearly be difficult to negotiate with any sort of garden machinery or by people who may have limited mobility. One useful way to get the best of both worlds is to combine the two and build a stepped ramp, which will allow a greater degree of manoeuvrability than a steep, continuous flight of steps, but takes up less room than a single ramp.

Materials for steps and other changes of level must, above all, be strong and durable, and for this reason the most popular are bricks, stone and concrete. Wood is also popular, but it must be adequately treated against rot before use. Building single steps and low or minor retaining walls, not more than 20–30cm (8–12in) high, on gently sloping ground is probably within the scope of anyone who has a basic understanding of construction techniques and an aptitude for do-it-yourself. Large flights of steps, high retaining walls, and retaining walls on steeply sloping terrain, however, will almost certainly require more expertise, and you may need to enlist professional help if your design involves these features. Where there are major changes of level, it is also worth thinking about safety, and you may find it necessary or desirable to install, for example, a handrail or a low wall along one or both sides of steep flights of steps or long ramps.

You should also consider the appearance of high retaining walls and large flights of steps, which can be quite dominant visually, particularly if your garden slopes upwards and away from the house so that all the vertical faces of the changes of level are visible. If this is the case, you will need to decide whether you want to make a positive feature out of these faces, or whether it would be better to attempt to disguise or screen them in some way. If you decide to opt for the positive approach, you should build your steps or walls using materials and in a style that reflect the theme of the rest of your garden – whether it is formal or informal, modern or old fashioned. A mixture of different materials, such as old brick and flint, either whole or 'knapped' – that is, cut to expose the black centre – can be particularly attractive in these circumstances. Remember, too, that retaining walls and steps do not necessarily need to be in straight lines all the time, and you can introduce curves and other shapes, where appropriate, to add more interest to the features.

On the other hand, reducing the impact of such structures can be achieved fairly simply and effectively by planting trailing plants in the soil just behind the top of the wall, so that the stems hang down and conceal its face. You can also attach wires and trellis direct to the face to support climbers that are planted at the foot of the wall. A third solution is to have a combination of both trailing and climbing plants, which should, in theory, cover the wall in half the time. Retaining walls and step risers can be built from wood, which can be in the form of round or sawn

Retaining walls made from treated logs are excellent for displaying a range of plants

Key to planting

 1 *Juniperus sabina* 'Tamariscifolia'
 2 *Cornus alba* 'Aurea'
 3 *Cotoneaster* x *suecicus* 'Coral Beauty'
 4 *Skimmia japonica* 'Rubella'
 5 *Weigela florida* 'Foliis Purpureis'
 6 *Genista lydia*
 7 *Spiraea japonica* 'Gold Mound'
 8 *Festuca glauca*
 9 *Vinca minor* 'Argenteovariegata'
10 *Euphorbia polychroma* 'Candy' (syn. *E. p.* 'Purpurea')
11 *Juniperus horizontalis* 'Blue Chip'
12 *Miscanthus sinensis* 'Morning Light'
13 *Geranium wallichianum* 'Buxton's Variety'
14 *Salix helvetica*
15 *Helianthemum* 'Henfield Brilliant'
16 *Heuchera micrantha* var. *diversifolia* 'Palace Purple'
17 *Molinia caerulea* ssp. *caerulea* 'Variegata'

Railway sleepers and gravel can be used to make reasonably inexpensive steps. Wood used in structures such as this must be treated before use to protect it from rot. Remember, too, that the treads must be wide enough to permit easy and safe access.

logs, or even second-hand railway sleepers if these are available. The beauty of wood is that, because it is a natural material, it will blend into a garden much more readily than, say, brick or concrete, and you can, of course, change its colour with stain to tone it down and therefore reduce its impact.

Fences, trellis, screens

As garden features, fences, trellis panels and screens are often thought of as being purely functional items that are simply used for marking boundaries, supporting climbing plants or for obscuring views of unsightly objects. This notion

has affected the quality of the design, and sometimes the construction, of these features, which are often not given the consideration they deserve. However, with a little thought and effort, they can be turned into attractive and worthwhile elements in their own right as well as being able to perform their more basic functions within the garden.

The most popular materials used for the construction of fences and such like are wood (both hard and soft), metal (usually wrought iron and mild steel) and, in a few limited cases, plastic. Brick, concrete and stone can sometimes be used to build the posts or piers between which panels made of the other materials can be fixed, and this

Wooden trellising, which is widely available and relatively inexpensive, is the perfect way to increase the height of a screening fence and provide the ideal support for climbing plants of all kinds.

mixing of materials can sometimes result in features that are both interesting and attractive.

Free-standing structures such as these rely mainly on the strength of the supporting posts or piers for their stability, especially fences made from solid panels, which can be subject to quite extraordinary forces from strong winds on occasion. Such posts need to be securely fixed in the ground, usually to a minimum depth of 45cm (18in), but in soft, light or permanently wet soil this depth may need to be increased still further. In heavy, hard and stony ground, it is possible to backfill the post hole with a well-rammed mixture of stones and soil to achieve a good fix, but otherwise posts should be concreted in position. Brick, stone or concrete piers or posts, provided they are well built and laid on adequate solid concrete foundation pads and provided with a

A fence need not be only a convenient way to indicate the boundary between gardens. A decorative fence can become a striking feature, as here, where it creates a dramatic backdrop for the imposing urns.

capping or coping on top to finish off, should be virtually maintenance free and should last almost indefinitely. Wrought iron or steel posts, even though they may be well painted initially, can eventually succumb to rust unless you are able to have them galvanized beforehand. If this is not possible, they will need to be rubbed down and re-painted every few years if rust begins to appear. Wooden posts, particularly those made from softwood, are more likely to deteriorate than any other type, and you will need to treat them thoroughly with an appropriate preservative before setting them in the ground. Some timber yards will pressure-treat wood for you, and this is a much more effective and longer lasting way of preserving timber than painting or staining it by hand. Hardwoods, such as oak or elm, are naturally more durable and longer lasting than softwood, such as pine or larch, but even they will eventually deteriorate, and for the extra cost and effort that might be involved it is probably worth treating, at the very least, the sections that are to be buried in the ground.

Individual styles of fencing are almost without number but you will find that nearly all fences are based on one, or a combination, of the following:

* Panel fencing: a prefabricated panel is fixed directly to, or between, two posts or other form of upright support.
* Post and rail fencing: the fencing, whether it is made from panels or individual boards, laths or planks, is fixed to two or more horizontal rails, which are attached to vertical supports.
* Post and wire fencing: this is similar to post and rail fencing, but the horizontal rails are replaced by tensioned wires, which might be plastic coated for appearance or galvanized for longer life. This type of construction is most suitable for use with flexible plastic or metal mesh type fencing (such as chain-link or chicken wire), which is fastened at fairly close intervals to the wires with special clips or small twists of wire and also, if necessary, to the posts, for extra strength.

You can, of course, attach trellis panels to the face of walls or even to existing solid fence panels

Use fastigiate trees, conifers, tall grasses, such as *Miscanthus*, and bamboos to break up the horizontal lines of walls and fences. Vigorous climbers with bold leaves, such as *Vitis*, will quickly provide leafy cover and mask the wall or fence

so that they can support your climbing plants and wall shrubs. Ready-made panels for this purpose are available in a range of shapes, sizes and

Basic fence types

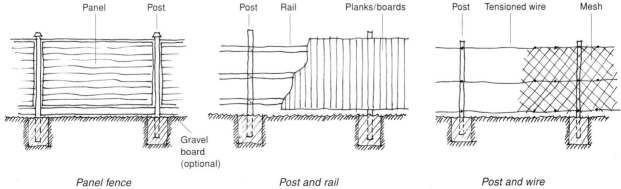

Panel fence   Post and rail   Post and wire

materials, not only in softwoods and hardwoods but also in wrought iron and even plastic. Some of these shop-bought panels are rather lightweight in structure, and you should consider using them as support only for annual climbers, such as sweetpeas, or for climbers that are slow growing or that have a delicate habit with little weight. Vigorous climbers, such as vines and honeysuckle, can exert a lot of weight and stress, and for plants such as these a heavier duty type of panel should be used. For the greatest strength, you should fix these to walls with plugs and screws rather than just with masonry nails, which can gradually work loose in time, especially if the quality of the wall behind is doubtful.

Hedges

As garden features, hedges are sometimes maligned and, for this reason, are often underused. With a little careful thought and planning, however, they have the potential to make a valuable contribution to your garden in many ways.

The most popular use for a hedge is as a boundary, in the same way that you might use a fence or wall, although the impact of a hedge is obviously not as immediate as that of a man-made structure, unless, of course, you are prepared to pay more to buy larger, more mature hedging plants and thereby gain a couple of years' growth. Hedges need not be confined to the perimeter of a garden, however, and wherever you need to create some sort of division or screen within a garden, a hedge in one of its many forms can often be the most sensible, attractive and cost-effective solution.

Apart from the relatively modest initial outlay, one of the great attractions of hedges over walls or fences is the fact that virtually anyone can create a hedge with only a minimum of help and guidance. In addition, because a hedge is composed of living plants, whose appearance will change with the seasons, it tends to bring a more sympathetic and natural aspect to the garden than the relative harshness which an unchanging brick wall or row of fence panels can introduce.

The fact that a hedge is growing can also add to its attraction if you try to think of it as a solid mass, rather like a sculptor's block of stone, which you can adapt to suit different purposes, or even moods, using nothing more than a pair of garden shears or an electric hedge trimmer. In terms of cost, hedges compare well, at least initially, with man-made structures, although the final cost will depend as much as anything on the choice of species and the planting density that this will require – container-grown evergreen shrubs and trees, such as yew (*Taxus* spp.) or

Hedges need not be merely green boundaries. They can also be used to frame views and to draw attention to other garden features

holly (*Ilex* spp.), for example, are likely to be considerably more expensive than bare-rooted species such as privet (*Ligustrum* spp.) or shrubby honeysuckle (*Lonicera nitida*).

Although hedges can be quite flexible in the way that you are able to determine their ultimate size and shape, it is important that you choose a variety of plant that has the degree of vigour and habit of growth that are compatible with your needs so that you can get the best results from the hedge in the long term and be saved from

Herb gardens are traditionally edged with low hedges of box (*Buxus sempervirens*). The slow-growing, small-leaved variety *B. microphylla* 'Compacta', which will scarcely achieve 30cm (1ft) in height in 30 years, is especially suitable for edging.

unnecessary work and wasted time. For example, if you wanted to create a low-growing, formal hedge to go around a small herb garden an ideal choice would be dwarf box (*Buxus sempervirens* 'Suffruticosa') or *Euonymus fortunei*, both of which are slow growing, have small leaves and

Plants for hedging

The following lists include plants for different heights of hedge. Some are grown for their foliage, while others are grown for their flowers.

Low hedges: less than 60cm (24in) high
Berberis buxifolia 'Nana'
Berberis thunbergii 'Atropurpurea Nana'
Buxus sempervirens 'Suffruticosa'
Euonymus fortunei (varieties)
Cotoneaster microphyllus var. *thymifolius*
Lavandula angustifolia 'Hidcote'
Lavandula angustifolia 'Nana Alba'
Potentilla fruticosa 'Red Ace'
Potentilla fruticosa 'Tilford Cream'

Medium hedges: 60–120cm (2–4ft) high
Berberis thunbergii f. *atropurpurea*
Berberis thunbergii 'Aurea'
Buxus sempervirens
Buxus sempervirens 'Elegantissima'
Cotoneaster conspicuus 'Decorus'
Ilex aquifolium (varieties)
Lavandula x *intermedia* 'Grappenhall'
Ligustrum ovalifolium 'Argenteum'
Potentilla fruticosa 'Katherine Dykes'
Potentilla fruticosa 'Princess'
Rosa 'Bonica'

Tall hedges: 1.2–1.8m (4–6ft)
Buxus sempervirens
Carpinus betulus
Cotoneaster lacteus
Cotoneaster simonsii
Elaeagnus x *ebbingei*
Fagus sylvatica
Fagus sylvatica Atropurpurea Group
Ilex aquifolium (varieties)
Photinia x *fraseri* 'Red Robin'
Prunus laurocerasus
Pyracantha (varieties)
Rosa glauca
Rosa rugosa
Taxus baccata
Thuja plicata 'Atrovirens'

are naturally dense – all ideal qualities for what you have in mind. Something coarser and more robust – *Rosa rugosa*, for example – would be almost impossible to keep at this small size, however, because of its tremendous vigour and wayward habit, and in trying to keep it under some sort of control you would be continually cutting off all the flowering shoots.

Hedges are, of course, composed of plants – in this respect they are the same as a shrub border or rose bed – and, as with ornamental plants, to get the best results from them you need to keep the plants adequately supplied with moisture and nutrients to achieve healthy growth. It is, therefore, important that the ground is prepared as thoroughly as for any ornamental planting, particularly when you bear in mind that your closely spaced hedging plants will be competing strongly for the available moisture and nutrients within a limited space. It is essential to ensure that the soil is completely weed free, and you can improve its overall quality and condition by the addition of bulky organic matter, such as rotted farmyard manure or garden compost, and slow-acting fertilizers. Watering immediately after planting and at regular intervals thereafter is equally important, and mulching the soil with bark, garden compost or an artificial material, such as black polythene, will be an aid to both moisture retention and in keeping the soil free of weeds.

Hedges grown purely for their foliage effect can be trimmed as required, either when they are actively growing or just before growth is about to start in early spring. Use hand or powered shears to achieve the best finish with coniferous hedges and other types with small or soft leaves and stems. For varieties of plant that have large, leathery leaves, such as common laurel (*Prunus laurocerasus*), or strong, heavy stems, such as *Rosa rugosa*, use secateurs or a sharp knife for a neater pruning cut. Shears and trimmers will not necessarily cause such hedges any harm, but the appearance as a result of such trimming is usually unsatisfactory because the damaged leaves turn brown before they fall and look unsightly. Flowering hedges need to be pruned or trimmed with a little more thought so that you do not make the mistake of removing the wood that is about to flower. In general, hedges that flower early in the year – forsythia, for example – should be pruned immediately after flowering by cutting out all or a proportion of the old, flowering wood, while those that flower on new wood later in summer, such as roses, can be pruned harder in late winter or early spring. In both cases, however, if you trim flowering hedges too frequently you will risk cutting off the majority of the flowering wood at some stage. For this reason, if for no other, flowering hedges are generally more effective and flower better if they are allowed to put on more growth than those grown only for their foliage. Flowering hedges, therefore, need more room in which to develop.

Pergolas and arches

It is worth including pergolas and arches in your garden design for several reasons:

- ✳ They can be used to frame a particularly attractive view or focal point.
- ✳ They can link different parts of a garden.
- ✳ They are useful for dividing a garden into two or more separate areas, where a wall or fence would be too solid for the purpose.
- ✳ They can provide excellent support for a wide range of climbing plants.
- ✳ They can be used to introduce height into a garden where a tree or another solid object would not be suitable.
- ✳ They can instantly transform a garden, or part of a garden, for what is often a modest cost.

You can select from quite a wide range of materials to build your pergola or arch, depending on the chosen style or theme of your garden. These materials include wood (both hard and soft), metal, brick and stone, although the brick and stone are more usually found used in a combination with either wood or metal. It is even possible to find examples made from recycled plastic, made to look like wood, which are completely maintenance free.

Although you may come across many elaborate and complicated pergola and arch designs, the most effective designs are often the simplest, particularly if you bear in mind that an expensive ornamental arch that is completely hidden by luxuriant climbers is going to look exactly the same as a much simpler, cheaper arch that is completely hidden by the same luxuriant climbers.

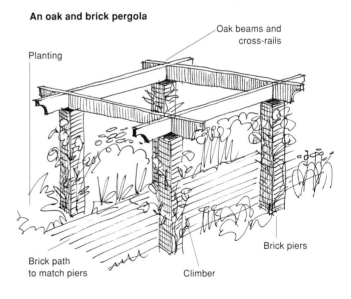

An oak and brick pergola

Oak beams and cross-rails

Planting

Brick piers

Brick path to match piers

Climber

In general, you will probably find that structures made from softwood are the least expensive to buy and construct, whether they are made from square-edged, sawn timber or from simple round, rustic poles with the bark still attached. It

Left: A pergola is not a difficult feature to build. This example, made from standard-sized timbers, incorporates ready-made trellis panels, which provide additional support for climbers. All the wood has been stained the same colour.

Below: An unusual and eye-catching black-painted metal archway is a perfect support for the rambling rose *Rosa* 'Adélaïde d'Orléans'.

is essential, however, whatever your choice, that any parts of a wooden construction that come into contact with the ground should be well treated with a suitable timber preservative or stain. Ideally, you will get the best results by using wood that has already been pressure-treated at the sawmill, and this will last for many years. Remember that if you have to cut this type of timber after it has been treated, you will have to apply extra preservative or stain to the newly exposed faces. Hardwood, such as oak, is also an excellent material to use, although its main drawback is its relatively high cost compared with much cheaper softwood. However, hardwood is naturally much more durable, and you do not need to treat it as thoroughly to prevent rot as you would a softwood.

Metal arches and structures are also usually more expensive than the equivalent designs in softwood, and you should paint them with a suitable metal primer, followed by one, if not two, coats of an exterior quality gloss paint that is suitable for the purpose. Be careful when you are fixing these into the ground, because even tiny chips to the paint may expose the bare metal beneath and allow rust to take hold. The best treatment for structures made from wrought iron or mild steel is to have them galvanized and then powder-coated to your desired colour. These processes are specialized and can be expensive, but the finished quality is excellent.

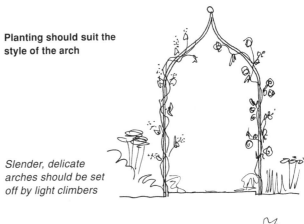

Planting should suit the style of the arch

Slender, delicate arches should be set off by light climbers

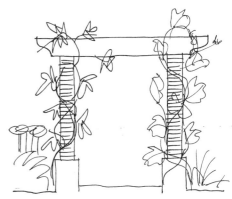

Heavy, solid structures need more vigorous climbers with large leaves

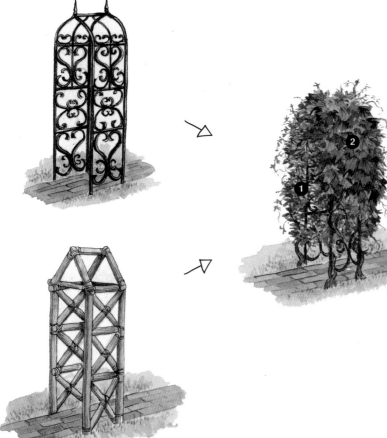

Two different styles of ornamental arches, before and after planting. If they are heavily planted, both the wrought iron and rustic arches will eventually have the same effect

Key to planting
1 *Lonicera periclymenum* 'Belgica'
2 *Vitis vinifera* 'Purpurea'

Brick and stone piers that are used to support wooden or metal overhead beams will need adequate concrete foundations, but, provided that the brick or stone you have chosen is frost resistant and well laid, they will need no further treatment or maintenance and should last you indefinitely. This method of construction for arches and pergolas is probably the most expensive because of the large amount of labour that it entails, particularly if you use a hardwood such as oak to make the horizontal cross-beams and rails, but the finished structure should not only last a lifetime but will look splendid.

A summerhouse need not look out of place in even a small town garden. The comparatively large gravelled area prevents the design from looking too cluttered.

Garden buildings

Garden buildings can range from tiny lean-to greenhouses, which are barely large enough to stand up in, to large, purpose-built summerhouses in which you can hold a dinner party. Whatever their size, they are elements of a garden design that are all too often placed with little thought of how their purpose and appearance will affect the rest of the garden. For simplicity, these buildings can be divided into two main categories: those that are purely practical or utilitarian, such as basic aluminium greenhouses and wooden sheds, and those that are much more ornamental in appearance, such as summerhouses and gazebos.

Buildings that are purely functional should ideally be sited in the most convenient place for their purpose, so that a greenhouse would be most useful and effective if it were placed in a sunny part of the kitchen or vegetable garden, while a shed for bicycles, toys and the winter storage of garden furniture would be better if it were located close to the backdoor of your house or somewhere near the patio. However, to be cost effective, many examples of this type of utility building look extremely basic, partly because of the way they are designed and partly because of the materials used to construct them, and their functional appearance often means that placing them in the most convenient and practical positions makes them not only obtrusive but also even eyesores. To get round this problem you will have to decide at an early stage which aspect is going to be the more important to you – appearance or convenience. If, as is often the case, the answer is not immediately obvious, you need to try to achieve a compromise. This might mean, for example, building a trellis screen around your shed on which you can grow vigorous, leafy, possibly evergreen, climbers in order to camouflage it. Alternatively, you might have to place the greenhouse in a position that is not absolutely ideal from the plants' point of view, and this might mean that, although not all of your tomatoes will ripen, the greenhouse itself will be at least partly out of the main line of sight from the sitting room window.

Summerhouses and gazebos, although fulfilling definite roles, are also ornamental by their nature

Positioning garden buildings

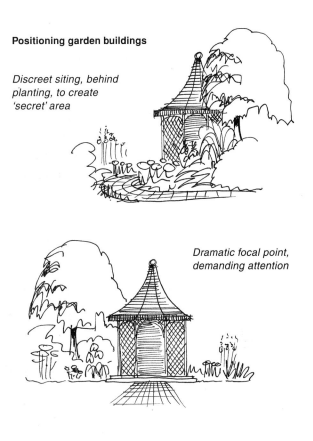

Discreet siting, behind planting, to create 'secret' area

Dramatic focal point, demanding attention

Bringing the summerhouse forwards a little, gives the garden a new dimension by creating a 'hidden' area beyond it, which could be used for a statue or other feature

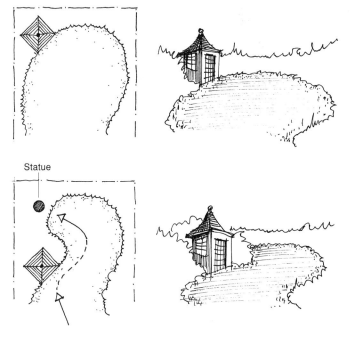

Statue

The same plants can be used to create very different results

This arrangement allows room around the gazebo and gives a feeling of space while drawing attention to the gazebo itself. The impression of space is enhanced by raising the paving beneath it

Here, by closing in the same planting and by keeping the paving low, there is a much greater sensation of privacy and enclosure

and, as such, they can be used in a design to make a positive contribution to the garden as features in their own right. Deciding to draw attention to them deliberately is more a matter of choice than of absolute necessity, and they can be equally effective whether positioned in full view as a focal point or tucked away in a secluded, private corner as a surprise. Whichever approach you choose, any garden building will be far more effective where room is left around the sides and back of it for generous planting, which will act as a natural, sympathetic frame and backdrop.

The cost of garden buildings, whatever their purpose, can vary tremendously according to their size, style and the materials used. Many sheds and greenhouses, for example, are available in standard sizes and in kit form, which makes them economical compared with similar buildings that

may need to be specially made. Small, simple models, such as a basic wooden garden shed, can usually be assembled relatively easily, but large, complicated designs, such as a brick summerhouse with a tiled roof, will probably require professional expertise and assistance at some stage in the construction process.

All types of garden buildings will last longer and look better if they are erected on a solid, level base, to which they can be anchored if necessary for greater strength and stability. For utility buildings, a base of mass concrete or of plain concrete flags bedded onto a compacted layer of hardcore is usually quite adequate when keeping the cost to a minimum is more important than the general appearance. Ornamental summerhouses and gazebos really deserve a base that is more attractive and appealing, however, and you may want to consider York stone flags, old bricks laid in a herringbone or basket-weave pattern, or any other material that will complement the structure and be in keeping with other areas of paving and materials elsewhere in the garden. Garden buildings made from softwood will need regular treatment with stain or preservative to prevent the timber from rotting and to keep it looking good, and you could select a colour that is used on other timber features elsewhere in the garden. Hardwood structures may not need treating merely to prevent rot setting in, but they will nevertheless look and weather better if they are stained occasionally. Better still, treat them regularly with wood oil, which will enhance the natural colour.

Beds, borders and planting

Plants, regardless of whether they are tall, stately trees or tiny alpines, are the finishing touches in a garden, and with the huge range of varieties that is now available from nurseries and garden centres there can hardly be any situation for which suitable plants cannot be found.

Before you make your final choice of individual plant varieties, you need to take an overall view of your garden design and make sure that you are happy with the basic purpose of each bed, border or group of plants. One particular grouping of plants may need to be wholly practical – a clump of tall evergreen shrubs to screen the compost area, for instance. On the other hand, the purpose of a planting might be more symbolic – for example, two trees on either side of a path to create the illusion or suggestion of an arch or gateway leading into the garden beyond. At the same time as deciding on the purpose of the individual plants or groups of plants that you have selected, you should also consider the garden as

Even in small gardens the careful placing of a tree or large shrub can create an illusion of secrecy and hidden space

Using plants for different effects

Tall shrubs for screening

Trees used to create a 'gateway'

being an overall composition, which needs an underlying structure in the same way a book or painting does. You can achieve such a structure by carefully placing trees and large shrubs, especially evergreens, in key positions to form a permanent, large-scale framework within the garden. Into this overall scheme, you can add smaller plants and garden features, such as containers and ornaments. Without these larger, woody plants, many gardens would be flat and uninteresting, especially in the winter months when the smaller, deciduous shrubs and most perennial plants will be either mere skeletons or non-existent. Small gardens may need only one small tree and three or four large evergreen shrubs to create a more than adequate framework or structure, whereas larger gardens will usually need proportionately more and larger plants to achieve the same effect.

Having established the purpose – practical or aesthetic or a combination of the two – of your various planting areas, you will want to begin selecting individual plant varieties that are not only going to help you achieve the desired visual effect but that are going to be healthy and thrive where they are planted. There is no point, for example, in planting a tree that will screen an unsightly view when it is 5 metres (16ft) tall, if the ground conditions where it is planted will not allow it to grow to that height. In order to avoid this kind of disappointment and to make your planting a success, you must choose plants that are well-suited by nature to the particular physical conditions in which they are being expected to grow – for example, a dry, acid soil in shade – or you must eliminate or change the conditions to suit the particular needs of the plants, whatever they may be. Of these two approaches, the former is to be preferred wherever possible, if only from the point of view of convenience, whereas the latter should be attempted if there are no sensible alternatives or, possibly, where the effort and cost required to make the changes are not considered excessive in relation to the benefits you will ultimately gain from them.

Trees in lawns make excellent specimens, but the grass beneath will suffer or even die, especially beneath an evergreen such as yew (*Taxus*)

Make a feature of the tree by using log edging to create a slightly raised area beneath the crown, covered with bark and emphasized with a seat

Key to planting
1 *Elaeagnus* x *ebbingei*
2 *Corylus maxima* 'Purpurea'
3 *Miscanthus sinensis* 'Zebrinus'
4 *Geranium* x *oxonianum* 'Wargrave Pink'
5 *Hydrangea macrophylla* 'Blue Wave'
6 *Juniperus virginiana* 'Sulphur Spray'
7 *Luzula sylvatica*
8 *Euonymus fortunei* 'Emerald 'n' Gold'
9 *Leucanthemum* x *superbum* 'Wirral Supreme'

It is impossible to overstress the importance of complete and thorough ground preparation for any planting areas, especially in new gardens, where you may encounter all manner of problems. This may be the best, if not the only, opportunity you will have to thoroughly dig over,

Applying a layer of mulch in newly planted beds and borders not only helps to retain moisture in the soil but will also act as a weed suppressant. A mulch of a material such as bark chippings generally looks more attractive than bare soil.

clean and improve the soil, to check the quality of drainage and generally get the beds into good shape while there is nothing to impede your progress. Any problems in these areas that are not tackled at this early stage will almost certainly be infinitely more difficult and inconvenient to sort out once the garden is planted and established. It is always almost irresistible to try to fill up a plot of bare soil with plants as soon as possible, to see a little bit of colour and interest, but there is a great danger that in doing this you might cut corners for short-term gain and pay the price later on with problems such as badly water-logged lawns or borders infested with perennial weeds, such as ground elder.

Once they are planted and beginning to become established, most woody plants – that is, trees, shrubs and conifers – and perennials will grow better and keep in good health if they are given additional food in one form or another from time to time during the growing season. There are many types of proprietary fertilizer now available that will do this job and that are quick and convenient to apply. Such fertilizers are usually added directly to the soil by way of powders, granules or as liquids diluted with water. Some of these liquid forms can also be conveniently sprayed directly onto plant foliage for a quicker effect. However, the addition to the soil of organic matter, such as home-made garden compost, leaf mould or rotted farmyard manure, is even better since it not only provides nutrition to the plant roots over a relatively long period but it will also improve the physical structure of the soil, whether it is clay or sand, and increase its moisture- and nutrient-holding capacity. As a further bonus, a thick layer of well-prepared compost applied to the soil's surface makes an excellent mulch for keeping weeds at bay and is also gradually broken down into the soil, thereby improving its structure.

Lawns

Although it is one of the simplest of all garden features, a well-tended lawn can make all the difference to a garden. A sparse, weedy patch of rough grass can, however, completely spoil the appearance of what might otherwise be an attractive plot. One of the commonest reasons for the failure of many lawns to live up to the gardener's expectations is the fact that they are not treated with the same degree of care and respect that might be given to expensive shrubs or trees, even though their potential value in a garden, especially relative to their cost, is probably greater than any other single feature. Paying attention to a few basic details, most notably in the preparation stages before the turf is laid or the seed is sown, can provide you with the basis for a long-lived, healthy and attractive lawn that will complement the rest of your garden.

Whether you choose to turf or seed the area that will be the lawn, it is vital to prepare the ground as thoroughly as if it were going to be a shrub bed or herbaceous border, and while this

---

Planting in a restricted area

When planting space is limited, the correct selection of plants is more critical than in any other type of garden. Wherever possible, you should choose varieties that will provide either an extended period of flowering interest or that will contribute in other ways as well as flowering – for example, with additional winter stem colour, berries and fruits, autumn leaf colour or handsome, striking evergreen foliage. Plants that will thrive in the shade or in dry conditions caused by larger shrubs and trees are also invaluable for underplanting so that you can make the best use of all the available planting areas.

Although a lawn requires more regular and frequent attention than any other garden feature in terms of mowing and maintenance, a well-tended lawn pays dividends. If you have children who will use the lawn for playing, choose one of the harder wearing utility mixes of lawn seed.

might at first glance appear to be unnecessary work, the long-term benefits will make it worthwhile. You should, therefore, dig over the area to be grassed, forking out any rubbish, debris and all weed roots and then roughly grade it to the approximate finished levels that are required. The soil should then be trodden down and re-raked to achieve a more accurate level, raking off or knocking down high spots and moving soil around to fill in low ones. Once you are generally happy with the level, it will pay you to leave the area alone for a while, possibly several weeks, which will not only allow any weed seeds in the soil to germinate but will also give pieces of

perennial weed root left behind time to sprout leaves, so that both types can then be eradicated. During this 'fallow' period, the soil will have time to settle, and you will be able to see if there are any low or high spots that you have missed. When you have eliminated this flush of weeds, you should rake and roll the lawn area once or twice more to achieve a final smooth, firm, level bed that is free of stones and any other debris, leaving a fine tilth ready for seed sowing or turf laying. At the time of the final raking, you can also add a fertilizer – choose the appropriate type, depending on whether you are going to seed or turf the lawn – which will help in the early establishment of the grass. The timing of all these operations can be quite critical to the ulti-mate success of your lawn, and you should work on the basis that lawns, whether grown from seed or turf, are best sown or laid in mid- to late spring or early to mid-autumn because, at these times of year, both soil temperatures and moisture levels are more or less ideal for both methods.

Select the type of grass seed or turf according to the level of wear and tear and quality of finish that you want or need. In doing this, remember that perennial rye grass, in its various forms, is hard wearing and usually has good winter colour. It is, however, quite coarse and requires frequent cutting to keep it looking respectable. Finer grasses, such as fescues and bents, are not usually quite so hard wearing as rye grass and can sometimes look a little sad in winter. They do make a neater lawn though, are generally more tolerant of drier, poorer soils, and can be cut less frequently than lawns that are made from the more vigorous grass types.

In terms of cost, and all other things being equal, a turfed lawn will invariably be more expensive than one grown directly from seed. The main advantage of turf over seed, however, is that it is possible to use the lawn almost as soon as the turves have rooted into each other and into the soil below, and in an ideal situation, depending on the time of year, this could be within three to four weeks of being laid. Seeded lawns, on the other hand, may require a complete growing season before the grass seedlings are strong enough, and have knitted together sufficiently, to take anything other than light or infrequent use.

The other distinct advantage of turf over seed is that once it is laid, turf will prevent any weed seeds still present on or near the surface of the soil from germinating and becoming established. In a seeded lawn, the soil effectively remains bare until the grass has germinated and has grown sufficiently to cover it – during this period, weed seeds also have the opportunity to grow, although most such weeds will be eliminated after the grass has been cut once or twice.

Once your lawn is established, regular mowing while the grass is actively growing, from spring to autumn, will help to keep it neat and dense. Removing the grass clippings when mowing will help to prevent a build-up of thatch (dead vegetation), which can encourage pests and diseases, but by doing this you will also be removing nutrients that would, in the normal course, be returned to the soil when the grass leaves rotted down. These nutrients need to be replaced, therefore, and you can do this by feeding the lawn with a proprietary lawn dressing or fertilizer in spring and again in autumn, at which time you should also rake the lawn with a spring-tine rake to remove dead grass, moss and any thatch that may be present. Regular rolling will help to keep the turf smooth and level, which will allow closer cutting, and discourage moss, which can tend to become established in shady or damp areas and quickly takes over from the grass.

Water features

Almost every garden can be enhanced by the addition of water in one form or another, whether it takes the form of a dramatic, formal cascade with many fountains or a tiny wooden half-barrel, containing a miniature waterlily and standing on the patio next to the backdoor. Water will always bring an extra, undefinable quality or dimension to a garden, and it is worth making a little extra effort to include a water feature in one form or another in your own design for that reason.

Whatever material you use to construct your water feature, it must, above all, be completely waterproof, and it must also be made from a

Water always brings an indefinable character to the garden, and a wall-mounted spout such as this takes up little room while providing the perfect environment for lush foliage plants, including ferns.

material that is not going to rot or deteriorate with age, which would make it prone to leaks. There are three main ways of constructing most water features, and your choice will depend partly on your budget and partly on your level of skill:

+ Rigid, pre-formed shapes.
+ Flexible pond liners.
+ Purpose-built concrete or brick ponds.

The most foolproof of the three methods is to use a rigid, waterproof container, which might be an off-the-shelf, pre-formed fibreglass or plastic pond or something even simpler (and possibly cheaper), such as a plastic cold water tank, which you would get from a builder's merchant. If you want your pond or feature to be set flush in the ground, it is necessary only to excavate a generous hole, make the bottom of this firm and level and then, once the container is in place, carefully backfill around it with fine soil or sand to make sure that the sides are fully supported before it is filled with water. Do use a spirit level to check that the top edges of your tank or container are level before adding water – if the top edges are not absolutely level, the effect will be one of water apparently on the slope, which can be quite disturbing to the eye. If you intend to keep fish, it is worth avoiding metal containers, which could

A raised pond made out of railway sleepers and a flexible liner, with a wooden board edge for seating

Key to planting
1. *Spiraea japonica* 'Gold Mound' or *S. j.* 'Golden Princess'
2. *Phormium tenax*
3. *Viburnum plicatum* 'Mariesii'
4. *Ligularia dentata* 'Desdemona'
5 *Elaeagnus* x *ebbingei*
6 *Iris pseudacorus* 'Variegata'
7 *Picea pungens* 'Hoopsii' or *P. p.* 'Koster'
8 *Miscanthus sinensis* (or a variety)
9 *Juniperus sabina* 'Tamariscifolia' or *J. horizontalis*
10 *Nymphaea* 'Marliacea Rosea'
11 *Caltha palustris* var. *palustris* 'Plena'

contaminate the water and prove toxic to the fish, unless, of course, you are able to seal them beforehand with a couple of coats of proprietary bituminous or other suitable sealant.

The second method, and probably the most popular, is to line a hole in the ground with a flexible liner. This can be anything ranging from a piece of builder's polythene to heavy gauge, butyl rubber of a quality that may be suitable for lining reservoirs. With almost all pond liners you will get what you pay for – the cheaper, thinner liners are usually less resistant to wear and tear and have a shorter life than the better quality, more expensive types, mainly because, unless they are completely immersed in water, they will gradually degrade through constant exposure to the ultraviolet rays from sunlight and become brittle and weak. Constructing a pool with a flexible liner requires more care and effort than installing a rigid container. First, the excavation must be 'masked' with a layer of soft sand, old carpet underlay or a proprietary matting so that the liner cannot be punctured by underlying sharp stones. Then, the edge of the pond liner must be fixed and concealed, and this is most usually achieved by laying a narrow path on top of it, around the edge of the pond, using paving slabs, bricks or stone laid on a wet bed of cement–sand mortar.

Raised ponds and water features can also be built using pond liners. If you choose to do this, you use the liner to cloak the inside of a rigid box structure, which might be made from brick, concrete, stone or even wood. Remember that this structure must be strong enough to withstand the water pressure behind it. One of the main attractions of this arrangement is that you can then use the edge of your pool as a seat.

The third method of building a water feature is to construct a strong, purpose-built, rigid structure from bricks, concrete blocks and/or

Positioning an informal pond

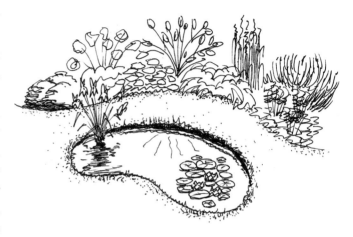

Small, informal – or natural – ponds may look lost and out of keeping when they are placed in isolation

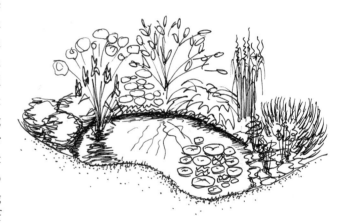

Incorporating the pond into the edge of a bed or border provides a stronger background and is also good for wildlife

concrete. This can be made completely waterproof by either sealing it with a suitable pond paint or else by applying a fibreglass skin, which is both waterproof and flexible. This type of structure, while probably being the most difficult and expensive to create, will make the best and most durable water feature if built correctly, whether it is set into the ground, is raised above it or is a combination of the two.

The safety of small children around water is always a concern, and one way to get round this is to create a 'safe' water feature. In simple terms this involves placing a small tank in the ground as in the first method, covering it with metal re-inforcing mesh, strong enough to take the weight of your chosen feature, placing the feature on this and covering the rest of the mesh with small rocks, cobbles or shingle. A submersible pump in the tank is used to move the water up into the feature – a bubble fountain or drilled boulder, for example – and it then trickles back into the tank to be recycled.

A millstone water feature

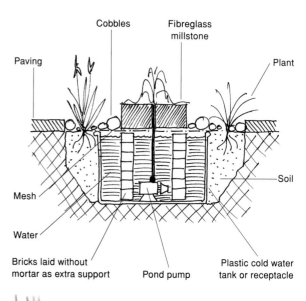

Key to planting
1 *Carex pendula*
2 *Juniperus squamata* 'Blue Star'
3 *Cornus alba* 'Elegantissima'
4 *Iris sibirica*
5 *Viburnum tinus*
6 *Miscanthus sacchariflorus*
7 *Hosta* 'Honeybells'
8 *Euphorbia characias* ssp. *wulfenii*
9 *Astilbe* x *arendsii* 'Fanal'

Containers

One of the most fascinating aspects of container gardening and one that attracts many of its devotees is the fact that virtually any plant can, at some stage of its life, be grown in a container, regardless of its ultimate natural size. Traditionally, many varieties of annual bedding plants, such as pelargonium, lobelia and petunia, make excellent seasonal container displays, usually from late spring or early summer to the first frosts of winter. The use of herbaceous perennials, shrubs and even small trees, such as hostas, azaleas and Japanese maples, for a more permanent or long-lasting effect in pots and tubs is rapidly gaining in popularity. A third type of plant that can also be successfully grown in containers is the edible kind, particularly salad crops and herbs. Soft fruit, such as strawberries and blackcurrants, and even some varieties of apple are also suitable for container culture.

Where and when to use containers is often determined by personal taste, but they really come into their own as a growing option where space for traditional planting is limited or where there is no garden at all in the recognized sense – for example, on the balcony of an apartment or flat. The question of what to use for growing the plants in is unimportant, because virtually any receptacle that will hold an adequate amount of suitable soil or compost can be used. Terracotta and stone pots will look more attractive and complement other planting better than, say, recycled tin cans and old plastic buckets, but, provided that there are adequate drainage holes at the bottom and there is no risk of the soil or compost being contaminated by the fabric of the container, almost anything will suffice.

In addition to plastic, stone, terracotta and wood pots and troughs, hanging baskets and window boxes are the most traditional types of

Container gardening

The following list illustrates a few examples of different containers and the materials from which they are made.

Plastic pots
- Ordinary pots, bought from garden centres and nurseries, are plain but relatively cheap.
- Moulded and ornamental pots, sometimes made to look like terracotta but available in other colours, are cheaper and lighter than the real thing.

Terracotta
- Mass-produced plain varieties cost more than plastic pots and they are readily available; the cheapest ones, however, may not be frostproof.
- Ornamental, heavily decorated, larger pots are heavy and more expensive than plain versions. Hand-made pots, which are elegant and expensive, are also sometimes available in extremely large sizes.

Wood
- Oak half-barrels, which are available in various sizes, are quite economical.
- Square and rectangular planters, made from pressure-treated softwood, compare well in price with terracotta pots.
- Hardwood planters – the Versailles type – are elegant and long lasting but expensive. They are available in both natural and stained finishes.

Metal
- Not readily available off-the-shelf, although some reproductions, based on antique lead urns and the like, are being made.

Stone
- Generally more expensive than most other kinds, stone pots are heavy, but extremely durable and improve with age. They are usually available as urns and troughs.

container. However, many other, less obvious objects can be put to good use, including:

Antique chimney pots
Old wooden wheelbarrows
Galvanized watering cans
Enamel buckets
Car wheels (with a bit of work!)
Porcelain WCs
Enamel and stone sinks
Rocks or large boulders with holes
    in the centre

Probably the main difference to be aware of between growing plants in containers and in the open ground is the limited amount of space that is available for root growth and moisture retention in any but the largest of containers. To try to compensate for this, it is worth using the best quality proprietary compost, which can be either soil-less or loam-based, and sometimes even a mixture of the two, to provide the best possible conditions for adequate root development. A loam-based compost will be much heavier than the equivalent volume of soil-less compost, and you should bear this in mind if you need to move your containers around. Frequent watering is also essential to the success of any container planting, and with few exceptions you should never allow the rootballs of plants in containers to become bone-dry or frozen solid.

When annuals are planted in containers, the young plants are inserted into new compost at the beginning of each season so that there is a regular renewal of the growing medium. However, woody plants and perennials, which are to remain in their containers for a long period, will eventually become pot-bound or too large for their allotted space. When this stage is reached you have to make the choice between either repotting or potting on the plant. Repotting involves knocking the plant out of its

Containers provide an excellent way of creating seasonal focal points, as illustrated by this terracotta chimney pot planted with summer-flowering annuals.

container, teasing out and cutting off a proportion of the old, matted rootball and replacing the plant in its original pot or container, using fresh compost to take the place of the soil or rootball that you have removed. Repotting is a technique that is usually resorted to when the plant or the container has reached the maximum size that you can reasonably cope with. For large containers, when repotting is impractical, an alternative is to top dress by scraping off a layer of old compost from on top of the existing rootball, usually no more than 25–50mm (10–20in) deep, and replacing it with fresh. Potting on, or replanting, on the other hand, is simply a process of moving the plant into the next available size of container until you reach a stage where it becomes either impractical or unnecessary to move it into anything larger, after which repotting or top dressing can be used as above.

It is common to fill pots and containers with too many plants in order to achieve an instant effect of maturity, especially when you are using annual bedding, and you may find that the food value of your compost becomes seriously depleted well before the end of the growing season so that your plants begin to suffer. You will, therefore, need to supplement the nutrition, and this can be achieved by sprinkling soluble fertilizer on to the surface of the compost so that it is watered in, by regular liquid or foliar feeding or by inserting proprietary granules of controlled-release fertilizer into the pot, which should provide food for a full season. Whichever type of

Containers are a useful way of controlling invasive plants such as mint or, as here, variegated ground elder (*Aegopodium podagraria* 'Variegatum').

fertilizer you use, make sure that its chemical composition is suitable for the type of plant you are intending to grow, which will depend on whether the main attraction is the flowers, the fruit or the foliage. However, if you have a mixture of these plants in a single container you should use a general-purpose fertilizer, which will provide a balanced diet, as it were, for the best overall results.

Ornaments and garden furniture

Garden ornaments, rather like household ornaments, can be very personal objects, and using them allows you to put your own final touches to a garden. The range of subjects suitable for use as ornaments is extensive, and almost anything, from sculptures to statues, sundials to bird tables, and even individual rocks or pieces of driftwood as mementoes of an enjoyable holiday, can find a home in your garden.

Although the selection of ornaments will ultimately be determined by your own individual taste, they are more likely to be effective and add an extra dimension to the garden if you can choose them to suit the particular setting in which they will be displayed. For example, an antique, stone figurine might be more at home in a cottage-style or old-fashioned garden than an abstract, stainless steel sculpture would. Similarly, a bright orange, glazed urn could strike a discordant note if it is placed among a herbaceous border where the colour theme deliberately revolves around pale blues, yellows and whites. Heavily ornamented, large or intricate ornaments are usually best placed in isolation – in the centre of a lawn, for example – or against a plain, contrasting background such as a yew hedge. Simpler or smaller objects on the other hand, such as beach cobbles, are often better displayed in groups and can be enhanced by allowing low plants to creep over and among them.

Placing ornaments

Key to planting
1 *Kniphofia* 'Ada'
2 *Acanthus mollis*
3 *Leucanthemum* x *superbum* 'Wirral Supreme'
4 *Lavandula angustifolia* 'Hidcote'

Place a pale coloured, intricate piece of sculpture or ornament against a plain, dark background, such as a yew hedge

Place plain, dark ornaments against a pale, busy background. Note that the colour of the lavender flowers picks out the colour of the pot

A glorious wisteria provides the perfect frame for the ornamental wrought iron seat. Wisterias are not self-clinging and require support so that their flowers can be seen at their best.

Create a succession of focal points that are not all visible from a single place

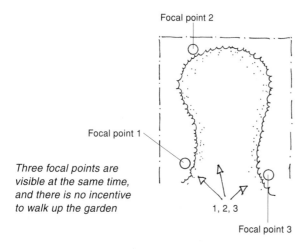

Focal point 2

Focal point 1

Three focal points are visible at the same time, and there is no incentive to walk up the garden

1, 2, 3

Focal point 3

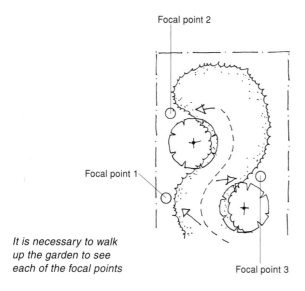

Focal point 2

Focal point 1

It is necessary to walk up the garden to see each of the focal points

Focal point 3

Placing ornaments at the most obvious or natural focal points is a basic principle of garden design and an effective way of using them, but you can often use them to equal effect by putting them in less likely situations – for example, positioning a stone frog so that it pokes out from beneath an evergreen shrub – to create an unexpected element of surprise or humour. Do make sure, though, that your chosen ornaments are suitable for outdoor use or that you take suitable precautions to safeguard them if they are not. Wooden objects, for example, are likely to rot, especially if they are placed directly on soil or they will become overgrown with mosses and algae if placed in shady, damp places. You may also find that some terracotta pots and figures are not completely frostproof and will need to be brought into a frost-free place over winter or, if they are left outside, be adequately protected with sacking and polythene.

Garden furniture must first and foremost be suitable for its intended purpose, and it should, therefore, be practical, comfortable and, of course, affordable. The style and material of your chosen furniture can, however, have a significant effect on how it looks in the garden and also on how much room it might take up. For example, a two-seater bench made out of delicate, white-painted wrought iron will appear to be much lighter and actually take up less space on the ground than an equivalent bench made out of heavy, dark-coloured hardwood. Your selection of furniture must, therefore, take into account the space that is available in the part of the garden where it will be used, such as on the patio or beneath an arbour, or, if necessary, you might have to make the areas larger to accommodate your choice.

Apart from the amount of room that it will take up, the appearance of any garden furniture should be considered, not just in terms of your own personal likes or dislikes, but also in the way it can influence, or be influenced by, the garden around it. Matching your furniture to a theme in your garden, whether it is to a particular colour, style or material, is probably the ideal way of ensuring that it is seen as an integral part of the overall design and not just an afterthought, and in small gardens especially, where space is at a premium, this approach can be vital to the success of your design.

Shape and proportion

How do you know if something is a square, a rectangle or some other shape altogether? The simple solution, of course, is to measure it and draw it on a piece of paper. But at what point does this shape start to become long and thin, or maybe shallow and wide, rather than just being a rectangle? Unfortunately, there is no simple mathematical formula to show you that what appears to be a nicely proportioned garden 15 metres wide by 30 metres long (50 x 100ft) suddenly turns into a long, thin, awkwardly shaped garden just because it happens to be 31 metres long and 14 metres wide (102 x 46ft). What happens in reality is that your eye looks at the garden and quickly receives certain visual information, which it passes on to your brain, and the message that it cleverly sends to you is that 'this garden looks long and thin to me'!

What is significant about this rather simplified statement is the fact that your brain is able to reach its conclusion based on only a small amount of quite straightforward information – just a few straight or curved lines – and this gives a major clue as to how you might be able easily to manipulate a shape, whether it is an entire garden plot or just a small part of it, to make it appear different by concealing those lines that send a certain kind of message to your brain and introducing new ones that send a different kind of message.

Let us look at a simple example. Imagine that your present garden is formal, an effect that results from the fact that your beds and borders are straight-edged and square. It would be a simple matter to change the edges of these planting areas into long, flowing or sinuous curves, and in doing so completely transform the appearance of the garden into an informal one. You can control

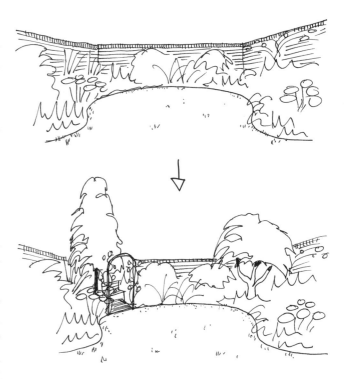

Corners can be dull areas, but it is possible to create interest by placing features that not only act as focal points but that disguise the angles where fences or walls meet

various effects in the garden by changing shapes, which are really nothing more than the spaces or areas enclosed by straight or curved lines. As we have already seen, square, angular or geometric shapes tend to be associated with formality, while random, undefined shapes suggest a feeling of informality. One way of explaining why this might be would be to consider two island beds, one a perfect square, the other an irregular, curved shape. Your eye is able to identify the four corners of the square and is easily led by the straight lines that connect them, in two directions only, from side to side or front to back. The curved bed, on the other hand, has no corners,

Right: The dense planting in the borders and the meandering shape of the lawn successfully disguise the rectangular shape of the garden. The effect is heightened by the focal point of the tree in the far corner.

Below: The grass path leading to a stone urn provides an axis on either side of which are identically shaped beds. The symmetry and formality of this arrangement is underlined by the box edging enclosing what might otherwise be a random collection of plants.

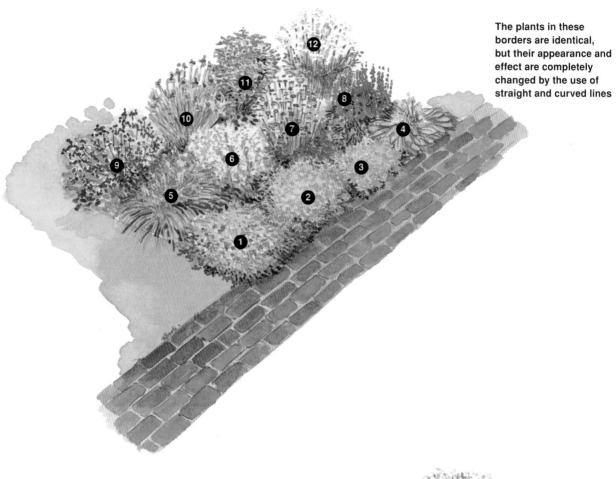

The plants in these borders are identical, but their appearance and effect are completely changed by the use of straight and curved lines

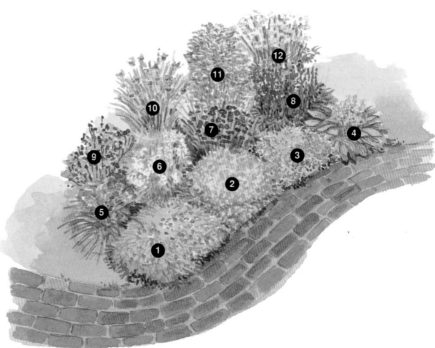

Key to planting

1 *Geranium* 'Johnson's Blue'
2 *Euphorbia polychroma*
3 *Aster novi-belgii* 'Lady in Blue'
4 *Hosta* Tardiana Group 'Halcyon'
5 *Hemerocallis* 'Stella de Oro'
6 *Phlox paniculata* 'White Admiral'
7 *Anchusa azurea* 'Loddon Royalist'
8 *Astilbe* x *arendsii* 'Bressingham Beauty'
9 *Heuchera* 'Rachel'
10 *Iris pallida* 'Variegata'
11 *Solidago* 'Cloth of Gold'
12 *Leucantheumum* x *superbum* 'Snowcap'

ends or other obvious starting points, and your eye is moving in ever-changing directions as it follows the curve around. This helps to explain why there is such a contrast between regular and irregular shapes and suggests a useful way of using different shapes for different purposes.

We have already noted the value of the way in which the relative proportions of some garden features, whether they are solid objects, such as trees, or flat spaces, such as paved areas or lawns, can be manipulated to change mood or atmosphere. Proportion is also valuable in another way that is more to do with providing balance in different areas of the garden. For example, if there was a large summerhouse in one corner of your garden with several tall trees and shrubs around it, and in the opposite corner there was only a tiny ornamental pot enclosed by a few low perennials, the effect would be unbalanced because of the difference in scale – or relative proportions – between one corner and the other. In planting schemes, in particular, the proportion between individual plants, or groups of plants, can make a significant difference. As an example, imagine a large, mature guelder rose (*Viburnum opulus*)

A large shrub will appear badly proportioned if it is accompanied by a single, small plant

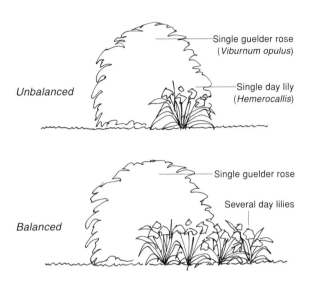

planted next to a single day lily (*Hemerocallis*). At maturity, the discrepancy in size between them would be immediately obvious, with the guelder rose being absolutely dominant. However, if you were to plant another nine or ten day lilies of the same variety, the relative proportions of the two would be radically changed, and there would be much greater balance between them.

Using plants' habits to accentuate a design

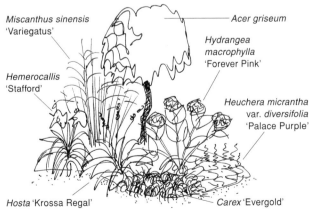

Plants with contrasting, varied habits lend themselves to informal designs

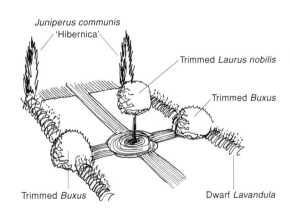

Use plants with naturally uniform, neat habits to emphasize formality in a design. Alternatively, choose varieties, such as box (Buxus) and yew (Taxus), which can be maintained as regular shapes by clipping

Quick and easy transformations

So far we have looked at the various man-made and natural features that can be used in gardens and have highlighted the various basic principles that can be applied to create a worthwhile and attractive garden design from them. The assumption has been that, working within your own constraints, which will be dictated by the space, money and time you can devote to the project, you will at some stage end up with a completely redesigned or revamped garden. However, what should you do if your circumstances are such that you are either unable or unwilling to undertake what might be potentially major garden works or alterations but nevertheless still feel unhappy with your garden, which might need a lift or boost? How can you quickly achieve what may seem a major impact with the minimum effort and outlay on your part?

There are two main ways to make a difference. The first of these is by modifying some of the features that are already in the garden; the second is to add one or two extra features to the existing layout. There is no reason, of course, why you should not do both. The starting point is to make a list of all the aspects of your garden that you are unhappy with – that is, your 'dislikes' – in order of their importance or irritation value. Taking each item on the list in turn, you need to identify the best way in which it can be improved – that is, does it require a modification or an addition?

For example, you might wish to emphasize the informal nature of your garden, which at present is marred by a perfectly straight concrete path running down the centre of the garden to the greenhouse. Replacing the offending path with a gently curving one, at the same time using a more sympathetic material such as an old brick, could completely change the effect.

Another typical example might be if you find the view from your garden unattractive or offensive – a view of the distant office block, say. In these circumstances you will need to add some form of screening by planting a carefully positioned group of small trees or large shrubs or by building a garden structure, such as a trellis, fence or a pergola planted with climbers, to block out the offending eyesore.

You will see that, in both of these examples – one the modification of an existing feature, the other the addition of something new – a fairly simple and relatively inexpensive change has solved a problem that may have seemed much greater than it really was and has resulted in a much improved garden and a happier gardener!

It may be, however, that the reason for your dissatisfaction is not so much a visual one as something more practical – the beds or borders adjoining the lawn are so tightly curved or wavy that mowing the grass is both time-consuming and difficult. Making the curves longer, and

Although this small town garden is over-looked by neighbouring houses, the climbing roses have been used to create a secluded spot for a small sitting area.

Privacy in the town garden

In many gardens there is always the chance that you will be overlooked from adjoining gardens or houses – quite possibly from more than one direction – and a degree of privacy can therefore sometimes be quite desirable or even essential. This can usually be achieved by the careful positioning of walls, fences and hedges along the boundaries that separate your garden from those of your neighbours. There are occasions, however, particularly in densely built-up areas of towns and cities, where being overlooked is a serious problem and where the garden boundary might actually be the wall of a two-storey building, and it would be impossible to screen such a wall in the traditional way. You will, therefore, need to identify the particular areas of your garden where privacy is needed – such as a patio or terrace – and build a screen around that particular area rather than against or near to the offending wall.

therefore effectively shallower and simpler, will do much to eliminate the source of irritation and also save valuable time, which you can use to enjoy the rest of the garden. Incidentally, the best way to achieve just the right curves is to run the mower fairly close to, but not right up against, the junction of the lawn and the border, taking a line that is comfortable for you to follow, and then you can simply re-shape your border edge to match that line.

There may also be occasions when taking something away from a garden can be as effective as adding something. Old fruit trees that are past their prime, bearing little or no fruit or that are canker-ridden and unsightly, with lots of die-back, are a common feature of many older and neglected gardens. Removing these trees will give you an opportunity to replace them with another healthy, ornamental tree of your choice or to open up the garden to other possibilities, such as creating space for a new border. Alternatively, the new space could become the location for a gazebo or summerhouse or you might reveal a previously undiscovered and attractive view that you could enhance in another way.

Opposite: **What was a fairly bland, uninviting corner with traditional straight-edged lawn and narrow borders has been transformed by simply covering the entire area with shingle, and adding some strategically placed plants and a small bench. The addition of a few stepping stones leading to the sitting area makes the corner more inviting**

Key to planting
1 *Miscanthus sacchariflorus*
2 *Elaeagnus pungens* 'Maculata'
3 *Potentilla fruticosa* 'Tangerine'
4 *Persicaria affinis* 'Superba' (syn. *Polygonum affine* 'Dimity')
5 *Berberis* x *ottawensis* 'Superba'
6 *Pinus mugo* 'Ophir'
7 *Caryopteris* x *clandonensis* 'Heavenly Blue'
8 *Phormium* 'Sundowner'
9 *Rosa glauca* (syn. *R. rubrifolia*)
10 *Cotoneaster* x *suecicus* 'Coral Beauty'
11 *Fargesia murieliae* (syn. *Arundinaria murieliae*)
12 *Ilex aquifolium* 'Silver Queen'
13 *Viburnum opulus* 'Aureum'
14 *Hydrangea serrata* 'Preziosa'
15 *Juniperus virginiana* 'Grey Owl'

Using screening to obscure eyesores and create privacy

Placing a screen near the offending objects (left) requires much greater height than placing it nearer to the viewer (right)

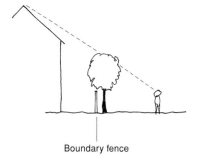
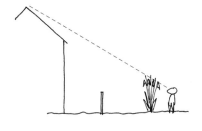

Boundary fence

Tall objects close to or even on your garden boundary are almost impossible to screen directly (left), so screen or enclose only the most important part of your garden (right)

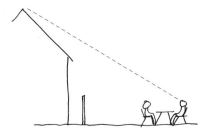
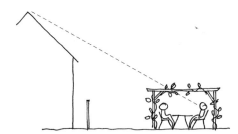

Traditional border and lawn

Gravel transformation

91

Ideas for quick transformations

Following are some suggestions and ideas for quick transformations that will almost certainly improve your garden for a minimum of cost, time and effort.

✴ Place individual features to act as focal points in positions that you can identify as needing some interest, such as a corner between two fences – arches, statues, seats and similar objects are all suitable.

✴ Cover areas of old, unsightly concrete or tarmac with pea shingle or stone chippings to create an attractive surface on which to stand pots, tubs and ornaments.

✴ Cover areas of poor, thin or patchy grass with a piece of mulching fabric or membrane, pinned down with hoops made from galvanized fencing wire. Plant through the fabric with a selection of shrubs, perennials and grasses, and mulch with shingle, stone chippings or ornamental grade bark for a low-maintenance finish.

✴ Screen particularly annoying or unsightly views and objects with groups of trees and

Containers can transform otherwise plain areas. Perennials, such as *Phormium* 'Sundowner', can be combined with less permanent bedding plants, such as busy lizzies (*Impatiens*).

shrubs for a natural effect or construct a trellis fence or pergola for a more immediate solution.

* Straight paths, especially those that run right down the middle of the garden or parallel to the boundary fence, can be unattractive and overdominant. Replace them with paths that are gently curving or that run in a zigzag fashion or diagonally to create more interest.

* Bland, uninteresting patios and areas of paving can be brightened by placing on them a selection of tubs, pots and other containers, planted with perennials and shrubs, including some evergreen varieties, as well as annuals, such as pelargoniums and lobelia, to provide interest all year round. You could introduce ornaments among the containers, such as large pebbles, small statues or unusually shaped pieces of wood or rock.

* In mixed borders of shrubs and perennials or beneath deciduous trees, plant spring-flowering bulbs, such as snowdrop, aconite, crocus and early narcissus. These will flower, grow leaves and die down again before they are overshadowed when the larger perennial plants above them come into leaf.

* In overcrowded shrub borders, cut down and grub out about every third plant, especially those that are past their best. This will create space into which the remaining shrubs can grow and allow them to develop into a better shape as well as improving their flowering potential. The bare soil that this exposes can be planted with perennials and low, ground-cover shrubs, which will not hinder the growth of the larger specimens.

* Once your beds and borders are free of weeds, mulch them with dark, ornamental grade bark chippings – this not only conserves moisture but helps to prevent the germination of annual weed seeds – and it also looks good, too.

Ideas for focal points

Many gardens may fail in terms of general appeal because they lack a focal point or points, which can be used to attract attention and create extra interest in a garden. Whatever you choose as a focal point, remember that it does not need to be large or overly dramatic – indeed, you could argue that a focal point that is too large or dramatic will completely dominate the view of a garden at the expense of other smaller, but nonetheless equally interesting, features. In a typical garden, the introduction of two or three points of interest, such as a statue, a small water feature and an arch that have been carefully placed so that you see them in a succession as you walk up the garden, rather than having them all in view at the same time, can make an enormous difference to the overall appearance for what is often a relatively modest cost and amount of effort on the part of the gardener.

This list of ideas for focal points is not intended to be fully comprehensive because almost anything can, in theory, be used to attract attention – even an old enamel bath planted with pelargoniums. Nonetheless, there are plenty of suggestions to enhance your design.

Water features

Water in all its forms makes a striking feature in any garden. Still water can be used to reflect an attractive tree or statue positioned behind a pool. Moving or running water can be placed to catch the sunlight and introduce movement to the garden. The sound of running water is refreshing and relaxing, and a suitable place would be near a quiet arbour or sitting area.

Specimen plants

Individual plants may be chosen for their striking flowers, their dramatic foliage or for their overall

When water is used to reflect striking features, such as a tree with autumn colour, make sure that the water body is oriented along the line of view and not across it to maximize the reflection

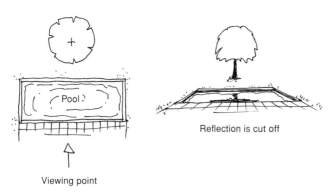

Reflection is cut off

Viewing point

Viewing across a body of water

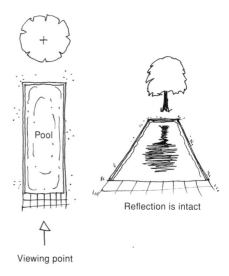

Reflection is intact

Viewing point

Viewing along a body of water

In long or large gardens there will usually be sufficient room to create a worthwhile stream, meandering gently between its source and the pond into which it flows

Upper pool

Stream

Lower pool

In small or shallow gardens make the stream longer and more of a feature by creating acute changes of direction in a zigzag fashion so that the water has to flow further

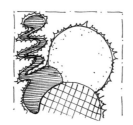

shape. Potentially large plants, such as trees and some more vigorous shrubs, can be placed in isolation, such as in the centre of a lawn. Smaller species may be more effective when they are seen against a backdrop of green foliage to set off their particular characteristics. A specimen of the golden-leaved *Choisya ternata* 'Sundance', for example, might be the perfect solution for planting in an otherwise dull corner bed.

Herb garden

You may have already included a large herb garden or area for growing herbs in your overall garden design and would not, therefore, regard it as a focal point for the purposes of this exercise. However, a tiny herb garden – a small circle of a metre (yard) or so across – can make a focal point, forming part of a stone or brick patio or set into the centre of a larger circle of gravel or paving.

Topiary

Although it can take some time to develop, a piece of topiary can make a striking feature and point of interest, whether it is planted in the ground or in a large container. As with specimen

If space is limited, break up areas of low planting (right) and provide focal points with climbers on poles and obelisks, or use plants that are naturally narrow and fastigiate

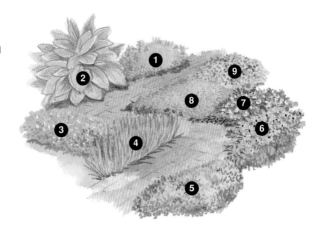

Key to planting
1 *Geranium* 'Johnson's Blue'
2 *Hosta fortunei* var. *aureomarginata*
3 *Euphorbia polychroma* 'Candy' (syn. *E. p.* 'Purpurea')
4 *Iris* 'Green Spot'

5 *Juniperus squamata* 'Blue Star'
6 *Rudbeckia fulgida* var. *deamii*
7 *Helianthemum* 'The Bride'
8 *Vinca minor* 'Atropurpurea'
9 *Thymus vulgaris*

10 *Juniperus scopulorum* 'Skyrocket'
11 Sweetpeas on cedar-wood obelisk
12 *Miscanthus sinensis* 'Variegatus'
13 *Rosa* 'Albertine'

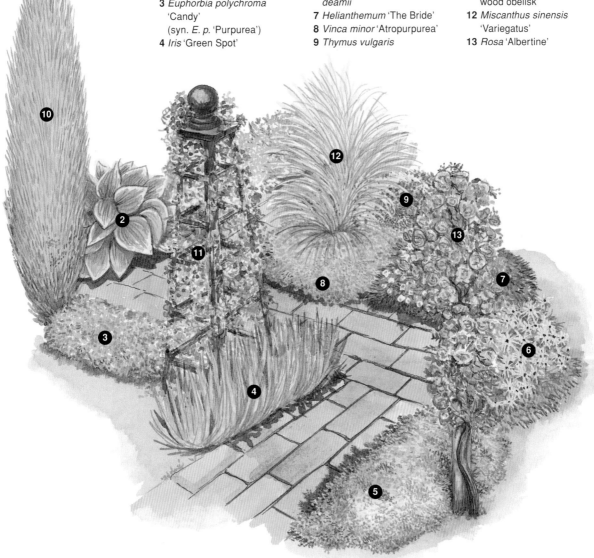

plants, topiary works best when it is seen against a contrasting background that will reveal its colour or shape to the best effect.

Urns, pots and other containers

Containers of all types are ideal for use as focal points, provided they are not too heavy, because they can then be moved around to suit your preferences or to reflect seasonal changes within the garden. Large containers can be placed on their own on a patio or near to the backdoor. Smaller containers look better in groups of three or more. Use hardy perennials and shrubs for greater general interest. Some containers are so ornamental that they do not need to be planted!

Arches and pergolas

Excellent for creating height wherever the garden may seem a little flat, arches and pergolas look even more effective when they are positioned for a definite purpose, not simply to create a focal point. For example, where a path joins a patio is an obvious position for an arch, while a pergola would look good over a shady sitting area away from the house.

Ornamental garden buildings

Summerhouses, gazebos and arbours can make outstanding focal points, although the position of the largest of these structures is as likely to be determined by practical as aesthetic reasons. Remember, too, that the view from the buildings is as important as the view of them.

Garden seats

Garden seats are not only practical but can be used as focal points when they are not actually being used. Seats placed in the open, away from plants, buildings or garden structures, are less likely to be used than those tucked into borders, beneath trees or under a small gazebo or arbour.

A small statue will be a delightful focal point, which will be seen to best effect against planting that does not compete with it for attention.

Statues and sculpture

The obvious place to position a statue or sculpture is in the centre of a circular or square lawn or on the corner of a patio, so that it does not get in the way but can be viewed from the sitting room window. Place them against a dark or plain background, such as a yew hedge, or an evergreen shrub, such as a laurel.

Bird tables and bird baths

What might at first glance seem rather ordinary objects can prove to be valuable additions to a garden if they are in the right position. Ideally, bird tables and baths should be reasonably near to, and in view of, the house. You will not only enjoy the sight of birds eating and bathing, but remember that by encouraging them into your garden, they will probably be doing you a favour by eating caterpillars, slugs and other undesirable visitors at the same time.

Sundial

A sundial can be categorized as a statue or sculpture in terms of its visual appeal, but to be practical it needs to be set in a completely open position so that is in sun all day. The most appropriate place, therefore, is in the centre of a lawn or paved area.

This sundial makes an elegant and very effective focal point.

97

Individual rocks and boulders

Like containers or statues and sculptures, individual rocks and boulders can, if they are particularly large and dramatic, be placed in isolation or positioned in groups of smaller pieces.

They are probably most effective when they are placed in gravel or among low ground-cover plants, to give the impression of being partly buried. Rocks and boulders laid on smooth, unyielding surfaces, such as flagstones, can look artificial.

Placing rocks and other features

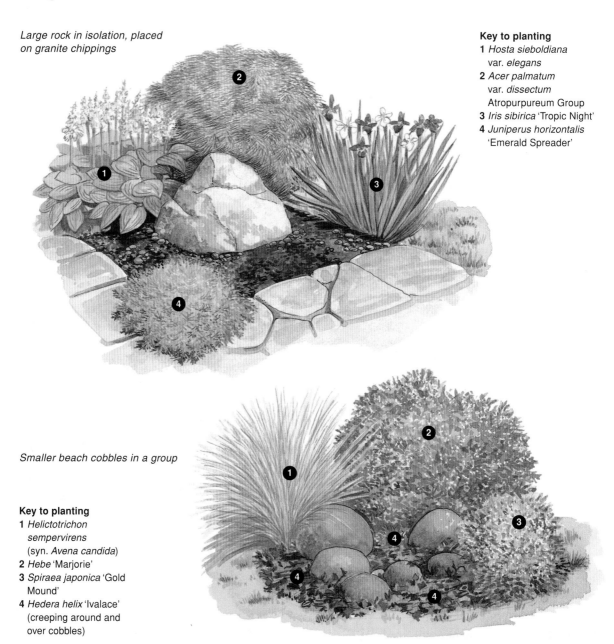

Large rock in isolation, placed on granite chippings

Key to planting
1 *Hosta sieboldiana* var. *elegans*
2 *Acer palmatum* var. *dissectum* Atropurpureum Group
3 *Iris sibirica* 'Tropic Night'
4 *Juniperus horizontalis* 'Emerald Spreader'

Smaller beach cobbles in a group

Key to planting
1 *Helictotrichon sempervirens* (syn. *Avena candida*)
2 *Hebe* 'Marjorie'
3 *Spiraea japonica* 'Gold Mound'
4 *Hedera helix* 'Ivalace' (creeping around and over cobbles)

Design solutions for problem areas

There are probably few gardens, new or existing, that do not have at least one problem that creates difficulties out of all proportion to its size or extent. Some of these problems are likely to be of a visual nature – for example, an ugly fuel tank may be positioned in full view of the sitting room window – or it may be something more practical or fundamental, such as a badly drained area of soil where plants do not thrive or may even die because of the poor ground conditions. Whatever the problem, until you tackle it head on, you are never going to be completely happy with your garden.

Both new and existing gardens may have some problems in common, but each type of garden can also have individual difficulties that are specific to the type. Older, established gardens often contain mature trees and shrubs that have outgrown their position, are badly shaped, cast heavy shade over smaller plants beneath them or create excessive dryness and deplete the soil's nutrients with their extensive root systems. In a brand new garden – that is, a bare plot before it is laid out and planted – the topsoil provided may be of poor quality or of insufficient depth, builder's rubbish may be buried or the drainage is poor because the soil was badly compacted when the house was being built.

Whatever type of garden you have, it is important to identify both the nature and the extent of each particular problem so that you can come up with the right solution. A problem that occurs above ground is relatively easy to identify, but problems resulting from conditions below ground are not always easy to spot immediately, and you may need to dig a series of small trial holes and observe your garden over a long period so that you can fully assess the nature and extent of a problem.

In the remainder of this chapter a number of common gardening problems are described. These problems occur in all types of gardens, and there is a description of the possible reasons or causes for them as well as some suggested solutions. Some of the solutions may solve more than one problem, while equally there are some problems that may have more than one solution.

Soil problems

The soil is waterlogged, damp or sticky and wet in all beds and borders throughout the garden, and water appears in holes as they are dug.

Cause
Generally high natural water table.

Solutions
✳ Raise the finished level of soil in the affected beds and borders by mounding them.

✻ Use retaining edges made from treated timber, bricks or other durable material to create raised beds, backfilling with additional good topsoil, which has been improved with sharp grit and organic matter.

✻ Select and plant varieties of trees, shrubs and perennials that will thrive in wet, boggy areas, such as willow (*Salix*), dogwood (*Cornus*), astilbe and hosta.

✻ Reduce the level of the water table within your garden by installing a system of land drains, provided that this can be connected to an appropriate outlet to take the water away.

A garden with a high water table

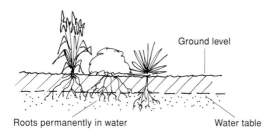

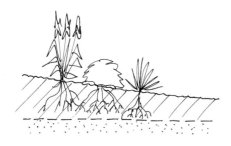

Mound up the soil to minimize the effects

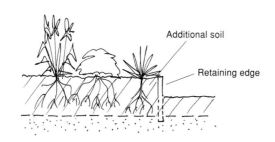

Create a raised bed with a retaining edge

The soil is waterlogged, damp or sticky and wet in just one or two low spots.

Cause

The water table is just close enough to the surface in these places to create wet ground conditions.

Solutions

✻ Raise the level of the ground at these points with sufficient soil to reduce the effect of the water table.

✻ Excavate at these points to below the water table and create a natural pond or wet area suitable for wildlife.

✻ Plant with suitably moisture-tolerant trees, shrubs or perennials.

A localized wet spot

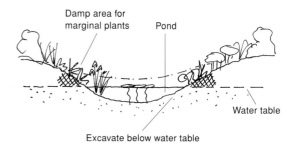

Take advantage of a permanently wet part of the garden to create a natural or informal pond. Even the smallest pool will have space for a waterlily.

Damp country gardens

Lack of moisture can often be a prime considera-tion in some town garden designs, but the opposite can be true of country gardens, especially in naturally low-lying areas, such as those adjacent to rivers, streams and ponds, or where, for geological reasons, there is an unusually high natural water table. You can tackle excess ground water in one of two ways. First, view it as undesirable and unnecessary – which it may indeed be if your soil is permanently waterlogged and soggy – and eliminate it by means of field drainage, which, over a large garden area, can be a major and costly exercise. Alternatively, you can adopt a different approach and turn it to your advantage by planting up the area with trees, shrubs and other plants that will positively thrive in moist ground. An extension of this might be to excavate into the ground below the natural water level, and by so doing create a natural pond or series of ponds, surrounded by wet areas of marginal planting.

Water takes a long time to drain away.

Cause
A compacted layer of soil, especially found in gardens of new houses or wherever the ground has been heavily trampled.

Solution
✶ Dig through the affected area to relieve the compaction, which may require digging to more than a spade's depth.

Cause
The subsoil may be heavy, impervious clay.

Solution
✶ You will need to install land drains connected to a soakaway, ditch or surface water drain to take away surplus water.

Cause
If the problem is localized, it may be caused by builder's materials buried below ground.

Solution
✶ Thorough digging may uncover the likely cause – a sheet of buried polythene, for example, can act like an underground pond.

Solving the problem of poor, 'unnatural' draining

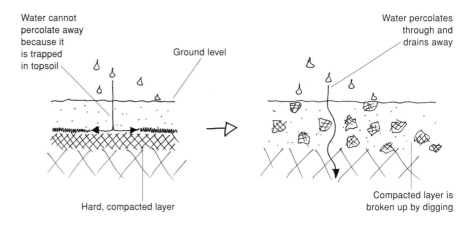

Poor drainage caused by compaction

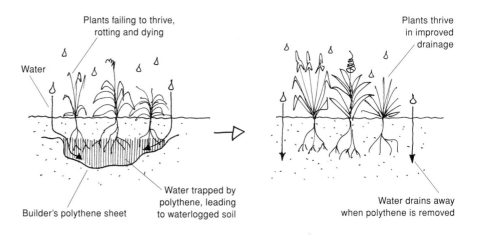

Poor local drainage caused by buried obstructions

Terraces are the ideal solution to gardening on a steeply sloping site. Building retaining walls and, if necessary, importing quantities of topsoil into your garden will be expensive, and you should also consider the timing of the various stages of the planned design so that contractors have easy access to complete the work.

Soil erosion makes it difficult to establish plants because there is rapid water run-off and exposure of roots.

Cause
A steeply sloping garden.

Solutions
✶ Create level or gently sloping terraces by building retaining walls and edges to hold back soil.

✶ Where terracing is not practical, mulch planting areas with thick layers of coarse grade bark, which is heavy enough to stay in place without being blown around or being washed off by rainwater.

✶ Plant low, evergreen ground-cover plants such as ivy (*Hedera*) and periwinkle (*Vinca*) and peg down the long shoots to encourage more rooting into the soil and so stabilize the soil surface. You

103

can combine this with mulching for an even better solution.

✱ Use a porous pipe or seep hose watering system laid in planting areas to provide slow, gentle irrigation that will not run off down the slope. Burying such a system among the plants is even better because it not only encourages deeper rooting but also reduces moisture loss by evaporation from the soil's surface.

The soil, although not waterlogged, is generally sticky and heavy to work, but becomes hard and baked in hot, dry weather.

Cause
A high proportion of clay in the soil.

Solutions
✱ Dig organic matter, such as well-rotted farmyard manure, garden compost or leaf mould, into the soil, preferably in the autumn. This will improve the soil's structure and encourage earthworm activity, increasing aeration, which is necessary for good root growth.

✱ If natural, organic matter is not available, mulch with a proprietary soil conditioner, which will gradually break down into the soil and improve fertility.

✱ Fork sharp grit into the top 30cm (12in) of soil to help open up the structure and prevent surface compaction, which can lead to poor drainage, lack of aeration and increased evaporation in hot, dry weather.

✱ Add ground limestone or chalk where the soil pH is low (less than pH 7.0) and where lime-hating, ericaceous plants, such as rhododendrons or camellias, will not be grown.

Frequently, the above solutions will be more effective if they are used together, in combination, rather than singly.

Plant problems

It is difficult to establish planting beneath or between trees and large shrubs.

Cause
The competition from the existing roots deprives smaller, newer or shallow-rooting plants of both moisture and nutrients.

Solutions
✱ Plant with suitable drought- and shade-tolerant ground-cover shrubs and perennials. Make sure that these are well watered on a regular basis for at least the first season.

✱ Use a mulch of bark, shingle or pebbles to cover the bare soil and do not plant anything, leaving the mulch itself as the ground cover.

✱ Thin out or remove some of the trees and shrubs to let in more light and moisture. Remember to grub out any roots and to improve the soil with fertilizer and compost before replanting the area.

✱ Provide a permanent irrigation system, which can be turned on manually when required or by an automatic timer set to give regular waterings while you are on holiday.

Opposite: **Establishing planting in an existing border**

Key to planting

1 *Prunus lusitanica*	13 *Viburnum opulus* 'Compactum'
2 *Malus* 'Royalty'	
3 *Acer platanoides*	14 *Persicaria affinis* 'Donald Lowndes'
4 *Betula pendula*	
5 *Berberis darwinii*	15 *Leucanthemum x superbum* 'Snowcap'
6 *Rosa* 'Bonica'	
7 *Kerria japonica* 'Pleniflora'	16 *Mahonia aquifolium* 'Apollo'
8 *Aucuba japonica* 'Crotonifolia'	17 *Aconitum* 'Bressingham Spire'
9 *Viburnum tinus*	18 *Hemerocallis* 'Pink Damask'
10 *Juniperus horizontalis* 'Turquoise Spreader'	
11 *Cornus alba* 'Spaethii'	19 *Heuchera micrantha* var. *diversifolia* 'Palace Purple'
12 *Iris* 'Jane Phillips'	

Before thinning – shady with bare soil

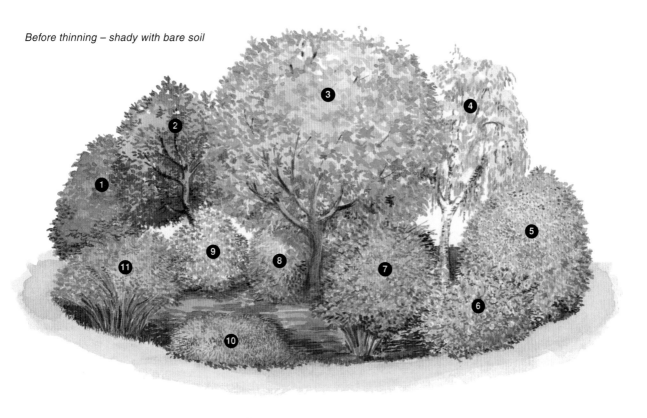

*After thinning – more light and moisture are available
to grow a wider selection of plants*

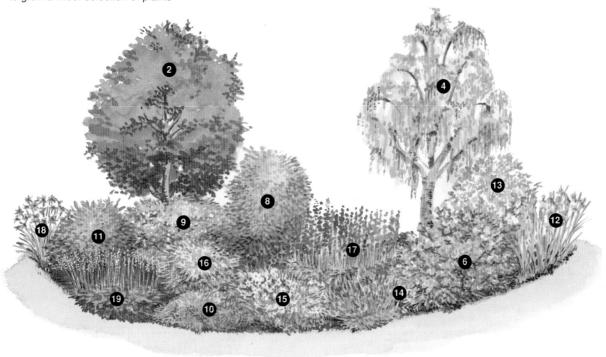

Climbers and other wall plants look weak, sickly and generally lack vigour.

Cause

The soil is dry because the plants are in the rain shadow of a wall or fence.

Solutions

✳ Plant the climbers and wall shrubs further out from the base of the wall, away from the effect of the rain shadow, and train them back to trellis or wires on the wall.

✳ Use drought-tolerant plants, incorporating extra compost in the soil when planting, and mulch them to prevent excess moisture loss and to keep the roots cool.

✳ Provide irrigation, which might be to individual plants by means of a drip system or more general in the form of sprinklers or a seep hose.

✳ Where the border is quite narrow, lay any adjacent paving or grass areas so that they gently slope towards, rather than away from, the bed to throw any rainwater onto the planting area, so providing some additional natural irrigation when it rains.

Solving the problem of dry soil near fences and walls

Dry town gardens

An often unforeseen aspect of gardening in towns, especially where gardens are hemmed in by buildings, roads and other hard surfaces, is that any rain falling onto these surfaces will be channelled away through the drains and sewers rather than being allowed to percolate directly into the ground where it falls. This can, and usually does, result in a general lowering of the water table in these areas, and this means that there is less water available for plants. In your garden design for such a site, you should pay even more attention to plant selection, making sure that you choose varieties that are drought tolerant or that are deep rooted enough to reach any ground water below.

Alternatively, you might want to consider installing some form of irrigation system for part or all of your garden, especially if you particularly wanted to grow some varieties of plant that might not otherwise thrive in the naturally drier conditions. It would, in any case, be a good idea to improve the moisture-retaining capacity of the soil by the addition of generous amounts of organic matter and by mulching heavily after planting.

You should also bear in mind that large buildings or structures can create a rain shadow in the lee or shelter of any prevailing wind, and it is worth taking time to observe your garden to find out how extensive such an influence might be and to select your plants accordingly or to install an irrigation system.

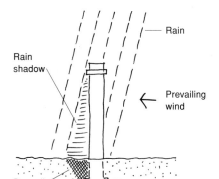

Plant climbers out of the rain shadow and train them back to the wall

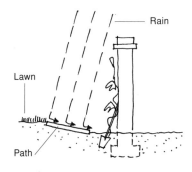

Slope the path towards the bed to direct rain water towards the plant

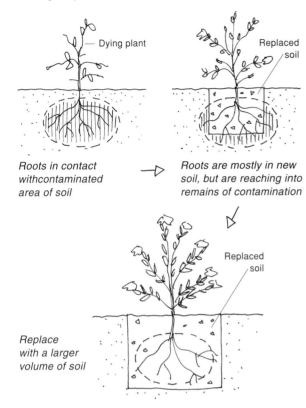

Roots in contact with contaminated area of soil

Roots are mostly in new soil, but are reaching into remains of contamination

Replace with a larger volume of soil

Replaced soil

Plants are dying in just one or two spots in the garden of a new house.

Cause

Buried builder's rubbish just below the root zone might be causing dryness or waterlogging by interfering with the natural water movement.

Solution

✻ Dig down until the offending problem is uncovered, and remove it.

Cause

The soil has been contaminated by diesel, white spirit or other substances used by the builder having been tipped onto the soil.

Solution

✻ Dig out the affected area and replace with fresh soil before replanting. If plants are still affected, the contamination may well be more extensive, downwards as well as sideways, and you will need to replace a larger volume of soil.

The garden is heavily infested with weeds.

Solutions

✻ Systematic and regular hand weeding as soon as weeds appear will eventually result in clean soil, but with persistent weeds this can take months. However, where weeds are among existing plants this might be the best solution. Destroy all weeds removed to prevent the possibility of the spread of seeds or reinfestation from tiny pieces of root left in the ground.

✻ Treat the weeds with an appropriate herbicide according to the type of weed and the circumstances. Note that some soil-acting herbicides may persist in the ground for many weeks or months after application and these should, therefore, be used only as a last resort. Wherever possible, use only those types of herbicide – known as systemics – that rely on direct contact with the plant leaves and stems and that are rendered inactive on contact with the soil.

✻ Cover the weedy area with a sheet mulch, such as black polythene or old carpet underlay. Weigh the mulch down with bricks initially to prevent strong rooted weeds, especially perennials such as docks and thistles, from pushing it up off the ground. Compost or bark as a mulch may suppress small annual weeds but will not cope with established perennials.

Mulching to kill existing weeds

Existing perennial and annual weeds

Mulching fabric, such as black polythene or old carpet

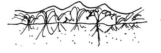

Well-established weeds will tend to push up the fabric

Weigh the fabric down with bricks until the weeds are dead

107

Plants generally lack vigour, producing small, pale or yellowish leaves and poor flowers.

Cause
The soil is dry, light and poor in nutrients.

Solutions
✻ Dig in organic matter, such as garden compost, rotted manure and leaf mould, at every opportunity to improve both the moisture-holding capacity and the nutrient value. If necessary, add a general fertilizer in spring, lightly forked in at the recommended rate, and liquid or foliar feed plants in summer to keep them strong and healthy. This is particularly valuable when the soil is dry and the plants might be under stress.

✻ Mulch all planting areas with a thick layer of coarse bark or gravel, which will help to keep the soil cool and prevent excess moisture loss by evaporation from the soil surface, leaving more available for the plants themselves.

✻ Consider installing a simple irrigation system, preferably of a type such as a porous pipe, which can be buried a few centimetres below the surface to encourage deeper rooting, and reduce moisture loss by evaporation.

Landscaping problems

An unattractive distant view or object detracts from the rest of the garden.

Solution
✻ Screen the view or object with trellis, fencing, a wall, tall shrubs or trees, or possibly a combination of any of these. The key to success in hiding anything from view is to place the screening material as near as possible to the viewer, not to the object to be screened. In this way a relatively low barrier can effectively hide quite a substantial unsightly object in the far distance.

An effective and comparatively quick way of hiding an unsightly building is to erect a screen of wooden panels, which can be used to provide support for climbing plants and shelter for tender container-grown subjects.

Animal damage

One small, but nevertheless important, aspect of gardening in the countryside is the potential threat from rabbits, hares and deer, which can cause damage to plants, ranging from superficial nibbling to complete grazing down to ground level. Where damage is likely to be minor and only occasional, you might feel that it is not worth taking any action. However, regular, serious 'pruning' may be sufficient to encourage you to protect plants, either individually or in groups, with one or more of the various types of tree guard or fencing that available for the purpose. You should make adequate provision for such a contingency, not only in the way that you design your garden but also in the budgeting for it.

Outbuildings or an old garden wall are unattractive, but they are not in sufficiently good condition to support climbers on wires or trellis fixed directly to them.

Solution

✶ Create an independent screen of wires or trellis to be planted with climbers by placing free-standing posts in the ground, positioned a short distance in front of the buildings or wall but not actually touching them, and fixing the wires or trellis to the posts.

Screening a dilapidated outbuilding with posts and horizontal wires to support climbers

Key to planting
1 *Clematis montana*
  var. *rubens*
2 *Hedera colchica*
  'Sulphur Heart'
3 *Lonicera pericylmenum*
  'Belgica'
4 *Vitis coignetiae*

109

Lawn problems

When you mow the lawn, localized spots are left where the grass appears to be longer or it is cut too low in places and 'scalps' the surface.

Cause
An uneven lawn, with small humps and hollows.

Solution
✶ Skim off the turf from any high and low spots of the lawn using a small, sharp spade or a special turfing iron. Move soil from the high spots to the low spots to make them level and even, replace the turf and firm down by laying a small board or plank on top and treading on it – do not tread directly on the turf with your feet because this will create more unevenness.

Lawn edgings

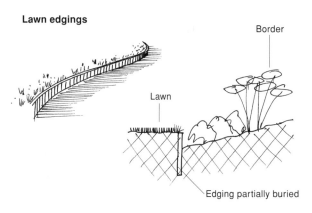

Border

Lawn

Edging partially buried

Proprietary flexible lawn edging

Unstable, crumbly lawn edges are difficult to keep neat and trim.

Cause
The soil is very light and sandy and has little structure.

Solutions
✶ Use a special plastic or metal lawn edge to provide support or make your own edging from long, thin, wood strips, 7.5–10cm (3–4in) deep, fixed with small wooden stakes at intervals. Make sure that all wood is treated.
✶ Lay a course of bricks, tiles or small flagstones around the lawn to create a level mowing edge that gives stability and makes mowing easier.
  Note: any rigid lawn edge should be fixed or laid so that its top is approximately 13mm (½in) below the level of the lawn to prevent it catching on the lawn mower blades.

Cause
Soil at the perimeter of adjoining beds or borders is scraped away too deeply from the lawn edge.

Solution
✶ Make sure that the soil level is just low enough to allow you to use your edging shears and no more. Alternatively, fix a permanent lawn edge as described above.

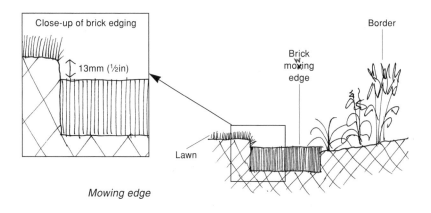

Close-up of brick edging

13mm (½in)

Brick
mowing
edge

Border

Lawn

Mowing edge

Right: Mowing is made much easier and far less time consuming if an edging of bricks or small paving stones is laid around the edge. Remember that a mowing strip must be set slightly lower than the lawn itself if it is to be useful.

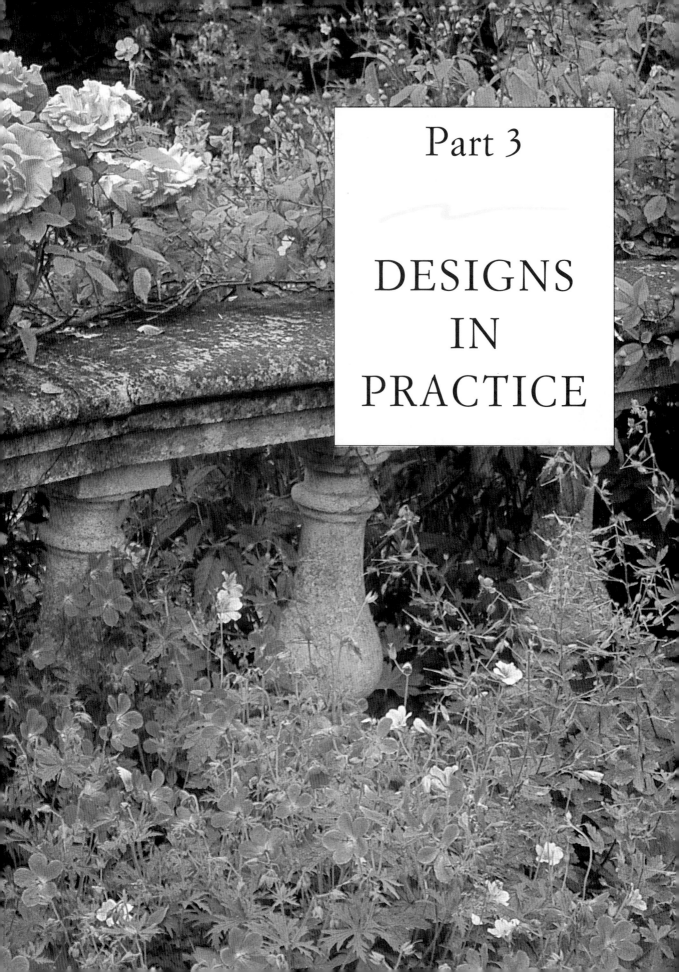

Part 3

DESIGNS IN PRACTICE

Styles of garden

In reality there are many styles of garden. Some of these can be easily defined and are quite recognizable – the cottage garden, for example – but others may not be as easy to define. What is it, in fact, that gives a garden a style? Is it the way that it looks, the way it performs or functions or a combination of the two? This is a question that could take up a whole book on its own to answer. However, for first-time or less experienced gardeners, it is more important to be able to create a worthwhile, individual and attractive garden that they are happy with than to spend valuable gardening time thinking about the finer points of form or function in a garden!

In this chapter we look at a range of garden 'styles'. This list is not intended to be – indeed it cannot be – completely comprehensive, but you will see that it covers a broad spectrum of fairly typical situations and circumstances, which will be familiar to a wide audience of gardeners.

Low-cost and starter gardens

In many respects, the criteria employed to create low-cost and starter (or first-time) gardens are similar. Not the least of these criteria is the distinct possibility that a first-time garden owner is also probably going to be a first-time home owner and is, therefore, likely to be doing any

gardening, at least within the short term, to a tight budget because most of the available cash has gone into the house.

A garden, in some ways, is much like a car, in that you not only have to pay money to buy it initially but you will also continue to pay during its lifetime, or for at least as long as you own it, to maintain it in a good, roadworthy condition. The point that you need to bear in mind is to try and avoid false economies by making bad decisions at the outset, because these decisions may ultimately lead to greater expense and general problems later on. An example of this might be if you were to buy some topsoil that is cheaper than normal. Unless you happen to know and accept the reasons why the soil is being sold cheaply, you might unknowingly find yourself with a garden full of pernicious, obstinate weeds choking your valuable shrubs and perennials to death a year or two later. Knowing and accepting the implications of a decision that you make to save money is not the same as not knowing and finding out too late – to your cost.

It is all too easy to let the cost of putting together a garden get out of hand, especially when you see the wide range of plants, garden features and other garden-related items that are so temptingly displayed in garden centres and nurseries. However, the importance of drawing up a design that not only meets your family's

particular gardening and outdoor needs but is also affordable must always be foremost in your thoughts. To that end it is vital that you agree a budget and stick to it, even if it means phasing the construction work to spread the cost.

One of the most effective ways in which you can keep the total cost of your garden under control is to resist the urge to cram it full of all sorts of unusual features. Instead, make the effort to design a layout that is simple in its style and that will prove to be uncomplicated to build. It is far more valuable, in terms of the overall results and the satisfaction you will derive from achieving your plan, to concentrate your time, effort and expense on producing a limited number of good quality garden features that harmonize with and complement each other than to spread your resources too thinly and ineffectively over a larger number of mediocre ones.

Sometimes the simplest designs are the most successful. The wooden decking and natural stone flags provide an elegant but unobtrusive background for the containers and garden furniture.

There is yet another reason – and one that will appeal not only to budget-conscious but also to first-time gardeners – for making sure that a garden design is kept simple both in concept and content, and that is that it will be much easier to build and plant a simple garden in the first instance. A complicated, intricate design is likely to require a great deal of skill and experience to implement. The advantages of adopting a straightforward plan are twofold: first, you may feel sufficiently confident to carry out some or even all of the work yourself, which means that you may not need to employ professional help but be able to make do with just a spare pair of hands; second, even if you do find that you need

Provided they are not subject to heavy wear, gravel paths are an attractive and economical alternative to paving stones. The golden tone of the gravel has been chosen to harmonize with the warm yellows and oranges of *Hemerocallis* 'Prima Donna', *Dahlia* 'John Street', *Erysimum* 'Gold Flame' and *Arctotis* x *hybrida* 'Apricot'.

help, a simple design is going to require less labour – skilled or unskilled – and also probably fewer materials than a more complicated one, and so you will still make savings.

Guidelines for low-cost and starter gardens

Patios and paving

✶ Keep the shapes of paved areas simple for ease of construction.

✶ Make patio sizes and path widths a multiple of the brick or flagstone size, so that you do not need to cut them.

✶ Use a material such as gravel or stone chippings for covering areas that will not be subject to heavy or frequent use.

✶ Lay paving slabs or bricks on a sand bed. It is easier and more convenient for do-it-yourself purposes because if any mistakes are made, the paving can be easily and quickly lifted and relaid with no mess or old mortar to clean off.

✶ Check that your selected paving material is non-slip. Some of the cheaper concrete flags can be slippery, and therefore quite dangerous, when they are wet.

Lawns and grassed areas

✶ A lawn grown from seed is generally cheaper than one created from from turves – but the same, thorough ground preparation is necessary for both types if the lawn is to become successfully established and hard wearing.

✶ Grass as a ground cover is probably cheaper than any other type of cover, so make your lawns and grass areas generous to reduce the size of other, more expensive areas, such as shrub beds and borders, and use simple shapes that are easy to look after.

Planting

✳ Concentrate your planting in just two or three relatively generous areas to achieve maximum effect, rather than spreading the plants thinly all over the garden, which will cost the same but give a greatly diminished effect.

✳ Try to avoid planting varieties requiring specialized or particular growing conditions – rhododendrons and camellias, for example, require lime-free soil – and choose plants that are tolerant of a range of soils and situations.

✳ Spread the cost of your planting by doing a proportion each season and taking two or three (or even more) years to complete it.

✳ Select plants that are easy growing and require either little, or simple, maintenance.

✳ Choose varieties that each give a long period of interest, whether from flowers, stems, berries or leaves, or even better, a combination of these.

✳ Plant perennials that can be easily lifted and divided into several pieces for replanting to increase the area of your planting without additional cost.

Arches and pergolas

✳ If you are buying these in ready-to-assemble kit form, the simplest designs in softwood are usually more economical than other types of ornate design. Hardwood is more expensive than softwood, but is longer lasting.

✳ Treat softwood well with a suitable, plant friendly preservative, especially posts that are set in the ground.

✳ Piers and columns that are made from bricks, concrete blocks and stone will probably be more expensive and require greater skill and expertise to build, but they will last longer than wooden posts.

✳ Simple arch and pergola designs in wood make good do-it-yourself projects. Remember, though, that if you plant climbers they will eventually cover most of the structure, so the strength and overall proportions or size are more important than fiddly detailing or ornamentation, which will eventually be hidden.

✳ Where screening is necessary, combine a pergola with trellis panels by fixing the panels between the posts of the pergola. This will save on the cost of additional posts if you made the screen separately. Make sure that the pergola posts are the right distance apart first.

Water features

✳ Some small water features, such as bubble fountains and artificial millstones, are available in complete kit form, are simple to install and are relatively inexpensive to buy compared to the cost of a large pool and waterfall.

✳ Pools made from flexible liners are less expensive than those made from materials such as concrete and are not complicated to construct, particularly if you keep the shape simple, such as an oval or circle.

✳ The cheaper varieties of plastic or PVC pool liner may require more care in their installation, and they are not as durable or long lasting as the more expensive types of rubber liner.

✳ Fountains and other forms of moving water, such as streams, require the use of a submersible pump to circulate the water and you will need a convenient and safe electricity supply.

Walls and fences

✳ Walls can be relatively expensive to build and may require considerable skill and expertise during their construction, but they are virtually maintenance- and therefore cost-free once in place.

✳ Fences are more economical to build than walls of comparable height, and are generally well within the scope of the do-it-yourself enthusiast.

✳ Wooden fences, particularly softwood types, may require regular treatment with an appropriate preservative to prevent rot. Posts or any other wooden parts of a fence that come into contact with the ground will benefit from an extra application of preservative.

✳ Fence panels mounted between brick or blockwork piers rather than wooden posts are a good compromise, being less expensive to build than a brick wall, but with greater overall strength and requiring less on-going maintenance than a plain wooden fence.

Low-maintenance gardens

There are probably thousands of keen gardeners throughout the world who willingly devote every moment of their spare time to working in the garden, carrying out all sorts of gardening tasks, no matter how mundane or uninteresting they might be. Numerous gardeners spend hours browsing around garden centres, nurseries and other suppliers that might in some way be relevant or connected to their pastime. However, there are probably just as many, if not more, people who derive equal pleasure from being able to look at and be in their gardens, but who do not wish to be tied to them to them every spare minute of the day and who want to spend what can often be limited leisure time in other ways. For these particular gardeners, a garden that requires only a minimum amount of regular care and attention to keep it looking good will be not only an attractive proposition but probably a necessary one.

All other things being equal, a garden that is based on a simple design will be easier and less expensive to maintain than a similar sized one that is complex and is crammed with all sorts of features and ideas, no matter how attractive they may be individually. 'Simple' does not, however, have to mean unattractive, and many gardens of all types can be successful and attractive because of their simplicity of design.

Although there is no reason why a low-maintenance garden cannot be relatively inexpensive to build, a degree of investment in the early stages of developing such a garden will probably repay the cost in years to come. For example, you might decide to install an automatic irrigation system that could water the whole garden. The initial capital outlay for buying such a system and having it installed by a specialist irrigation contractor could be high, but it would almost certainly be offset by the long-term benefits that you would gain in terms of sheer convenience, of time saved by not having to water by hand and of better overall plant growth, leading to a garden that will mature much sooner than might otherwise have been the case.

You can apply this same cost-benefit principle to whatever features you intend including in your garden to help you to determine if the extra expense that you might thereby be incurring because you have chosen to use better quality materials or have employed sophisticated construction techniques, and possibly also employed specialist help to do so, is outweighed by your savings in the other areas that are even more important to you, such as time, convenience and physical effort.

Do not be misled into thinking that all low-maintenance gardens look the same. Virtually any style of garden can have its maintenance liability substantially reduced by applying just a few basic principles, which are more to do with the practicalities of gardening than with its appearance. Some garden styles do naturally lend themselves to almost minimal maintenance regimes, while others may depend on certain particular or special aspects of garden maintenance or management for their existence or appearance. An obvious example here is a formal garden, where the style or theme relies on the neat, closely cropped, symmetrical or geometrical shapes of edgings, hedges and topiary – all of which are potentially labour intensive to maintain. However, even here there is scope at least to reduce the amount of maintenance, if only on a relative basis – a simple way, for example, is to select a slower growing variety of hedging plant that will require only one cut or trim a year as opposed to the two or three cuts that more vigorous types require.

Guidelines for low-maintenance gardens

Patios and paving

∗ Lay flagstones and other paving materials on a bed of sand–cement mortar. Point the joints between the flags with the same mortar to make it completely maintenance free by preventing the accumulation of wind-blown soil, which would otherwise provide a haven for weed seeds.

∗ Informal areas of gravel paving are best if they are laid on a firm base of hardcore, blinded with sand. Use a proprietary mulching fabric if you are laying gravel directly onto soil, to prevent the soil and gravel from mixing and to keep it weed free by preventing seeds from germinating and by acting as a barrier to perennial weeds underneath.

∗ Use a retaining edge of treated wood, brick or other durable material to enclose gravel areas and to prevent the gravel from spilling over into adjoining areas, especially lawns, where any stones may cause injury or, at least, damage your mower.

∗ Brush fine, dry sand over any areas of brick or sett paving that are laid on a sand bed to fill any thin joints. For wider joints use a dry mix of sand and cement, which will eventually set and will prevent soil and weed seeds from becoming established.

Lawns and grassed areas

∗ Use turves for an instant effect and to make the lawn usable as soon as possible. Turfing will also eliminate the possibility of annual weed seed germination, which can be a problem in seeded lawns.

∗ In areas of grass that are likely to be little used, avoid vigorous rye grass mixtures of seed or turf that will require more frequent cutting. Use one of the low-maintenance mixes now available.

∗ Keep all your lawn areas as simple in shape as possible and avoid breaking up the grass area with individual trees or shrubs or tiny island beds, which can be awkward to mow around.

∗ Lay a mowing strip, made from bricks or small, narrow paving flags, around lawns to make edge cutting simpler.

∗ Consider installing a pop-up irrigation system for the best quality lawns on light soils, which may otherwise dry out excessively in hot weather.

∗ Avoid the use of grass in shady areas beneath overhanging trees, or where there are permanent shadows from adjacent buildings. Growth of grass in these situations can be weak, and moss and weeds will soon become established.

Underplant deciduous trees and tall shrubs with shade-tolerant, ground-cover evergreens. The bright spring foliage of the false acacia (*Robinia pseudoacacia* 'Frisia') is echoed by the glossy leaves of *Aucuba japonica* 'Crotonifolia', which is itself interplanted with ferns.

Planting

⋆ Make sure that your ground preparation before planting is of the highest standard so that the plants will grow healthily and cover the ground as quickly as possible.

⋆ Mulch all planting areas with, say, natural bark or shingle to keep them weed free and help retain moisture in the soil.

⋆ Use a high proportion of evergreens in your planting scheme. These will provide year-round foliage and act as their own ground cover.

⋆ Underplant taller deciduous shrubs and trees with spreading ground-cover shrubs and perennials that will thrive in the shadier, drier conditions beneath. Mix in some early flowering bulbs as well for extra interest.

✳ Generally, aim to cover all the bare soil with plants, bark, shingle or some other material to eliminate the need for weeding and reduce the watering requirement.

✳ Install an irrigation system, preferably controlled by an automatic timer, to eliminate the need for hand watering. Choose a system that allows you to water separate sections of the garden at different times and frequencies for the maximum flexibility. Plants in containers can be watered from the same system if required or supplied by means of their own separate drip system, which can be run from the same timer.

Arches and pergolas

✳ If you are using softwood for arches and pergolas, make sure that it is pressure treated. Such wood lasts much longer than wood that has been hand treated. Remember, however, that if you have to cut into wood after it has been pressure treated, you must paint any freshly exposed surfaces with additional stain or preservative.

✳ Hardwood is generally more durable and longer lasting than softwood, but hardwood posts set in the ground will still benefit from treatment with preservative.

✳ Wrought iron is a strong, long-lasting material, especially if it can be galvanized before it is painted. Paint applied by powder-coating is better than hand-brushed or sprayed gloss paint. Both galvanizing and powder-coating may have to be carried out by specialists, which will increase the overall cost.

✳ Piers and posts made from brick, stone or concrete blocks are virtually maintenance free once constructed and will last almost indefinitely. They are probably also the most expensive form of upright, because of the amount of labour required to build them.

✳ Kits for arches and pergolas, which use plastic-coated steel tube in their designs, are long lasting and quite simple to put together with the minimum of tools and equipment.

Water features

✳ Use features such as a millstone or bubble fountain where the bulk of the water is contained and concealed in an underground tank or sump in which leaves and debris cannot accumulate. If you are designing your own 'concealed' water feature, make sure that the submersible pump needed to operate the fountain is readily accessible for annual servicing.

A bubble fountain requires only a small area and is a safe way of introducing a water feature into a garden in which children will be playing. Electricity is required to drive the water through the system, but solar-powered units are becoming available, which obviate the need for expensive ducting from the mains supply.

✶ Concrete or concrete and fibreglass ponds – as long as they are well made and well designed – will last almost indefinitely and are probably the most durable of all water feature constructions. Remember to seal any concrete with a proprietary sealant before filling it with water to prevent contamination by lime from the cement, which could harm fish.

✶ Ponds with a large population of fish will be prone to algal blooms because of the amount of waste products produced. Avoid this by severely reducing the number of fish or by omitting them altogether. Alternatively, build in a specialist filtration system during construction, which will help to clarify the water.

✶ Where all other things are equal, deep ponds are less prone to rapid temperature fluctuations, which can otherwise reduce water clarity and encourage algae.

✶ Aquatic and marginal planting will improve water quality by reducing the nutrient content of the water, which, when high, can lead to problems with algae. Some varieties of submerged aquatic plants, such as hornwort (*Ceratophyllum demersum*), will also help to oxygenate the water, to the benefit of all life in the pond.

✶ When you are building a pond, make sure that you make provision for a drain for easy emptying, if required, later on.

Walls and fences

✶ Well-built walls made from brick, stone and concrete in its various forms will last almost indefinitely and are virtually maintenance free, although they are usually more expensive than fences of an equivalent size.

✶ You may need to obtain local planning consent for garden walls over a certain height, and in certain situations, such as in a conservation area, there could also be other restrictions. Check before any work is begun.

✶ Fences made from woven panels and other lightweight wooden constructions may be relatively inexpensive initially but will probably need on-going and regular treatment and maintenance to keep them in good shape.

✶ Fences made from hardwood will last longer than those made of softwood, and they can look good if allowed to weather naturally, without being stained.

✶ Wooden fence posts, particularly softwood types, will last much longer if they are pressure treated in advance at a specialist sawmill or timber supplier.

✶ Consider using concrete, brick or stone piers in place of wooden fence posts to eliminate the problem of rotting.

✶ Fix gravel boards – narrow planks – at ground level between fence posts, with the fence panels mounted directly above them. If any rot does occur, only the gravel board needs to be replaced, which will involve less cost and less work. Alternatively, use pressure-treated gravel boards.

Formal gardens

Historically, the development of formal gardens as we might recognize them today came about mainly through the use of various combinations of rigid, geometric shapes and lines and angles to create what were essentially mathematical patterns laid out on the ground. In many cases, these were exercises in pure design almost for its own sake. The consideration of basic practicalities, which nowadays in a modern garden would

The use of axes in formal layouts

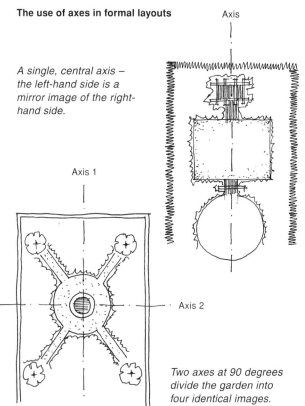

A single, central axis – the left-hand side is a mirror image of the right-hand side.

Axis

Axis 1

Axis 2

Two axes at 90 degrees divide the garden into four identical images.

This formal, symmetrical layout would be suitable for a large, traditional garden, but it could be easily adapted to suit a smaller plot by using half or even a quarter of the design.

probably be regarded as second nature, was almost certainly not a priority. Indeed, the scale of some surviving examples of this style of garden is quite impressive, especially when you consider that there were none of the mechanical or labour-saving aids available that we take for granted. Symmetry was a popular and widely used device, which added greatly to the overall geometric effect. In some of the simplest instances it might have involved a single central avenue or axis, with the garden on one side of this axis being a mirror image of the other. After this, the use of more than one axis opened up all sorts of symmetrical possibilities, much like the many images of a kaleidoscope, leading to increasingly compli-cated and in many ways artificial designs.

One notable characteristic of these older, formal gardens was the way in which plants often played a secondary role. They were usually heavily trimmed and artificially shaped and manipulated so that nature could not take its normal course, and they were used more as living, three-dimensional geometric shapes, whose purpose was rather to emphasize the architectural and mathematical nature of the garden than to provide botanical or horticultural interest.

Plants can be used to enhance the formal appearance of a garden

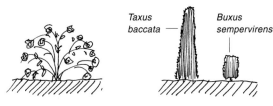

Taxus baccata — Buxus sempervirens

Loose hedges of plants such as roses are generally too informal because they cannot be kept neatly trimmed to shape

Hedges of yew (Taxus) and box (Buxus), for example, are suitable for formal garden because they can be trimmed tightly

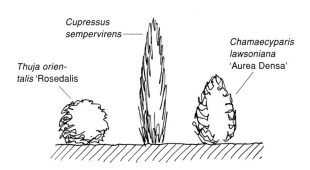

Cupressus sempervirens —

Thuja orientalis 'Rosedalis

Chamaecyparis lawsoniana 'Aurea Densa'

Some plants have naturally formal or geometric shapes without needing to be trimmed or pruned

Although the opportunities for creating modern formal gardens on the scale that was found centuries ago may now be few, the basic principals of such designs can still be applied to even the smallest of garden plots. What will be different, however, is that you will need, as in any style of garden, to consider more than just pure design theory. Your garden is going to be used in a variety of ways by you and your family, and a formal garden cannot afford to be different from any other garden in that it must work at all levels. If you decide that you like the idea of a formal style, you must come up with a design that will result in a garden that is attractive in appearance, is practical to use and can be achieved at a realistic cost to suit your own personal circumstances.

Of course, you do not have to design your whole garden in a formal manner any more than you would with any other styles, and there are certain instances, such as in a large, spacious garden or maybe in a long, narrow plot, where the most successful design solution will be for you to divide the garden into two or more separate, but nevertheless linked, spaces. This arrangement will give you an opportunity to keep to the same theme in each space, which will provide continuity and harmony, or to make each space deliberately contrast with the others. So you could, for example, have an arrangement whereby half of your garden is laid out informally, with generous sweeping curves and irregular shapes, filled with masses of plants and then, by merely stepping through a gap in a hedge that separates the two parts of the garden, find yourself in a severely formal area with restrained, organized and neat planting, providing a complete contrast of styles and mood to the garden on the other side of the hedge.

Guidelines for formal gardens

Patios and paving

✦ Use regular, geometric shapes such as squares, rectangles and circles or straight lines to define paved areas.

✦ Use straight paths to form axes, which can then be used to create varying degrees of symmetry.

✶ Emphasize the formal nature of your garden by laying any paving flags in a regular pattern, or bond, or by introducing repeated geometric patterns within a particular paved area.

✶ Gravel is a traditional paving material used in many formal gardens. Because it is relatively economical, it is a good alternative to large expanses of potentially expensive natural stone flags.

✶ Remember to allow in your layout enough uninterrupted paving space for more practical purposes – for example, standing out garden furniture or erecting a clothes drier.

Lawns and grassed areas

✶ Use shapes of lawn that will either match or complement the shapes of paving and areas of planting.

✶ Because lawns can make a vital contribution to the success of formal gardens make sure that the quality of your grass is at its best by good initial ground preparation and subsequent regular maintenance.

✶ Make sure that you keep lawn areas as generous and uncluttered as possible so that they can be used for recreational purposes as well as appearance.

✶ Use rigid lawn edgings or mowing strips around the lawns to keep their shape pristine.

Planting

✶ To emphasize formality, create beds that are mirror images of each other both in shape and content, symmetrically placed about one or more axes.

✶ Use neat, tightly clipped evergreen hedges to create boundaries and separate different garden areas from one another. Box (*Buxus sempervirens*) and yew (*Taxus baccata*) are two

Training plants against walls

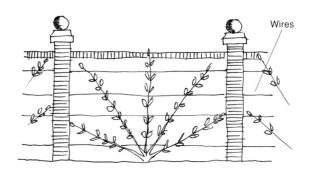

Train wall shrubs formally to emphasize the style of the garden

Evergreen shrubs can be trimmed into almost any shape to mirror a theme within the garden.

traditional varieties that still cannot be surpassed for this purpose.

✶ Another way to emphasize the formal layout of the garden is to keep your planting simple in style and content and to resist the urge to use lots of different varieties of plant.

✶ Where possible, choose plants that have a naturally formal or regular habit – whether it be globular, conical or columnar, for example – particularly for the structure planting of trees and large shrubs that will be necessary.

✶ Gravel or bark mulch can be used to set off the quality of individual plants and to keep down any weeds.

Arches and pergolas

✳ Most styles of arch and pergola, apart from rustic ones, are suitable for use in formal gardens.

✳ Take care to select a design for arches and pergolas that will suit the style of planting – light and elegant for use with small-leaved, delicate climbers, heavy and robust where large-leaved, vigorous varieties are to be grown.

✳ Square pergolas are especially effective when they are placed over the junction of two paths crossing at right angles.

✳ You can use a series of arches placed at regular intervals along a central path or avenue to create a tunnel effect, which can be made more emphatic by planting them with vigorous, large-leaved climbers, such as grape vines, which will cast lots of shade.

✳ Reflect or copy shapes that are found elsewhere in the garden when determining the style of your arch or pergola.

✳ Avoid the use of strong, brightly coloured stain or paint for treating arches and pergolas because it may detract from the simplicity and elegance of the structures.

Water features

✳ Create formal pools from circles, squares and rectangles – as single water bodies, using individual shapes, or by connecting two or more, making sure that there is at least one axis of symmetry.

✳ Finish off the edges of pools and water features with regularly shaped stone flags and bricks rather than with irregularly shaped pieces of stone.

✳ Raised pools and other water features can add an extra dimension to a formal garden, particularly when a fountain is included in the design.

✳ If space allows, sloping gardens provide an ideal opportunity to create a series of small, linked cascades, perhaps running down the centre of the garden into a long, narrow, canal-like pool.

✳ At the other end of the scale, small, wall-mounted water spouts can make attractive and interesting focal points at the end of a path or when viewed through an arch or gateway.

Walls and fences

✳ Brick walls make excellent boundaries for formal gardens, as do walls made from natural stone, particularly when laid in regular, even courses, rather than randomly built.

✳ High boundary walls are good for training shrubs and climbers against in a formal manner that suits the style of garden. This type of training is also an excellent way of saving space and of increasing the number of plants.

✳ Choose your wall materials carefully so that they match or complement any paving materials used elsewhere in the garden.

✳ High, long walls will need piers or buttresses for added strength, and these should be equally spaced to create a regular pattern.

✳ Simple, low-cost fences such as those made from woven panels and wooden posts, can sometimes be too crude where a more elegant formal design is required.

✳ Fences or screens made from wrought iron are appropriate for formal gardens, especially if they can be combined with brick or stone piers.

✳ Hardwood fences, particularly those incorporating highly decorative patterns and shapes, can be more suitable for use in a formal garden than plain, sawn, softwood types.

Plant lover's garden

If you are someone who has more than just a passing interest in growing or looking at plants and flowers, owning or at least having the use of a garden offers an ideal opportunity for you to pursue your interest. This may be limited, of course, by your own personal circumstances – for example, you might be constrained by the amount of space available for growing your favourite plants, or you might have plenty of room, but might be

Container-grown plants – here phormium and cordyline – and climbers – *Clematis* 'Gravetye Beauty' – increase the numbers of species that can be grown in even a small area.

prevented from exploiting the space fully because of your resources.

People can, of course, be plant lovers for different reasons. There are those who may just like plants for their own sake and are happy to cram their garden full of as many different varieties as possible, giving little or no thought to how the varying plants look *en masse*. You will also find those gardeners who care not just about the individual plants but about the relationships and effects that can be achieved with them, perhaps paying more attention to themes of colour or texture, and using them in much the same way as an artist might create a painting. Finally, there is probably a smaller section of the gardening population for whom the actual technicalities of growing, such as the propagation and cultivation of chosen plants, often of only one type, are more attractive than any overall aesthetic appreciation of the garden itself. This division is obviously convenient and somewhat oversimplistic, and there will inevitably be overlaps between each group. However, it does suggest that in essence there are three basic types of plant lover's garden, which might be summarized as follows:

* Gardens in which the various plants form part of an overall design and are seen as a total composition together with the other garden features, rather than as simply a collection of plants.
* Gardens in which plants are regarded primarily as a collection of individual species and varieties and the priority in the garden is to maximize the amount of space available for growing them, even if it is at the expense of the appearance of the overall layout.
* Gardens with a wholly horticultural purpose and in which, because of this, the priority is to ensure that there are adequate facilities for this purpose only – cold frames, greenhouses and potting sheds, for example. An overall garden design concept is not a consideration in this type of garden – if the gardens look attractive, it is more likely to be by default.

In reality, the third option is obviously a specialized application. It is not really representative and is probably of limited appeal to the vast majority of gardeners. However, it does raise an important issue, which can apply to any garden, regardless of its style or purpose, and that is, what effect, if any, will the way in which you develop your garden have if you wish to sell your house in the future? Overcomplicated garden designs or specialized and specific gardens may not appeal to many potential buyers, so it is worth thinking about your long-term intentions for the garden before deciding on such a limited design, which might later affect your ability to sell your house.

For the best results, it is important not to lose sight of the need to provide at least a basic design structure in your garden, even if this might mean including a variety of features and spaces that may seem to be of secondary importance, at least for your own purposes. Scaling down the size of your lawn or patio, for example, may have a relatively minor impact on the appearance of the overall design of your garden yet it will free additional space that can be devoted to more planting. However, if you were to omit the lawn altogether, although you will probably create lots of additional planting space, the lack of a grassy space will have a major impact both on the appearance and practicality of the design, and you should seriously consider whether it is really desirable. Imagine, for example, that your garden is full of plants and nothing else and that you decide to move. A potential buyer, who might have a family with young children, could immediately notice the lack of open space in the garden and be put off buying. Even a tiny patio and lawn would make the garden more attractive to the family.

The guidelines that follow are, therefore, aimed at the first, and probably most popular, type of plant lover's garden, which provides a happy compromise between plants, practicality and appearance.

Guidelines for plant lover's gardens

Patios and paving

∗ Circular patios, or indeed any other circular spaces, take up less room than square ones of the same diameter. A design with circles or a combination of circles and squares, will enable you to create comparatively more room to plant into.

∗ Gently slope areas of paving towards beds and borders that may be dry and that would benefit from extra water, so that the smallest amount of rainfall is directed to the soil and not wasted.

∗ Gravel can be used to create informal areas of paving and paths, provided they are edged to stop it spreading. If the gravel is laid over soil you can actually grow plants through it – using it as a mulch – as long as the plants do not obstruct the main thoroughfare.

∗ Leave finger-wide or slightly wider joints between flagstones unpointed, and fill them with soil covered with grit. This will give you the opportunity to plant tiny alpines, mosses and ferns. Make sure, however, that any plants are sited away from the main areas of foot traffic.

The use of space on the patio

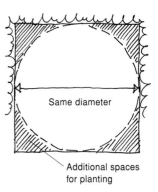

Circles are smaller in area than squares with the same diameter

Same diameter

Additional spaces for planting

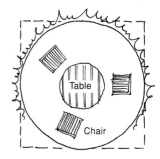

The corners of most square patios are not really used for garden furniture, so a circle may be just as useful.

Table

Chair

∗ Omitting individual flags or a few paving bricks will create spaces to take pockets of soil for small plants. Remember, however, to leave enough unbroken area of paving on which your garden furniture can be set out comfortably.

Creating planting pockets in paved areas

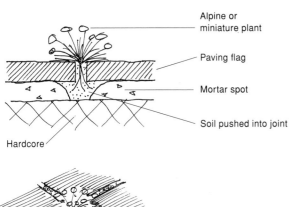

Alpine or miniature plant

Paving flag

Mortar spot

Soil pushed into joint

Hardcore

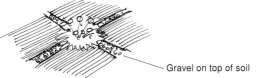

Gravel on top of soil

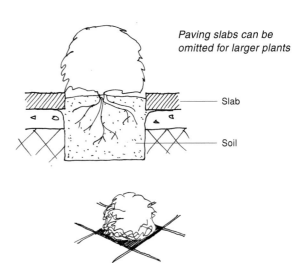

Paving slabs can be omitted for larger plants

Slab

Soil

Lawns and grassed areas

✶ Try to keep all grassed areas to a minimum size but do not overlook the important role that lawns can play in the overall design of the garden, both from the point of view of appearance and for practicality.

✶ As with patios, circles take up less space than other shapes of the same width, which leaves more room for planting.

✶ Consider creating a wildflower lawn or meadow, which can serve two purposes. The first, and obvious one, is that it can still be used as a lawn, although not to the extent of it being used as a football pitch every day. Second, it will give you the opportunity to grow wild plants in it for additional flowering interest.

✶ Spring- and autumn-flowering bulbs can be planted in a lawn or grassed area, provided that the areas where they are planted can be left uncut until the bulbs' leaves have died down sufficiently. Daffodils, for example, need about six weeks for the leaves to manufacture adequate resources in the bulb for the following year's flowers.

✶ Mix any grass clippings with garden and vegetable waste for recycling as compost, which can be used as a mulch, particularly around plants that benefit from good soil, such as roses, or dug deeper into the soil, as when putting in new plants.

✶ If your use of the lawn as a sitting or recreational area is likely to be infrequent, or even non-existent, consider alternatives to grass, such as a low or prostrate, evergreen, ground-cover planting. You will still have the general appearance of a lawn in terms of a flat, green area, but you will gain by reducing dramatically the amount of maintenance required.

Planting

✶ In gardens where space for plants is limited, try planting in tiers to maximize the room that is available. Within a narrow border you could plant two or three small trees with light foliage. Between these, you can put several deciduous shrubs that are tolerant of some light shade. At ground level, under and between the shrubs, you could then plant low ground-cover perennials, again choosing varieties that will take some shade and not require lots of moisture and mixing some small spring-flowering bulbs with them.

✶ Where plants provide the main interest in a garden there may be a tendency for you to plant them more densely than normal, in order to include as many varieties as possible. If this is the case, you must make sure that your initial ground preparation is of the highest standard and that adequate moisture and nutrition are provided for the plants throughout the growing season.

✶ Mulching all planted areas will help to keep down weeds as well as conserving moisture, and thus save time that can be spent on other, more enjoyable tasks.

✶ Make sure you have adequate facilities for disposing of, or recycling, plant waste, such as hard and soft prunings and grass clippings.

✶ Install an irrigation system for all or part of the garden to save time spent on hand watering.

Arches and pergolas

✶ As far as your garden design will allow, use every opportunity to introduce arches and pergolas, or other overhead structures, which are potential supports for climbing plants.

✶ When concreting in the posts for these structures, keep the amount of concrete to a minimum so that any climbers can be planted as close as possible to the posts themselves. For the best result, use formwork or shuttering to contain the concrete as you pour it.

✴ Fill in the gaps between the side posts of pergolas with trellis panels or horizontal wires to provide extra support and allow climbers to be trained sideways as well as upwards. Alternatively, plant additional climbers in the spaces between the posts.

✴ When any wooden structures that will be used to support plants are treated, make sure that the stain or paint you use is not toxic to plants (or indeed humans and animals).

✴ Some arch and pergola designs use materials, such as softwood, that need regular maintenance. These should, therefore, always be planted with climbers that will tolerate being cut down every few years without being killed or damaged so that you have easy access to the structure.

Water features

✴ As well as being attractive in their own right, water features can be used to extend the range of plants grown in a garden, by using aquatics, marginals and bog plants. The final selection will be determined by the type of water feature.

✴ The simplest of pools, made from a piece of pond liner or by using a prefabricated fibreglass or plastic shell set into the ground, can accommodate a range of aquatic and marginal plants. Variations in depth, including shallow marginal shelves, will allow you to plant a wider variety than a pool of a single, uniform depth.

A plant lover will want to include a variety of habitats, and a small raised pond will happily contain half a dozen aquatic as well as marginal species.

Shelter provided by walls and fences

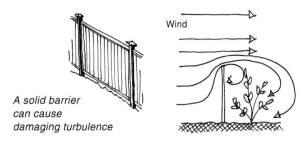

A solid barrier can cause damaging turbulence

A perforated barrier filters the wind with less subsequent damage to the plants

✗ You can create a bog garden next to a pool or elsewhere in your garden by burying a sheet of polythene or an off-cut of pond liner 30–40cm (12–16in) below ground. Puncture it with a fork to allow some drainage and backfill with a mixture of organic matter and heavy soil to provide a rich, moist bed.

✗ Even the tiniest of containers, such as an oak half-barrel, 45cm (18in) across, can be used to support just a couple of aquatic plants, such as a miniature waterlily.

✗ Well-planted pools, with a variety of aquatic and marginal plants, make an excellent habitat for frogs, toads and newts. In return, they will help control slugs and other unwanted creatures in your garden.

Walls and fences

✗ Boundary walls and fences provide good opportunities for growing a wide range of climbers and shrubs, and you should make full use of them. Make sure that there is adequate support in the form of trellis or wires fixed to the boundary structure for those climbers that cannot cling directly to a flat surface.

✗ Sunny south- and west-facing walls are warmer and more congenial to plants than colder north- and east-facing ones. Use them to advantage by growing choicer plants that would not thrive in the open or out of the sun.

✗ Solid walls and fences are not as efficient as perforated ones for creating shelter from the wind, and they can cause damaging turbulence in windy conditions. Walls and fences that are introduced to provide shelter are best made in an 'open' design, which will allow both air and light through to the benefit of plants behind.

✗ Most walls and solid fences have a dry side, or rain shadow, which is on the opposite side to any prevailing wind. In general, the higher the obstruction, the larger the dry area behind. You should consider this when selecting plants, and make sure your choice is appropriate for the dry conditions.

✗ Walls and fences of varying styles and heights need not be confined to garden boundaries and can be introduced into a garden to manipulate the microclimate of small areas for an express purpose, such as acting as a sun trap for the protection of tender plants or excluding the sun from an area to suit shade-loving species.

Family gardens

Designing a garden to meet the requirements of all the members of your family can be quite a challenge. Not only is each member of the family an individual, with his or her own personal tastes and preferences (which, to further complicate

Where providing space for recreation is a priority in a family garden, plants can be confined to raised beds and containers on the paved area around the house.

matters, may change with time and increasing age), but also, where space and finances are limited, you will discover either that you cannot physically fit into your garden all the ideas and features that your family would like or that you simply cannot afford all of them.

Obviously a compromise is needed, and the starting point to help you achieve this, as indeed it is with any garden, is to make two lists, one of your 'wants' – that is, of features such as a pond, arbour or herb garden – and the other of your 'needs', which are the more mundane but nevertheless necessary items, such as a shed or rotary clothes drier. Both of these lists should be made in decreasing order of priority, which will enable you to delete the least important items until you reach the stage where you are happy that you can both fit in and afford what remains, which will be the most important items.

If you bear in mind that your family's circumstances will change over time, a degree of forward planning can be helpful in achieving those compromises that are an essential part of most garden designs and in helping to avoid potentially wasteful or expensive mistakes. For example, although small children may need a large lawn area in the earlier years for running about, eventually their interests will change, and as they grow older they will probably be increasingly away from the house and garden. There will then be little need for an extra large lawn space. With some foresight, you can design your garden so that, in due course, part of the large lawn area can be used to build, say, a fish pond, which would not be practical or safe while the children are small.

You will probably find that the concept of working to a long-term overall design is of more value in a family garden than in any other kind. Apart from the flexibility that this type of

133

approach permits, it is also useful from the point of view of allowing you to control your costs. Because you are likely to need to begin with a simple garden layout and gradually add extra features, such as a pergola and pond, over a number of years, you will be able to spread the cost of developing your garden over a longer period, which in itself may be quite desirable and possibly even necessary.

Family life can be time consuming and hectic, and if your garden design actually creates extra outside work, particularly of the boring 'chore' variety, you are not going to be popular. Any design that you come up with should, therefore, take this into account and, wherever possible and affordable, you should try and incorporate ideas and techniques that will keep garden maintenance to the absolute minimum or that will, at least, eliminate the more mundane aspects of it, leaving instead only those tasks that are more pleasurable or indeed therapeutic, such as dead-heading the roses or picking vegetables.

A relatively simple design will go a long way to helping you achieve this, and it will also help you to make better use of all the available space, which is especially important in smaller gardens. Where possible, at least in the early years, avoid fragmenting and dividing the garden into too many small spaces or areas in an effort to fit in all your requirements because what will happen is that you may well end up with a cluttered and impractical design that satisfies no one.

Guidelines for family gardens

Patios and paving

✷ Make patios and other paved areas as generous as possible, so that there is plenty of room for a variety of outdoor activities that require clean, level, hard surfaces.

✷ Garden paths should be wide enough for a range of uses, such as walking, running, riding bikes and trundling wheelbarrows. Allow extra width where the path changes direction, to discourage corner cutting.

Increase the width of paths at corners

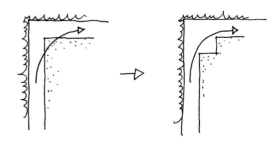

Narrow paths with sudden changes of direction can lead to corners being cut

Allow an extra paving area at the corners

✷ Avoid laying loose paving materials, such as gravel or stone chippings, in areas of heavy use where they may be easily displaced by running feet or spinning wheels.

✷ Rigid paving materials, such as flags or paving bricks, should be checked beforehand to make sure that they are non-slip, especially when wet.

✷ Wherever possible, lay areas of paving that will be subjected to heavy and frequent use, such as outside the backdoor, on a solid base of hardcore using a cement–sand mortar on which the slabs or bricks are bedded to prevent settling later on that might result in loose or uneven surfaces, which will not only look unsightly but could also be dangerous.

Lawns and grassed areas

✷ Make the lawn as large as possible, with room to accommodate a range of activities, and preferably keep the shape simple, avoiding narrow strips that would wear out quickly with regular use and be turned into mud baths or dust bowls.

Simple lawn shapes are easier to maintain

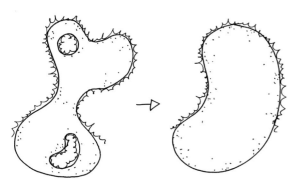

Wavy edged lawns and island beds look attractive but are not practical for general recreation

Keep shapes simpler – they are both practical and attractive

✶ For a lawn that is subject to frequent use, use a turf or seed mix that includes one or more of the dwarf varieties of perennial rye grass, which are relatively hard wearing but not quite as vigorous as the old-fashioned, taller types.

✶ Seeding a lawn will be cheaper than turfing. However, a turfed lawn will be usable much sooner.

✶ Install a rigid lawn edging or mowing strip, which will help to maintain the grass edge in a good condition and avoid damage where heavy use is inevitable.

Planting

✶ Keep planting areas bold and simple, rather than spread about in tiny beds and borders or even as individual plants set in the lawn. This will allow you to devote generous, uninterrupted areas for lawn and paving.

✶ In small gardens, use all the available wall and fence surfaces for planting climbers and trained wall shrubs, which will take up less space on the ground.

✶ If there are small children, check when you are purchasing plants to make sure that they are generally safe for use in your garden.

✶ Select durable, reliable shrubs, perennials and other plants that will regenerate easily if accidentally damaged and that will tolerate a wide range of soil conditions.

✶ Incorporate selected edible plants, such as herbs and salad crops, in your ornamental beds and borders where there is no space in the garden for a more traditional vegetable plot.

Arches and pergolas

✶ In both large and small family gardens, arches and pergolas are a good way to create additional room for growing ornamental climbers, edible

Usable lawn space

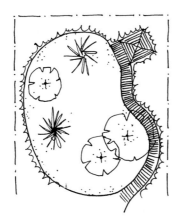

Left: Individual plants in lawns can make the overall area unsatisfactory for general family recreation

Right: Keep the lawn and patio areas as unbroken as possible to create the maximum possible usable space

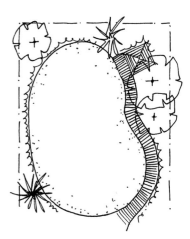

varieties, such as climbing beans, or cut flowers, such as sweetpeas.

✳ Arches and pergolas can be used to divide a family garden into separate areas or spaces without the need for a solid barrier, which, in a small garden, might be impracticable.

✳ To save on cost and to simplify construction, a row of two or more simple wooden arches can be joined together along their sides and tops with parallel wires or slender wooden battens. When planted with climbers, these will create a tunnel effect, much like a more expensive pergola.

✳ Simple, robust softwood structures, which are best pressure treated for a long life, are often just as effective as more expensive hardwood types, especially when you consider that they will eventually become covered with climbers, which will hide the structure anyway.

Water features

✳ Where there are going to be small children, water features should be chosen with safety in mind – a millstone or bubble fountain, for example – when the main body of water is securely concealed in an underground tank or sump. If you decide to have a pond, it should be properly secured by fencing of some sort, such as wrought iron railings with a lockable gate.

✳ Wall-mounted water spouts, such as a traditional lion's head mask, are another safe way of using water where there are children, and they can often be found for sale as complete kits.

✳ Where fencing is impracticable or too expensive, larger ponds can be made safe by laying heavy steel reinforcing mesh over them, even though this can be unsightly unless the pond is well-planted to hide the mesh.

Walls and fences

✳ Walls can make the securest and strongest garden boundaries, but they are also probably the most expensive way of doing so. Maintenance costs, however, can be minimal and a well-built wall should last indefinitely.

✳ Fences are usually more economical to build than walls, although they are not as strong overall and will require varying degrees of on-going maintenance, depending on their design and the materials used to construct them.

✳ Where the security of garden boundaries is important, any walls and fences should be designed in such a way as to make them difficult or impossible to climb over or through.

✳ Perforated screen block walls are relatively lightweight and do not have anything like the same inherent strength as an equivalent size wall made from solid brick or concrete blocks. They should not be used as a means of support for anything else, other than a couple of wires to support a delicate climber.

Shapes of garden

Although all gardens are individual, there are certain basic shapes of plot that seem to crop up on a regular basis, even though their sizes and proportions may vary from one garden to another. Even what might at first glance seem to be complicated shapes, can often be broken down into two, three or even more, simple and recognizable forms, which will ultimately prove to be valuable in the process of designing your garden, particularly if it doesn't conform to any of the basic shapes. Each of these shapes possesses certain characteristics that can influence a design for better or worse.

The five shapes described here – triangular, rectangular, corner (or L-shaped), wide and shallow, long and narrow – will cover a wide range of situations, and there is advice with each shape that will show you how to get the best out of each, using simple principles or ideas that, in most cases, can be applied regardless of the size of your garden.

Triangular gardens

If you were to take unusual garden shapes – that is, those that are not just a simple square or rectangle or some combination of the two – one of the most challenging from the point of view of garden design would be the triangle, especially the long, narrow variety. The main problem with this shape is the way that the two longer boundaries tend to funnel or channel your vision into the far, narrow corner, where they converge almost in a point, an effect that is made even more dramatic by the phenomenon of perspective. The apparent rapid decrease in the width of the garden caused by this odd shape will create a feeling of constriction or claustrophobia and lack of space, and the general result will be to make the garden appear or feel much smaller than it really is. When they are designing such a garden, many people unwittingly add to the problem by making their paths and borders run parallel to one or other of the longest boundary fences. Unfortunately, this only exaggerates the convergence effect. Similarly, people sometimes lay patios to face straight into the distant corner, with the same kind of result.

There are, however, three relatively simple and straightforward techniques that you can employ to help you overcome what can frequently be a tiresome and restrictive phenomenon in triangular gardens.

The first of these techniques is to break up the line of, or otherwise disguise, the garden boundaries, and in particular the point where the two longest boundaries meet, so that it becomes impossible for you to see directly into the corner or to follow the straight lines of the enclosing walls, fences or hedges.

Second, use a focal point, such as a summer-house, to draw attention in a particular direction, again usually away from the corner. If this is not practicable, the focal point should be brought well forward from the corner so that there is room behind for adequate tree and shrub planting to hide the junction of the boundaries at that point.

Disguising triangular gardens

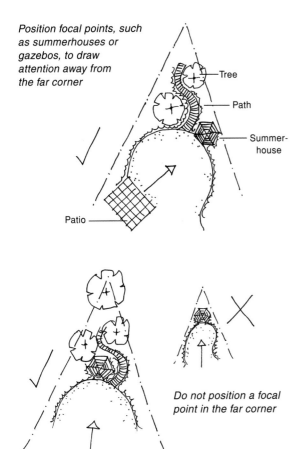

Position focal points, such as summerhouses or gazebos, to draw attention away from the far corner

Tree

Path

Summer-house

Patio

Bring forward the focal point and plant trees and shrubs behind it to hide the corner completely

Do not position a focal point in the far corner

Left: **Bold, large-leaved perennials and climbers will help to disguise the straight boundary walls of a triangular plot.**

Finally, the ground plan of paving, lawn, borders and other features should be laid out in a way that is in direct contrast to the triangular nature of the garden and that will divert your attention away from the boundary lines and the distant corner. If you are using straight lines for your path or lawn edges, say, make them run at angles to the boundaries, perhaps zigzagging backwards and forwards across the garden. Long, sweeping curves are equally effective, particularly where a circular theme is employed.

Rectangular gardens

Rectangular gardens, which, for the sake of this particular exercise, can also be taken to include square ones, might be said to be the most typical or commonly occurring of all garden shapes. However, the fact that it is such a frequently found shape does not necessarily make it any easier for you to create an interesting and individual garden design to suit your own needs. In some respects, in fact, you might find that the opposite is true. Because it is such a common shape, it is easy for newcomers to gardening to go out and find many poor examples of rectangular or square gardens that they might inadvertently use as a basis for their own designs, and in doing this, they are just as likely to perpetuate mistakes or pitfalls as they are to copy good ideas.

Probably the biggest trap that you may fall into when laying out a rectangular garden is to let the boundaries dictate the design. It is easy to make your lawn and patio rectangular or square or to have a straight path or paths running the length of the garden, parallel to the side fences or walls. What you are effectively doing is mimicking and emphasizing the square, box-like feel of the plot, and by doing this you are creating a garden that is completely lacking in surprise, interest or originality. The most straightforward solution to this problem, which indeed can be applied to all shapes of garden, is to disguise or hide the boundaries so that your garden appears not to have any at all. Because clues to its actual size cannot be perceived, you are freed from that particular constraint, which might influence your design. A dense covering of climbers planted on boundary walls and fences can be effective in hiding them, although if there is insufficient variation between the varieties they can actually end up looking flat, and they could even draw attention to the boundary instead of hiding it, especially if the selected plants are carefully trained along the top of the boundary fence in a horizontal line. It is much more effective if you can plant a mixture of large shrubs and trees as well as climbers, which will not only screen the

A winding path and borders with curved edges draw attention away from the long, straight boundaries of a rectangular garden.

structure of the boundary but will also break up the pronounced horizontal line that most boundary walls and fences produce.

The use of sweeping curves, particularly circles or part circles, when you are creating the plan is another device that can be effective in deflecting the viewer's eyes away from the straight sides of a garden because they constantly change direction. However, there may be instances when your design, for whatever reason, relies on straight lines rather than curves. These could be deliberately placed at angles to the boundaries – 45 degrees is a good angle to choose – rather than parallel to them, because your vision will be drawn away from the boundary lines, rather than directly along them. There is one exception to this particular approach, however, and that is when you have chosen to build a formal garden, which may actually be made more effective if you can emphasize the rectangular plot shape and use the straight boundaries as positive assets, by deliberately making your paths parallel to them and your patio or lawn rectangular in shape.

Simply turning shapes, such as a patio, through an angle can significantly influence the character of a garden and disguise its rectangular nature

Corner and L-shaped gardens

A corner plot, where the garden wraps around two adjoining sides of a house, may initially appear to be rather an awkward site to develop, chiefly because there seems to be no separation between front and back gardens in the accepted sense. Certainly, where you are looking for a greater degree of privacy, corner gardens can present more of a challenge, particularly as many such gardens occur at the junction of two roads. At the same time, however, the opportunities for creating an interesting and attractive garden can

be much greater than with a more traditional front and back arrangement. Because you are, effectively, combining both front and back gardens into one, there is a greater area and therefore more useful space and more scope for garden features, such as an additional sitting area, which can be tucked away into one of the corners. Although the visual effect of the boundaries may not be quite as dominant as in a simple rectangle, the same techniques can still be used to mask and disguise them. In addition, by turning your design through an angle of 45 or 60 degrees, you can open up opportunities to divide the garden from the corner of the house to the opposite diagonal corner of the garden if you feel that you would like a front and back layout.

L-shaped gardens, although they may be identical in both shape and size to corner plots, can offer different opportunities in some respects, largely because of how they come about. To all intents and purposes, they are just rectangular gardens but with an additional square or rectangle tacked on to the far end, away from the house on one side or the other. This extension of the

Left: The end of the plot is hidden behind the tall shrubs, but the path continues down the garden and suggests the presence of the space beyond. This is an ideal solution for an L-shaped garden.

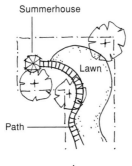

Above: Make the design of an L-shaped garden swing into the L to make the garden appear larger

retaining an element of surprise and mystery, because you would not really be sure of what lay just around the corner. This inviting approach to a design will work best if the boundaries of the garden are concealed as you would do in an ordinary rectangular plot, thus completely disguising the garden shape.

Wide, shallow gardens

In the strictest sense, wide, shallow gardens should really be included under the heading of rectangular, because that is often what they are. However, it is the fact that they are effectively turned on their side that makes them more of a challenge.

As with any rectangle, the design of these gardens can all too easily be influenced by the regimented square arrangement of the boundaries, and so the same techniques of disguising the boundaries and manipulating the space enclosed by them can and should be used to draw the viewer's attention away from the shape.

What can, and often does, cause particular difficulties, at least visually if not so much in practical terms, is the lack of depth, which unfortunately can be made to feel even more acute by the foreshortening effect of perspective, and can, in turn, make your garden appear to be even wider than it actually is. The far boundary wall, fence or hedge will accordingly appear close, and, depending on how long (or short) your garden is, the resulting feeling can be almost claustrophobic.

It is essential, first, that you plant up this far boundary with a mixture of trees, shrubs and climbers that will not only hide the vertical face, but that will also break up the pronounced horizontal line of the top of the fence or wall behind. The introduction of a false arch or pathway leading into the border along this boundary may

garden will probably not be visible directly from the house or from parts of the rest of the garden, and so there is lots of scope to develop a separate area that might take the form of a secret, ornamental garden into which you could escape, or you could use it to hide all the visually unacceptable items that are found in nearly all gardens – sheds and compost heaps, for example. On the other hand, the design of the garden could be arranged so as to lead you down and around into the 'extension', which might give the impression of it being a larger plot altogether while still

A tall evergreen, such as this conifer, will break up the strong horizontal lines of the fence.

Below: Disguising a wide, shallow shape

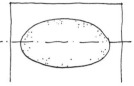

An oval lawn, with its axis running from left to right across the garden, will make it seem wider

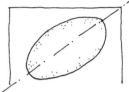

If the axis runs diagonally it will draw attention away from the extra width and shallow depth

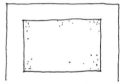

A rectangular lawn will serve only to emphasize the disproportionate shape of a wide, shallow garden

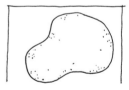

A curving, amorphously shaped lawn will help to disguise the garden's shape

suggest an entrance into more garden beyond, even though in reality there is nothing there.

What is as important, however, is for you to try and emphasize the longest dimensions of the garden, which are the diagonals running between opposite corners, in order to achieve a greater feeling of depth by drawing attention to them. You can do this by the technique of rotating any square and rectangular shapes in your design, such as a patio, through a suitable angle (not necessarily 45 degrees) so that the main view from it

144

is directed into one or other of the corners rather than at the nearest point of the far boundary fence. Then, in order to reinforce this, you can create focal points at each end of the diagonal or diagonals, which will provide further diversions for your attention.

The use of strong curves for making the shapes of lawns and patios, or serpentine paths as you would in a square or angular garden, is an excellent approach, and one of the most effective shapes is a circle, which is completely non-directional. An ellipse or oval can be equally effective, although in this case you must make sure that the axis of the ellipse is along one of the corner-to-corner diagonals and does not run directly across the garden from side to side, which could make it seem even wider.

Long, narrow gardens

The older, residential areas of many towns and cities are places where long, narrow gardens are most likely to be found, and they are particularly associated with terraced properties, which tend to have a fairly narrow frontage.

Although this shape of garden can often be equal to, if not greater in area than, a more traditionally proportioned rectangular plot, the overall dimensions of length and width can have a far more profound influence on the final design because of their relative proportions. The lack of width and the seemingly exaggerated length of these gardens can create a tunnel or corridor effect that, unless it can be suitably amended, will direct your gaze straight from one end of the garden to the other, leaving nothing to the imagination and even causing a slight feeling of claustrophobia. High boundary walls or fences are commonly found in this type of garden, and they serve only to accentuate the pronounced linear effect.

There are, however, two simple but effective ways in which you can overcome this apparent drawback and at the same time create a worthwhile garden. The first of these is to divide the garden into a series of two or three smaller spaces, which are still linked together but each of which has its own particular theme or function, which may or may not relate to the spaces on either side of it. The purpose of this is to prevent you from seeing directly down the garden, and the only way to find what is beyond is by actually walking through the separate spaces to see what lies ahead. It is not always necessary to use completely solid barriers, such as fences, walls or hedges, for this purpose. Often just the

Disguising a long, narrow garden

1 *Long, narrow gardens often leave nothing to the imagination*

2 *Sinuous, curving shapes disguise the length by providing continually changing viewpoints*

3 *An alternative is to divide the garden into two, three or even more almost separate compartments*

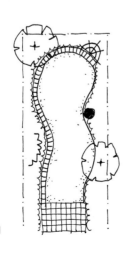

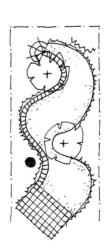

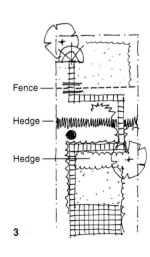

Fence

Hedge

Hedge

1

2

3

indication or suggestion of a screen, such as a free-standing trellis panel or maybe a group of tall bamboos, may be an adequate barrier. It is, in fact, important that an obvious link between the successive spaces is visible so that there is a sense of anticipation and interest as you proceed from one area to the next, otherwise you may well get the feeling that you are in a tiny and possibly claustrophobic garden, instead of what is actually a much larger one.

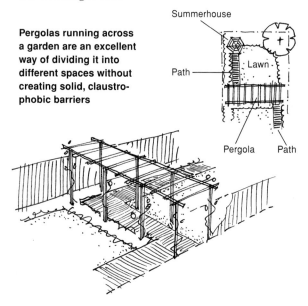

Pergolas running across a garden are an excellent way of dividing it into different spaces without creating solid, claustrophobic barriers

Summerhouse

Path

Lawn

Pergola   Path

The second way to tackle the problem of a long, narrow garden is strictly speaking a modification of the first, but it relies more on changing your angle of view as you progress down the garden. This can be achieved by, for example, putting in a long, serpentine lawn, which has carefully located features or groups of large plants placed on the inside of each bend, so that you cannot quite see beyond each bend until you have actually walked past it, and you only find out what is at the bottom of the garden after rounding, as it were, the final bend. If you do not want a lawn like this, you can use zigzag or meandering paths to create the same illusion, with a solid mass – whether living or man-made –

> ## Disguising the shape of your garden
>
> * Set square or rectangular patios and lawns at 45 degrees or another angle to the side boundaries.
> * Set paths to run at an angle to the garden boundaries, in zigzag or dog-leg style.
> * Make paths curved, meandering from side to side.
> * Fix trellis, pergolas and arches partially across the garden to interrupt the view and create almost separate compartments.
> * Use hedges, either evergreen or deciduous, to act in the same way as trellis.
> * Place groups of tall shrubs or trees at intervals in the line of sight to block views down or across the garden – this is particularly effective when used with informal curved paths and beds.
> * Use climbers and large shrubs, especially evergreen varieties, to disguise solid, formal boundary fences and to break up straight lines, particularly horizontal ones.
> * Carefully place focal points to draw attention in various chosen directions, positioning them so that they can be seen from different places in the garden.
> * Use shapes for lawns, patios and other flat areas that contrast with the shape of the garden.

at each change of direction, and at the same time, these will also divert your attention away from the severe boundaries, as would be the aim in a rectangular garden.

As in any garden enclosed by straight lines and right angles, you should endeavour to screen and break up the lines of boundary walls and fences using the same planting techniques that work in rectangular and other gardens.

The proportions of this long, narrow garden are cleverly disguised by the bold planting around the patio and the mixed border and arch across the centre of the plot.

Part 4

A SELECTION OF DESIGNS

In this final section we have taken the five styles already described – that is, low-cost and starter, low-maintenance, formal, plant lover's and family gardens – and have designed five gardens, one in each style. For each of these styles, there are five alternative designs that are based on the five fundamental garden shapes –

triangular, rectangular, corner (or L-shaped), wide and shallow and long and narrow. The dimensions for each of these garden shapes are shown below.

Altogether, there are 25 individual gardens, which you can copy, borrow ideas from or simply use as the inspiration for your own design.

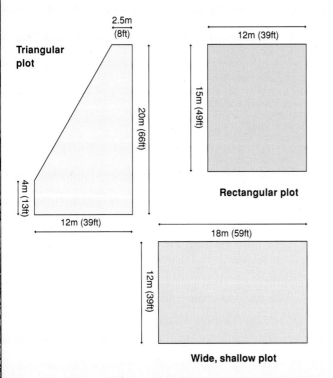

Triangular plot

2.5m (8ft)

20m (66ft)

4m (13ft)

12m (39ft)

Rectangular plot

12m (39ft)

15m (49ft)

Wide, shallow plot

18m (59ft)

12m (39ft)

Long, narrow plot

9m (29½ft)

22m (72ft)

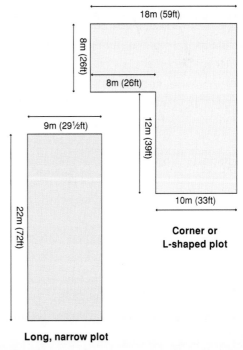

Corner or L-shaped plot

18m (59ft)

8m (26ft)

8m (26ft)

12m (39ft)

10m (33ft)

Low-cost and starter gardens

TRIANGULAR PLOT

This simple but effective and elegant garden design for a triangular plot, cleverly disguises the awkward nature of the site but at the same time leaves plenty of open, level space that is suitable for general garden recreation.

The patio of rectangular concrete slabs, which is angled to face the long boundary fence, provides easy access both directly onto the lawn and into the house by way of the patio doors. Large evergreen shrubs are planted in the small triangular bed behind the patio to create a soft, green backdrop. A small utility area, which is conveniently placed on the opposite side of the garden from the patio, and out of sight of the house, is screened from view by a combination of arches and trellis panels, which are planted with a mixture of climbers. This utility area is connected to the patio by a path, consisting of a single row of slabs, and a similar path leads round to the side of the house for access to the backdoor and the front garden.

At the far end of the garden, the narrowest point of the triangle is cut off by a trellis fence and gateway, and this creates a handy, concealed outside storage space for compost bins and any other garden objects that may need hiding. This storage area is connected to the patio by means of a curving, narrow gravel path. One end of this

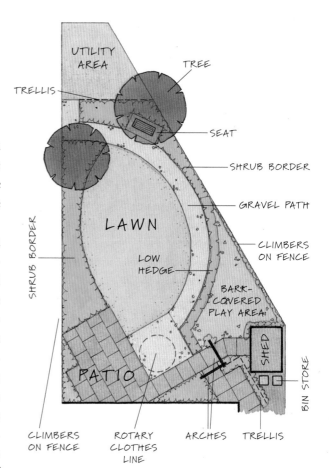

path is extended to form a small sitting area beneath a tree and the other end, nearer the house, forms a square large enough to provide room for a rotary clothes line, which is carefully positioned so as not to be in line with either the kitchen or sitting room windows.

The efficient use of space in the design of this garden allows for a small, almost self-contained play area to be created behind the shed, and although it is separated from the main garden by

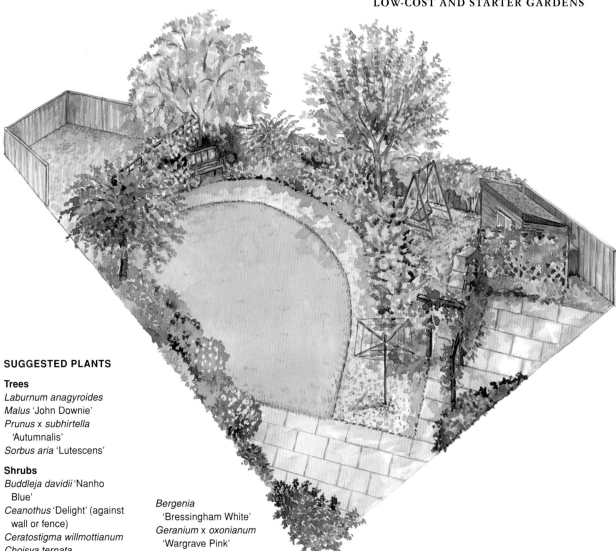

SUGGESTED PLANTS

Trees

Laburnum anagyroides
Malus 'John Downie'
Prunus x *subhirtella*
 'Autumnalis'
Sorbus aria 'Lutescens'

Shrubs

Buddleja davidii 'Nanho
 Blue'
Ceanothus 'Delight' (against
 wall or fence)
Ceratostigma willmottianum
Choisya ternata
Cornus alba 'Elegantissima'
Cornus alba 'Sibirica'
Elaeagnus x *ebbingei*
 'Limelight'
Hebe subalpina
Mahonia x *media* 'Winter
 Sun'
Philadelphus coronarius
 'Aureus'
Potentilla fruticosa 'Princess'
 (for hedge to play area)
Pyracantha 'Orange Glow'
Spiraea japonica 'Gold
 Mound' (for hedge to play
 area)
Viburnum davidii

Perennials

Achillea 'Moonshine'
Alchemilla mollis
Aster novi-belgii
 'Lady in Blue'
Bergenia
 'Bressingham White'
Geranium x *oxonianum*
 'Wargrave Pink'
Hemerocallis
 'Burning Daylight'
Leucanthemum x *superbum*
 'Snowcap'

Climbers

Clematis montana 'Alba'
Hedera colchica 'Sulphur
 Heart'
Jasminum officinale f. *affine*
Lonicera periclymenum
 'Serotina'
Rosa 'Schoolgirl'

Conifers and heathers

Erica x *darleyensis*
 'Silberschmelze' ('Molten
 Silver')
Erica erigena 'Irish Salmon'
Juniperus x *pfitzeriana*
 'Gold Coast'
Taxus baccata
 'Semperaurea'

a soft, low hedge of potentilla, it can still be easily supervised from the house or from anywhere else in the garden.

Most of the planting in this garden is contained within two simple, curved perimeter borders. A selection of trees and easy-care and reliable shrubs, both evergreen and deciduous, is interplanted with low, spreading perennials and ground cover to keep maintenance to a minimum. Climbers growing on the boundary fences are supported by horizontal wires, providing plenty of flower and foliage interest within a relatively modest space.

151

RECTANGULAR PLOT

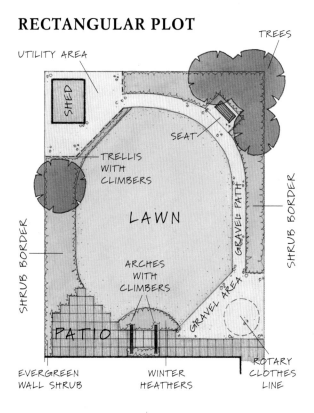

UTILITY AREA

TREES

SHED

SEAT

TRELLIS
WITH
CLIMBERS

LAWN

GRAVEL PATH

SHRUB BORDER

SHRUB BORDER

ARCHES
WITH
CLIMBERS

GRAVEL AREA

PATIO

EVERGREEN
WALL SHRUB

WINTER
HEATHERS

ROTARY
CLOTHES
LINE

A generous gravel area, retained by a low timber edge, provides plenty of space for a rotary clothes line, and it can also be used to stand out plants in containers for additional interest. This gravel area extends into a narrow path, which curves around in front of the bench seat and leads to a small garden utility area in the other far corner, where a shed and other basic gardening necessities are concealed from view by a screen of trellis panels covered in climbers. The planting theme in this design emphasizes the use of reliable medium and large evergreen and deciduous shrubs to form the basic structure, with perennials and dwarf shrubs planted between and beneath them for additional colour and also to act as ground cover. The choice of plants ensures that there is some interest in the garden all year round. All the boundaries are planted with climbers, which are trained onto wires and trellis panels, to provide extra flowers and foliage in what is a relatively small garden.

Vigorous climbers, such as honeysuckle and a clematis – here *Clematis* 'Comtesse de Bouchaud' – are a relatively inexpensive way of creating a quick, effective screen.

The design of this almost typical rectangular garden deliberately cuts off the corners so that the overall squareness of the plot is lost, and the slightly unorthodox lawn shape actually proves to be effective in providing a good-sized, usable recreation area, especially when it is combined with the surrounding paving.

To make construction easier, the square flagstones forming the patio are laid parallel to the house wall, but at the junction with the lawn the pattern is dog-toothed to create what is essentially a 45-degree angle to the paving, and this focuses attention on the bench seat in the opposite corner of the garden, beneath a small group of trees. A simple, matching flagstone path provides a link from the patio around the house, passing as it does so beneath two wooden arches, which help to suggest separate areas on the patio and which are emphasized by a small bed of winter heathers to one side of the arches.

SUGGESTED PLANTS

Trees
Betula pendula
Malus 'Royalty'
Prunus padus 'Watereri'
Robinia pseudoacacia 'Frisia'

Shrubs
Buddleja davidii 'Pink
  Beauty'
Caryopteris x *clandonensis*
  'Heavenly Blue'
Cornus alba 'Spaethii'
Cornus stolonifera
  'Flaviramea'
Cotoneaster x *suecicus*
  'Coral Beauty'
Deutzia x *kalmiiflora*
Elaeagnus pungens
  'Maculata'

Hebe pinguifolia 'Pagei'
Kerria japonica 'Pleniflora'
Mahonia aquifolium 'Apollo'
Philadelphus 'Manteau
  d'Hermine'
Pyracantha 'Soleil d'Or'
  (trained as a wall shrub)
Spiraea nipponica
  'Snowmound'
Viburnum tinus 'Eve Price'

Perennials
Achillea 'Fanal' (syn. *A.* 'The
  Beacon')
Aster novi-belgii 'Little Pink
  Beauty'
Bergenia cordifolia
  'Purpurea'
Hemerocallis 'Pink Damask'
Iris 'Jane Phillips'
Symphytum 'Goldsmith'
Veronica spicata 'Heidekind'
Vinca minor
  'Argenteovariegata'

Climbers
Clematis montana var.
  rubens
Clematis 'The President'
Hedera helix 'Oro di
  Bogliasco' ('Goldheart')
Hydrangea anomala ssp.
  petiolaris
Jasminum nudiflorum
Lonicera x *heckrottii* 'Gold
  Flame'
Rosa 'Meg'

Conifers and heathers
Erica carnea 'Foxhollow'
Erica carnea 'Springwood
  Pink'
Erica x *darleyensis* 'Darley
  Dale'
Juniperus squamata 'Blue
  Star'
Taxus baccata 'Repens
  Aurea'

153

CORNER PLOT

The extra space that a corner plot can offer compared with a more traditional back and front arrangement is used to good effect in this design.

Although the basic lawn shape closely matches the shape of the plot, it is turned through 45 degrees and in doing this completely changes the outlook of the garden by creating two triangular corners away from the front of the house. These areas provide ideal locations for an alternative sitting area and a play area. At the same time, the edge of the lawn creates a diagonal line from the corner of the house, and this provides a perfect opportunity to separate the garden into two distinct areas – one ornamental, one utility.

The broadly triangular patio, which is enclosed by the lawn, gets sun nearly all day because of its position on the corner of the house by the french windows. It is connected to the play area by a timber-edged, bark-covered path on one side of the lawn, and to the sitting area by means of a gravel path, which passes at one point beneath a climber-covered rustic arch on the opposite side. The play area is also covered in bark, and is separated from the lawn by a low, evergreen hedge.

The angular shape of the lawn provides an ideal opportunity for creating a large, separate utility and kitchen garden area down the other side of the house, and this is separated from the rest of the garden by the bark path and an informal hedge of mixed shrubs. An extension of the bark path positioned between the patio and the kitchen garden is made large enough to accommodate a rotary clothes line, which is conveniently placed close to the kitchen door for easy access and in a position that is sunny for a large part of the day.

Because of its position on the corner, the ornamental part of the garden could be overlooked from outside the boundaries, and planting

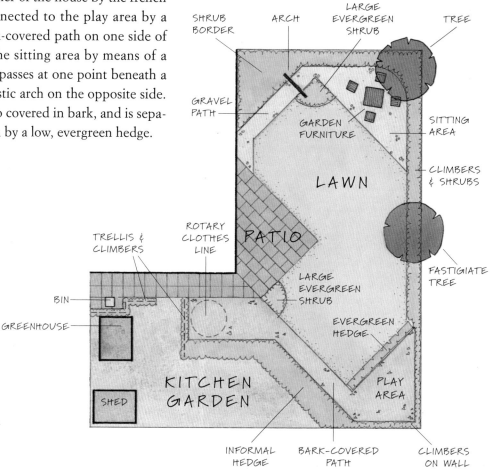

around this section is therefore of taller shrubs, with a particular emphasis on evergreens that will tolerate clipping or pruning as necessary, once they have achieved their required height, to keep them within bounds. A selection of mixed climbers growing on the boundary wall adds extra height and privacy as well as their own flower and foliage interest.

SUGGESTED PLANTS

Trees
Betula pendula 'Purpurea'
Malus x *zumi* 'Golden Hornet'
Prunus cerasifera 'Nigra' (syn. *P.* 'Pissardii Nigra')
Sorbus 'Joseph Rock'

Shrubs
Buddleja globosa
Cornus alba 'Aurea'
Cotoneaster horizontalis
Elaeagnus x *ebbingei*
Euonymus fortunei 'Emerald 'n' Gold' (for hedge by play area)
Hibiscus syriacus 'Oiseau Bleu' ('Blue Bird')
Ilex x *altaclerensis* 'Golden King'
Kerria japonica 'Pleniflora'
Mahonia x *media* 'Charity'
Philadelphus 'Beauclerk'
Prunus lusitanica 'Variegata'
Pyracantha 'Teton'
Rosa 'Pink Grootendorst'
Viburnum x *bodnantense* 'Dawn'
Viburnum tinus 'Eve Price'

Perennials
Aster novi-belgii 'Audrey'
Bergenia 'Wintermärchen'
Geranium ibericum
Hemerocallis 'Stafford'
Iris foetidissima
Lavandula angustifolia 'Nana Alba'
Miscanthus sacchariflorus
Miscanthus sinensis 'Variegatus'
Persicaria affinis 'Superba'
Veronica gentianoides
Vinca minor 'Atropurpurea'

Climbers
Clematis tangutica
Clematis 'Ville de Lyon'
Hedera canariensis 'Gloire de Marengo' (syn. *H. c.* 'Variegata')
Jasminum x *stephanense*
Lonicera periclymenum 'Belgica'
Rosa 'American Pillar'
Rosa 'Seagull'

Conifers and heathers
Erica carnea 'Springwood White'
Erica x *darleyensis* 'J.W. Porter'
Erica erigena 'W.T. Rackliff'
Juniperus horizontalis Glauca Group
Juniperus sabina 'Tamariscifolia'
Pinus mugo var. *mugo*

WIDE, SHALLOW PLOT

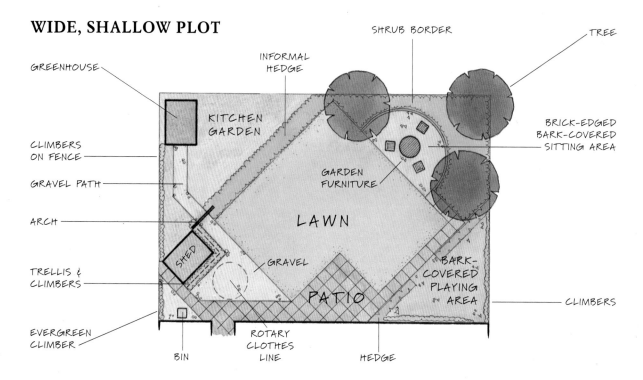

GREENHOUSE

INFORMAL HEDGE

SHRUB BORDER

TREE

KITCHEN GARDEN

CLIMBERS ON FENCE

GRAVEL PATH

ARCH

BRICK-EDGED BARK-COVERED SITTING AREA

GARDEN FURNITURE

LAWN

SHED

GRAVEL

TRELLIS & CLIMBERS

BARK-COVERED PLAYING AREA

PATIO

CLIMBERS

EVERGREEN CLIMBER

BIN

ROTARY CLOTHES LINE

HEDGE

In this garden, an L-shaped lawn is carefully and deliberately introduced as a central feature. Turning it through an angle of 45 degrees creates a series of angular spaces, and these help to disguise the shape of what would otherwise be an awkwardly proportioned and rather difficult plot. The small patio of square slabs, which is enclosed on two sides by the lawn, acts as a division between the utility garden to the left and the ornamental garden to the right, while being connected to both of them by slab paths. The right-hand path runs around the lawn and leads to a semicircle of gravel, which forms an alternative sitting area to the patio and acts as a focal point in that corner.

The triangle that is cut off between the patio and sitting area by this path makes an ideal play area. It is covered in chipped bark and is separated by a low, soft hedge from the rest of the garden. On the opposite side of the patio, a utility area of flagstones and gravel is conveniently situated with plenty of room for a shed, clothes line and bin store and with access to the front garden. There is a gravel path linking this area to a kitchen garden, which is screened from the rest of the garden and the house by an informal hedge of mixed deciduous and evergreen shrubs. A simple rustic arch provides a gateway through this hedge, and there is even space in the corner of the kitchen garden for a small greenhouse if wished.

In general, the planting throughout the garden is of reliable trees, shrubs and perennials, which have been selected for their ease of maintenance and to provide a degree of interest all year round. The informal hedge is allowed to grow to a height just above the fence level, so that this is not visible, and the corner behind the semicircular sitting area is similarly planted with tall shrubs and trees for the same purpose. Fences and walls within the ornamental garden are covered either with climbers or with wall shrubs, which have been trimmed and shaped to cover the flat surfaces against which they are growing.

SUGGESTED PLANTS

Trees
Betula utilis
Laburnum x *watereri* 'Vossii'
Prunus 'Pandora'
Sorbus aria 'Lutescens'

Shrubs
Brachyglottis greyi
Buddleja davidii 'Black
  Knight'
Cornus alba 'Kesselringii'
Cornus mas
Elaeagnus x *ebbingei* 'Gilt
  Edge'
Forsythia x *intermedia*
  'Lynwood'
Hebe pimeleoides
  'Quicksilver'
Ilex aquifolium 'Silver
  Queen'
Mahonia aquifolium
Potentilla fruticosa
  'Princess'
Pyracantha 'Mohave'

Rosa glauca
Spiraea x *vanhouttei*
Viburnum tinus 'Variegatum'
Weigela florida
  'Aureovariegata'

Perennials
Dicentra eximia
Doronicum 'Miss Mason'
Geranium macrorrhizum
  'Ingwersen's Variety'
Hemerocallis 'Stella de Oro'
Lavandula angustifolia

'Hidcote'
Rudbeckia fulgida var.
  sullivantii 'Goldsturm'
Vinca minor

Climbers
Actinidia kolomikta
Clematis 'Jackmanii
  Superba'
Clematis orientalis 'Bill

MacKenzie'
Hedera colchica 'Dentata
  Variegata'
Hydrangea anomala ssp.
  petiolaris
Lonicera japonica var.
  repens
Rosa 'Golden Showers'
Rosa 'Zéphirine Drouhin'

Conifers and heathers
Erica carnea 'Vivellii'
Erica vagans 'Lyonesse'
Juniperus horizontalis 'Blue
  Chip'

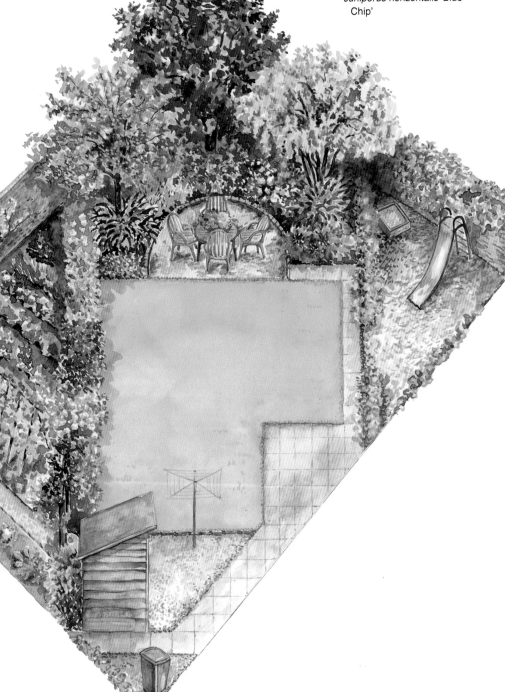

157

LONG, NARROW PLOT

Dividing this plot into a series of smaller connected areas makes a much more interesting and satisfactory design and eliminates the restricted view that is often to be found in such long, narrow gardens. The division relies on planting for its effect rather than the use of solid, man-made objects, and this style of approach complements the square, almost formal, manner in which the areas of the garden are marked out on the ground.

The main patio in front of the house is deliberately placed slightly off centre to allow just enough room on the other side of the garden to place a small shed, with space in front for a rotary

Annuals, such as marigolds, cleomes and dahlias are an obvious way of filling a space with reliable colour, but, combined with colourful and ornamental vegetables, such as cardoons, cabbages and ruby chard, they make a border both decorative and useful.

clothes line. Both of these are set on an area of gravel rather than more slabs in order to keep overall paving costs to a minimum. A small arch set against the house wall provides a suggestion of division between the ornamental patio and the utility area. A simple path of square flagstones runs beneath the arch, providing a link to the side passage and backdoor of the house.

Beyond the patio a specimen *Acer palmatum* f. *atropurpureum* partially obscures the view, and further on the rectangular lawn is separated by a border of mixed shrubs from a bark area behind it. This can be used as an alternative, more secluded space for sitting, or it can double up, if required, as a play area.

At the far end of the plot is a kitchen garden, again separated from the bark play and sitting area by an informal hedge of shrubs, but using varieties that will tolerate regular trimming in order to prevent too much encroachment into what is a limited area for growing vegetables

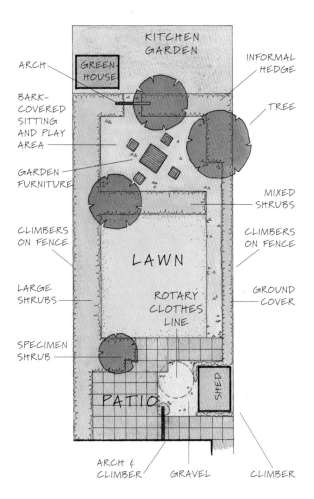

SUGGESTED PLANTS

Trees
Acer negundo 'Variegatum'
Betula pendula
Malus 'Evereste'
Sorbus aucuparia
  'Sheerwater Seedling'

Shrubs
Acer palmatum
  f. *atropurpureum*
Buddleja davidii 'Royal Red'
Ceanothus impressus
Choisya ternata
  'Sundance'

Cornus alba 'Elegantissima'
Cotoneaster x *suecicus*
  'Coral Beauty'
Euonymus fortunei 'Emerald
  Gaiety'
Forsythia x *intermedia*
  'Spectabilis'
Hibiscus syriacus
  'Woodbridge'
Leycesteria formosa
Mahonia aquifolium
  'Apollo'

Prunus laurocerasus 'Otto
  Luyken'
Pyracantha 'Harlequin'
Ribes sanguineum 'King
  Edward VII'
Rosa 'Buff Beauty'
Sarcococca confusa
Viburnum davidii

Perennials
Alchemilla mollis
Aquilegia McKana Group
Brunnera macrophylla
Euphorbia amygdaloides
  var. *robbiae*
Geranium phaeum 'Album'
Hemerocallis 'Bonanza'
Lamium maculatum 'Beacon
  Silver'

Persicaria affinis 'Superba'
Symphytum 'Hidcote Blue'
Vinca minor
  'Argenteomarginata'

Climbers
Actinidia deliciosa (syn.
  A. chinensis)
Clematis macropetala
  'Markham's Pink'
Clematis 'Rouge Cardinal'
Jasminum officinale
Lonicera periclymenum
  'Graham Thomas'
Rosa 'Meg'
Rosa 'Paul's Scarlet Climber'

Conifers and heathers
Erica erigena 'Golden Lady'
Erica erigena 'Irish Salmon'
Juniperus x *pfitzeriana* 'Gold
  Coast'
Juniperus scopulorum 'Blue
  Heaven'
Taxus baccata 'Fastigiata
  Aurea'

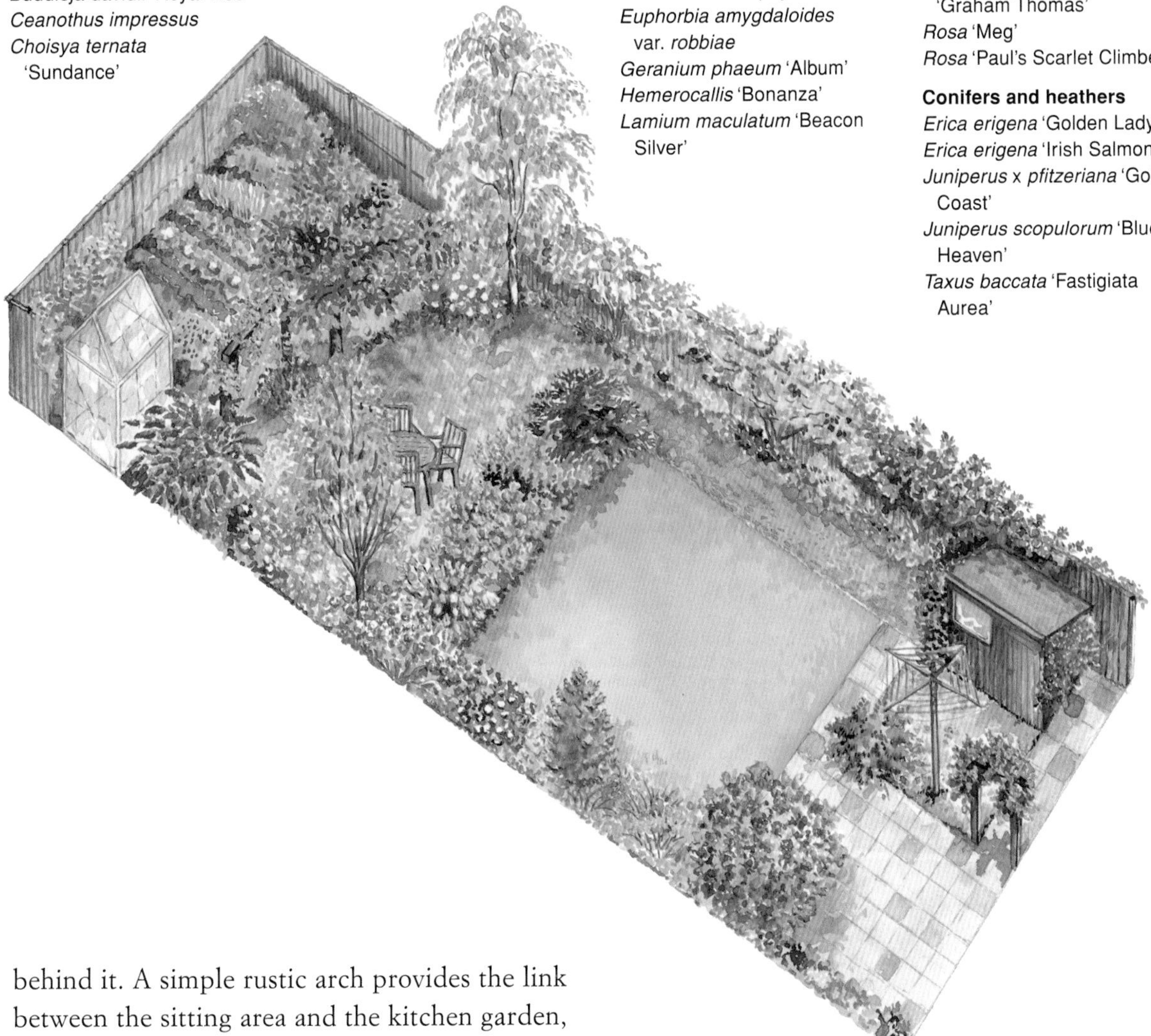

behind it. A simple rustic arch provides the link between the sitting area and the kitchen garden, where there is just enough space for a small greenhouse or cold frame.

The narrow areas of planting are built up in tiers in order to maximize what little growing space there is. Taller shrubs are underplanted with low shrubs and ground-cover perennials, which will tolerate the shade and the dryness caused by the larger shrubs and trees.

Low-maintenance gardens

TRIANGULAR PLOT

A striking combination of regular geometric patterns and informal curves in this design is most effective in hiding the fact that the garden is actually an awkward triangular shape.

The generous patio is rotated through an angle to face the far end of the garden, but what would otherwise be a distant view of the corner is then deliberately obscured by an attractive cedarwood gazebo with a shingle roof, set in a generous area of planting. A narrow curving path, one flagstone wide, sweeps around the right-hand side of the lawn, connecting the patio to the gazebo, and from there a second, brick-edged gravel path curves around and behind the gazebo to create the illusion of more garden beyond this point. This effect is given an added dimension by the combination of three arches straddling the gravel path, which give additional height. At the far end of the garden, the awkward, narrow corner is ideal as an outdoor storage area, and a trellis fence at the front, covered with evergreen climbers, completely screens it and the boundary fence behind it from view.

In the foreground, just off the corner of the patio, a low raised brick bed is lined with a pond liner and holds a millstone water feature, which is surrounded by beach cobbles. On the opposite side of the path from this is a utility area, housing a tool shed, a space for storing logs and a bin, which is enclosed and screened from view by a trellis fence planted with mixed climbers.

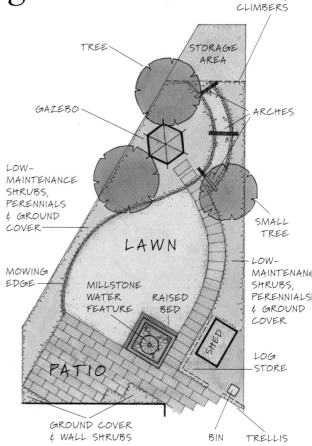

The lawn is entirely surrounded by a mowing edge composed of either paving flags or bricks, which are designed to make grass cutting much simpler and less time consuming.

Planting throughout the garden is of trees, shrubs, perennials and ground cover, and wherever possible varieties have been selected that require little or no regular maintenance. The beds are heavily mulched with bark chippings to suppress weeds and conserve moisture, but there is also a simple porous-pipe irrigation system, which is laid between the plants prior to mulching and which can be simply connected to an outside tap and turned on when watering is required during exceptionally dry spells.

SUGGESTED PLANTS

Trees
Acer negundo 'Flamingo'
Betula papyrifera
Malus floribunda
Sorbus aria 'Lutescens'

Shrubs
Berberis thunbergii 'Dart's Red Lady'
Ceaonothus 'Puget Blue'
Cotinus 'Grace'
Cotoneaster conspicuus 'Decorus'
Elaeagnus pungens 'Variegata'
Euonymus fortunei 'Golden Prince'
Ilex aquifolium 'Pyramidalis'
Osmanthus x *burkwoodii*
Potentilla fruticosa 'Abbotswood'
Prunus laurocerasus 'Zabeliana'
Pyracantha 'Orange Glow'
Rosa 'Nozomi'
Spiraea japonica 'Golden Princess'

Viburnum davidii
Viburnum opulus 'Compactum'
Viburnum tinus
Weigela florida 'Foliis Purpureis'

Perennials and grasses
Bergenia 'Sunningdale'
Brunnera macrophylla 'Dawson's White' (syn. *B. m.* 'Variegata')
Carex hachijoensis 'Evergold'
Euphorbia amygdaloides var. *robbiae*
Geranium x *cantabrigiense* 'Cambridge'
Hemerocallis 'Stella de Oro'
Hosta fortunei var. *aureomarginata*
Iris foetidissima
Lamium maculatum 'Roseum'

Liriope muscari
Miscanthus sinensis var. *purpurascens*
Symphytum 'Goldsmith'
Vinca minor 'Argenteovariegata'

Climbers
Actinidia kolomikta
Clematis armandii
Hedera colchica 'Sulphur Heart'
Hydrangea anomala ssp. *petiolaris*
Jasminum x *stephanense*
Lonicera henryi

Conifers and heathers
Erica carnea 'King George'
Erica x *darleyensis* 'Silberschmelze' ('Molten Silver')
Erica vagans 'Valerie Proudley'
Juniperus virginiana 'Sulphur Spray'
Pinus mugo 'Ophir'
Taxus baccata 'Semperaurea'

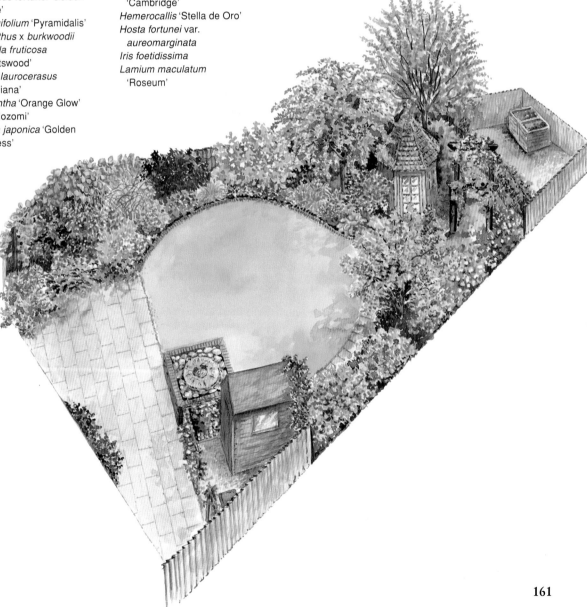

RECTANGULAR PLOT

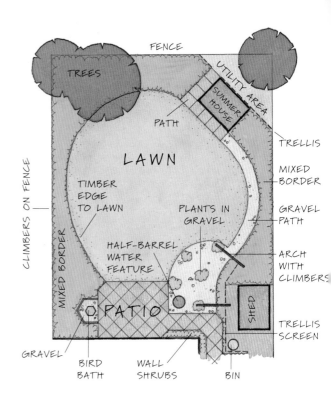

The shape of the lawn in this garden has been deliberately made into an ellipse in order to manipulate the overall design in two ways. First, its own strong shape provides a striking contrast to the straight lines and angles of the garden boundaries. Second, it helps to create extra depth in the far corners of the garden, which allows scope for greater areas of planting and the inclusion of other features of interest or necessity.

The patio is joined to the lawn across its full width, which is a convenient and practical arrangement allowing easy access between the two, and although the patio faces directly up the garden, it is the two far corners that will actually draw attention, one of them because it is densely planted and includes two ornamental trees, and the other because it is the location of a chalet-style summerhouse. Behind the summerhouse, the corner is ideal for use as a garden utility or storage area, with access from a narrow flagstone path along the far side of the summerhouse.

A domestic utility area consisting of a shed and bin store is completely screened off by wrought iron panels, which are planted with evergreen

and deciduous climbers. The patio itself, which is made from square flags, connects to a path that gives easy access to both the backdoor and the utility area. In the opposite direction the patio links with an informal, timber-edged gravel path curving gently up to the summerhouse. The patio and gravel path merge together in a larger area of gravel, on which is set a tiny, wooden half-barrel. Additional interest is provided by individual plants growing through the gravel surrounding it. Wrought iron arches in the same style as the trellis screen separate the flag paving, the water feature area and the gravel path beyond.

On the other side of the patio is a smaller gravel area, on which stands a bird bath. The gravel areas and lawn are edged with thin planks of pressure-treated timber.

A mixture of climbers is trained onto horizontal wires attached to the fence. The main planting areas incorporate a selection of trees, shrubs, perennials and grasses, to give year-round, low-maintenance interest. These are all planted through a mulching fabric which is pinned down onto the soil surface with wire hoops.

Wooden half-barrels can be easily made into small-scale water features that, once planted with miniature waterlilies and *Iris laevigata*, will require little attention.

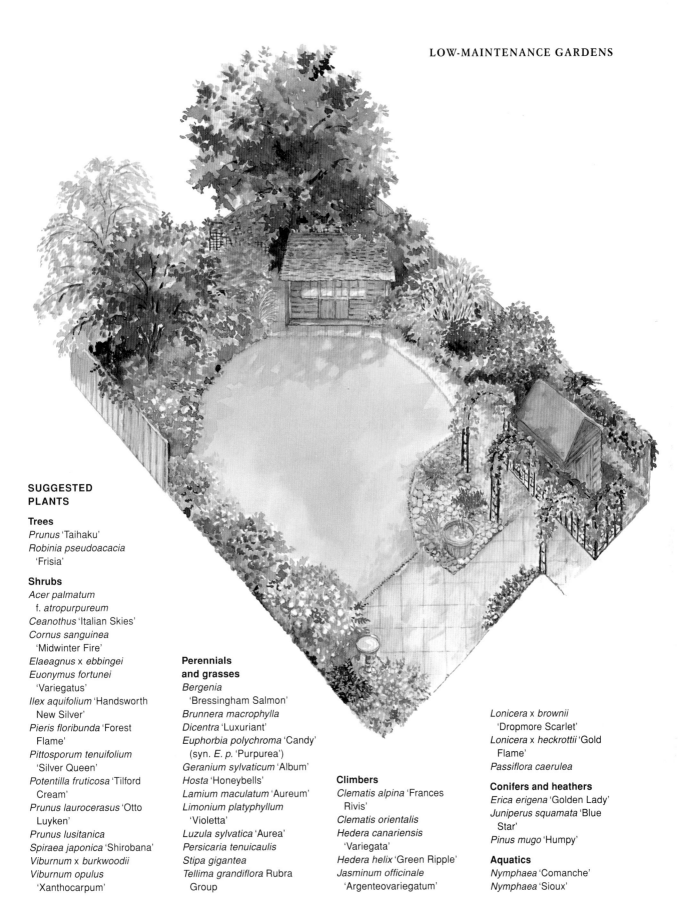

SUGGESTED PLANTS

Trees

Prunus 'Taihaku'
Robinia pseudoacacia
 'Frisia'

Shrubs

Acer palmatum
 f. atropurpureum
Ceanothus 'Italian Skies'
Cornus sanguinea
 'Midwinter Fire'
Elaeagnus x ebbingei
Euonymus fortunei
 'Variegatus'
Ilex aquifolium 'Handsworth
 New Silver'
Pieris floribunda 'Forest
 Flame'
Pittosporum tenuifolium
 'Silver Queen'
Potentilla fruticosa 'Tilford
 Cream'
Prunus laurocerasus 'Otto
 Luyken'
Prunus lusitanica
Spiraea japonica 'Shirobana'
Viburnum x burkwoodii
Viburnum opulus
 'Xanthocarpum'

Perennials and grasses

Bergenia
 'Bressingham Salmon'
Brunnera macrophylla
Dicentra 'Luxuriant'
Euphorbia polychroma 'Candy'
 (syn. E. p. 'Purpurea')
Geranium sylvaticum 'Album'
Hosta 'Honeybells'
Lamium maculatum 'Aureum'
Limonium platyphyllum
 'Violetta'
Luzula sylvatica 'Aurea'
Persicaria tenuicaulis
Stipa gigantea
Tellima grandiflora Rubra
 Group

Climbers

Clematis alpina 'Frances
 Rivis'
Clematis orientalis
Hedera canariensis
 'Variegata'
Hedera helix 'Green Ripple'
Jasminum officinale
 'Argenteovariegatum'
Lonicera x brownii
 'Dropmore Scarlet'
Lonicera x heckrottii 'Gold
 Flame'
Passiflora caerulea

Conifers and heathers

Erica erigena 'Golden Lady'
Juniperus squamata 'Blue
 Star'
Pinus mugo 'Humpy'

Aquatics

Nymphaea 'Comanche'
Nymphaea 'Sioux'

L-SHAPED PLOT

A conscious decision has been made in this garden to sweep the informal lawn right round into the foot of the L-shaped extension, giving the impression that the garden extends into an unknown and unseen area beyond, and the informality of the whole design is a key element in disguising the rather odd shape and rigid, angular boundaries.

The patio of random rectangular stone flags is set at an angle across the garden, and is substantially enclosed by plants on three sides, giving it a secluded and comfortable feel. This feeling is made even stronger by the two arches, which are linked together to form a pergola at one corner. Beneath this pergola, the stone paving extends on one side to a fuel and bin store, which is screened off by a wall, and also straight ahead to join a gravel and stepping-stone path. This path curves round to a prominent rock and water feature, which is set in a bed of gravel on the inside corner of the L. At this point, the path swings left to a utility area and kitchen garden, which is hidden behind a trellis fence, and also to the right, where it crosses the lawn to reach a black-painted metal gazebo in the opposite far corner. Beneath the gazebo is a bench seat set on a gravel-covered base.

Both the lawn and the gravel path are retained with a purpose-made, flexible edging, which fulfils the dual purpose of preventing the gravel from spilling onto the grass or soil on each side of the path and of helping to maintain the neat curves of the lawn, which are so important to the effect of the layout. In addition, the gravel is laid on top of a porous mulching fabric to prevent it from being trodden into the soil beneath.

Planting in this garden is predominantly confined to a perimeter border, which is given added

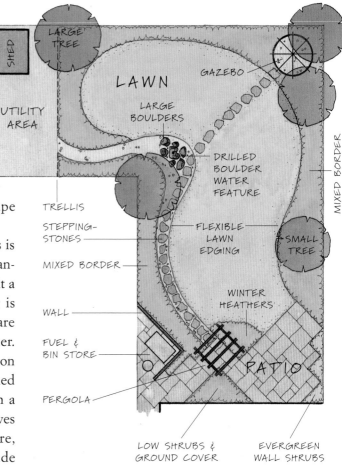

interest by the wide variation in depth, resulting from the lawn's irregular shape. The plants are a mixture of trees, shrubs, perennials and grasses, and they include several bamboos, which are particularly valuable in such a garden because their elegant, tall yet relatively narrow shapes are ideal for helping to break up the strong horizontal effect caused by the boundary fence and wall.

All the planting areas are mulched with composted, chipped bark to prevent the germination of weed seeds and to conserve moisture. Both the beds and lawn can be watered by a sprinkler irrigation system, controlled from an outside tap by an automatic timer, which can be programmed to control both the frequency and duration of watering.

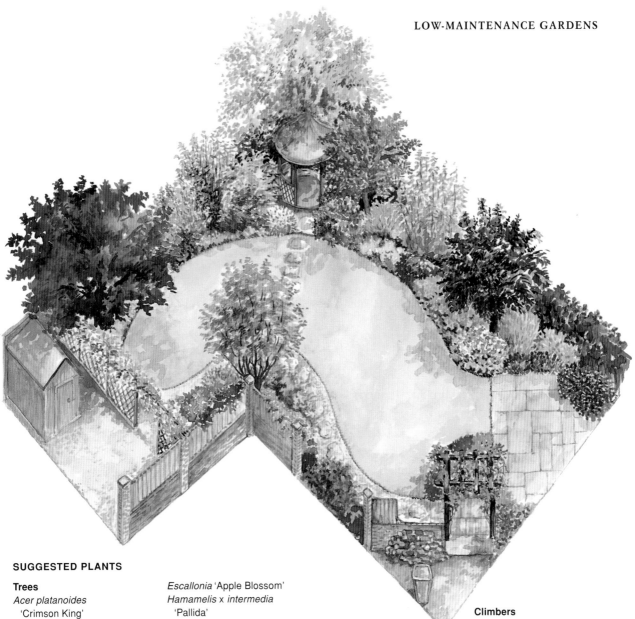

SUGGESTED PLANTS

Trees

Acer platanoides
  'Crimson King'
Betula utilis var.
  jacquemontii
Malus x *robusta* 'Red
  Siberian'
Prunus cerasifera 'Nigra'
Sorbus 'Joseph Rock'

Shrubs

Buddleja x *weyeriana*
  'Sungold'
Carpenteria californica
Ceanothus 'Blue Mound'
Chaenomeles x *superba*
  'Crimson and Gold'
Cornus stolonifera
  'Flaviramea'
Deutzia x *elegantissima*
Elaeagnus pungens
  'Dicksonii'

Escallonia 'Apple Blossom'
Hamamelis x *intermedia*
  'Pallida'
Kolkwitzia amabilis 'Pink
  Cloud'
Leycesteria formosa
Photinia x *fraseri* 'Red
  Robin'
Prunus cerasifera
Pyracantha 'Soleil d'Or'
Rosa rugosa 'Alba'
Spiraea nipponica
  'Snowmound'
Viburnum farreri

Perennials and grasses

Acanthus mollis Latifolius
  Group
Alchemilla mollis
Aster amellus 'King George'
Fargesia murieliae
Geranium renardii

Heuchera micrantha var.
  diversifolia 'Palace Purple'
Leucanthemum x *superbum*
  'Wirral Supreme'
Linum narbonense 'Heavenly
  Blue'
Miscanthus sacchariflorus
Miscanthus sinensis 'Strictus'
Pachysandra terminalis
Phyllostachys nigra
Pseudosasa japonica
Solidago 'Queenie' (syn.
  S. 'Golden Thumb')
Tiarella cordifolia
Tradescantia x *andersoniana*
  'Purple Dome'

Climbers

Actinidia deliciosa 'Hayward'
Clematis armandii 'Apple
  Blossom'
Clematis cirrhosa var.
  balearica
Hedera helix 'Buttercup'
Jasminum beesianum
Lonicera japonica
  'Aureoreticulata'
Vitis vinifera 'Purpurea'
Wisteria floribunda
  'Longissima Alba'

Conifers and heathers

Erica carnea 'Ruby Glow'
Erica x *darleyensis* 'Furzey'
Erica x *darleyensis*
  'Margaret Porter'
Juniperus chinensis 'Stricta'

165

WIDE, SHALLOW PLOT

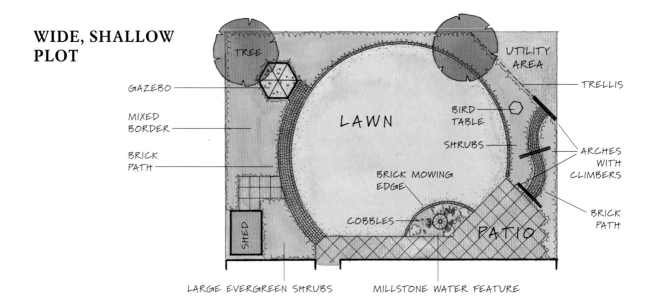

LABELS: TREE · UTILITY AREA · GAZEBO · TRELLIS · MIXED BORDER · BIRD TABLE · LAWN · SHRUBS · BRICK PATH · ARCHES WITH CLIMBERS · BRICK MOWING EDGE · COBBLES · BRICK PATH · SHED · PATIO · LARGE EVERGREEN SHRUBS · MILLSTONE WATER FEATURE

The almost circular lawn in this garden is not only a striking feature but also an effective way to distract attention from the odd proportions of the plot. The use of the lawn as a central theme leaves generous space in all four corners, which can be used to develop focal points, emphasize the diagonal views and, ultimately, make the garden appear larger than it really is.

The main axis of the garden is formed by the angled patio of square slabs which faces onto a hexagonal wooden gazebo in the diagonally opposite corner. At the opposite ends of the other diagonal axis are two utility areas. The far one is for general garden use, where compost bins and other unsightly objects can be stored. The near one, tucked behind the garage, is equipped with a shed, and there is adequate space for storing logs or coal. Connecting the patio to the triangular garden utility area is a meandering brick path, which is spanned by three wooden arches planted with climbers, while a diamond-patterned trellis fence separates the utility area from the shrub planting in front of it.

In the foreground, just off the edge of the patio, a nearly semicircular area of stones and gravel is enclosed by a brick edging, which also acts as a mowing strip at this point. A reproduction millstone placed over a concealed water tank below ground is set among the stones and forms a striking feature. At this same junction, the patio also joins a flag path, which runs along the house and leads to the other utility area behind the garage, before changing into a curving brick path, which leads around the left-hand side of the lawn to the gazebo in the corner.

The perimeter border varies greatly in depth, and this allows a wide range of different sized trees, shrubs and perennials to be planted. All of these are selected from varieties that will not only require little, if any, maintenance but will also provide year-round interest, and for this reason the layout includes a high proportion of attractive evergreen shrubs.

Planting is carried out through a porous mulching fabric, which is secured to the soil with hoops or staples made from pieces of heavy gauge, galvanized fencing wire. The fabric is concealed after planting with an ornamental mulch, which could be chipped bark, or you can use gravel or crushed stone, both of which are equally effective. The final choice will depend on your personal preference.

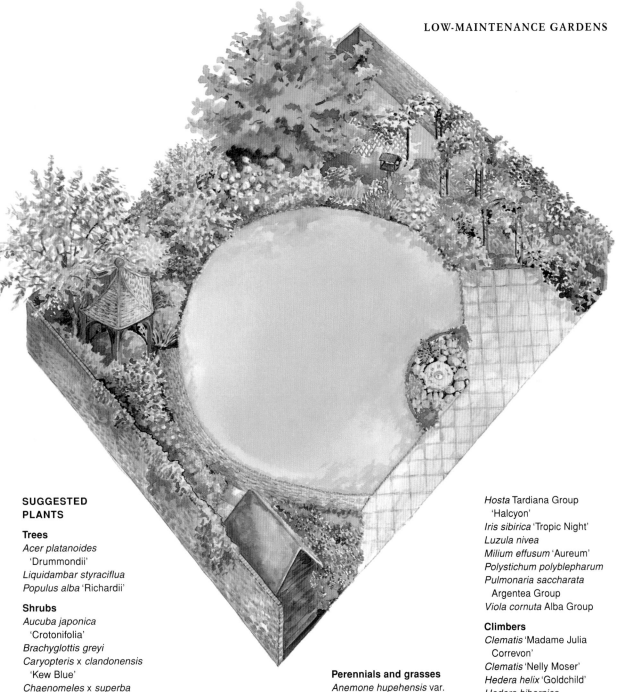

SUGGESTED PLANTS

Trees
Acer platanoides
  'Drummondii'
Liquidambar styraciflua
Populus alba 'Richardii'

Shrubs
Aucuba japonica
  'Crotonifolia'
Brachyglottis greyi
Caryopteris x *clandonensis*
  'Kew Blue'
Chaenomeles x *superba*
  'Pink Lady'
Cornus mas
Elaeagnus commutata
Escallonia rubra var.
  macrantha
Euonymus fortunei 'Emerald
  Gaiety'
Hebe pinguifolia 'Pagei'
Hydrangea paniculata
  'Grandiflora'
Ilex aquifolium 'Flavescens'
Kerria japonica 'Golden
  Guinea'
Ligustrum ovalifolium
  'Argenteum'
Photinia davidiana 'Palette'
Potentilla fruticosa
  'Katherine Dykes'
Rosa 'Suffolk'
Spiraea japonica 'Little
  Princess'
Syringa pubescens ssp.
  microphylla 'Superba'

Perennials and grasses
Anemone hupehensis var.
  japonica 'Bressingham
  Glow'
Aster amellus 'Rosa
  Erfüllung' ('Pink Zenith')
Coreopsis verticillata
  'Grandiflora'
Dicentra 'Snowflakes'
Eryngium variifolium
Euphorbia characias ssp.
  wulfenii
Euphorbia cyparissias
Geranium x *cantabrigiense*
  'Biokovo'
Hosta Tardiana Group
  'Halcyon'
Iris sibirica 'Tropic Night'
Luzula nivea
Milium effusum 'Aureum'
Polystichum polyblepharum
Pulmonaria saccharata
  Argentea Group
Viola cornuta Alba Group

Climbers
Clematis 'Madame Julia
  Correvon'
Clematis 'Nelly Moser'
Hedera helix 'Goldchild'
Hedera hibernica
Jasminum beesianum
Lonicera x *tellmanniana*
Schizophragma
  hydrangeoides
Trachelospermum jasminoides
Wisteria sinensis 'Alba'

Conifers and heathers
Erica erigena 'W.T. Rackliff'
Juniperus squamata 'Blue
  Carpet'
Pinus sylvestris 'Beuvronensis'
Tsuga canadensis 'Jeddeloh'

167

LONG, NARROW PLOT

The character of the design for this long, narrow plot is established not only by the use of a strong circular theme, which maximizes the open space available for recreation – that is, the lawn and patio – but also by the generally formal layout.

Having the crazy paving, semicircular patio running across the full width of the garden allows plenty of room to move the garden furniture around in order to make the best use of the sun. The same theme is repeated in the lawn, this time as a complete circle, and it is edged with brick to emphasize its perfectly geometric shape as well as making grass cutting easier. Like the patio, the lawn runs across the full width of the plot for maximum convenience and best use of the available space.

Beyond the lawn, a central rose tunnel or arch, constructed from a prefabricated kit of black PVC-coated steel tubing, focuses the view beneath onto a statue, which is set off by a rose hedge behind. A York stone path leads from the statue to both left and right, into a concealed space tucked away behind the hedge. Here are a hexagonal gazebo, built in the same style and materials as the rose tunnel in one corner, and a small tool shed in the other. This hidden area is mulched all over with gravel laid on top of a

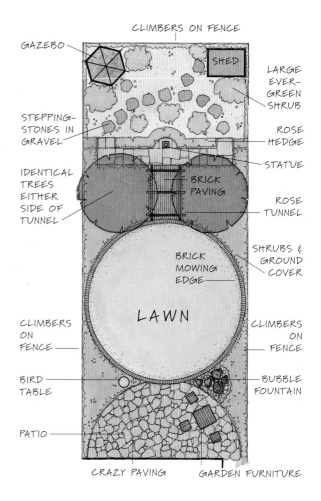

porous, weed-suppressing membrane or fabric, with individual pieces of York stone laid loosely on top and used as stepping-stones. The junction between the patio and lawn is emphasized by a bird table and bubble fountain, and these features provide additional foreground interest.

Planting consists predominantly of deciduous and evergreen shrubs, with a mixture of climbers trained onto, and completely covering, the boundary fence. The shrubs are generously spaced to allow plenty of room for them to develop into their natural size and habit, and the ground beneath and around them is either mulched with gravel or planted up with low or prostrate evergreen ground-cover plants to suppress weeds. As a final touch, and to reinforce the symmetry of this design, two golden false acacias (*Robinia pseudoacacia* 'Frisia') are planted on each side of the rose tunnel.

A gravel mulch is an effective way of keeping down weeds and of conserving moisture. Available in a variety of colours, this blue-grey gravel has been chosen not only to harmonize with the paving stones but to enhance the individual plants, including the erigeron.

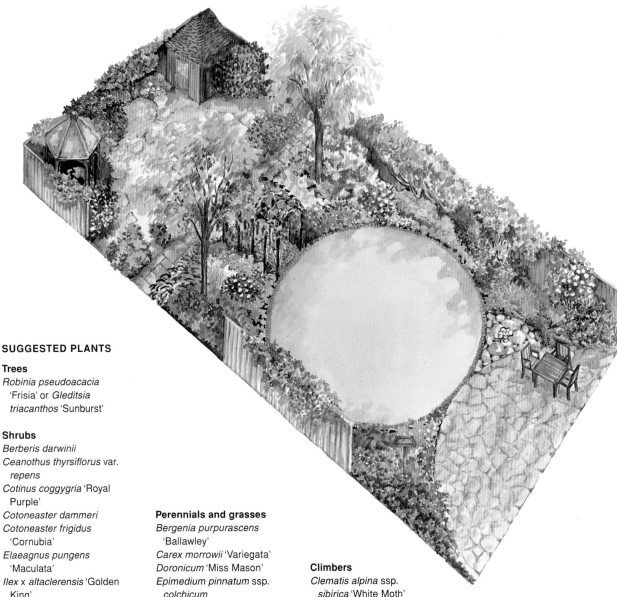

SUGGESTED PLANTS

Trees

Robinia pseudoacacia
'Frisia' or *Gleditsia*
triacanthos 'Sunburst'

Shrubs

Berberis darwinii
Ceanothus thyrsiflorus var.
repens
Cotinus coggygria 'Royal
Purple'
Cotoneaster dammeri
Cotoneaster frigidus
'Cornubia'
Elaeagnus pungens
'Maculata'
Ilex x altaclerensis 'Golden
King'
Ilex aquifolium 'Pyramidalis'
Osmanthus delavayi
Philadelphus 'Manteau
d'Hermine'
Photinia x fraseri
'Birmingham'
Pyracantha 'Mohave Silver'
Rosa 'Fru Dagmar Hastrup'
(for hedge)
Rosa glauca
Skimmia japonica 'Rubella'
Skimmia japonica 'Veitchii'
Spiraea 'Arguta'
Viburnum x bodnantense
'Deben'
Viburnum tinus 'Purpureum'

Perennials and grasses

Bergenia purpurascens
'Ballawley'
Carex morrowii 'Variegata'
Doronicum 'Miss Mason'
Epimedium pinnatum ssp.
colchicum
Euphorbia amygdaloides
var. *robbiae*
Geranium macrorrhizum
'Ingwersen's Variety'
Geranium renardii
Helleborus argutifolius
Liriope muscari
Luzula sylvatica 'Marginata'
Persicaria affinis 'Donald
Lowndes'
Polystichum setiferum
Divisilobum Group
Saxifraga 'Wada'
Vinca minor 'Alba Variegata'
Viola riviniana Purpurea
Group

Climbers

Clematis alpina ssp.
sibirica 'White Moth'
Clematis montana
'Elizabeth'
Hedera colchica 'Dentata
Variegata'
Hedera helix 'Chicago'
Lonicera x brownii
'Fuchsioides'
Passiflora caerulea
'Constance Elliot'
Rosa 'American Pillar'
Rosa 'Iceberg'
Rosa 'Maigold'
Rosa 'Meg'
Rosa 'Paul's Scarlet
Climber'
Rosa 'Schoolgirl'

Conifers

Juniperus communis 'Green
Carpet'
Juniperus horizontalis
'Hughes'
Taxus baccata 'Summergold'

169

Formal gardens

TRIANGULAR PLOT

One of the major challenges of designing a formal garden to suit a triangular or otherwise oddly shaped plot is in trying to establish a degree of symmetry within what is an asymmetric area. This particular design gets around the problem by dividing the garden into several smaller and simpler areas, which are easier to handle individually, rather than trying to do it all in one go.

The largest of these areas consists of a rectangular lawn, with the principal axis running parallel to the longest boundary of the garden – that is, from end to end. A York stone terrace in front of the house joins a path leading down the centre of the lawn, and there is a central feature of a statue standing on a circle of York stone paving. Beyond this statue, the view focuses on an arch carved out of a tall yew hedge across the garden, and behind this is a wrought iron gazebo, which can just be glimpsed through the arch.

To the left-hand side of the lawn, just off the edge of the terrace, is a separate rose garden around a wooden pergola, and York stone paving beneath this pergola connects back onto the lawn at the far end.

Beyond the yew hedge, the gazebo becomes the start of a new axis, running to the far end of this smaller area and forming part of a system of narrow gravel paths, which are used to divide up a small kitchen garden into separate planting areas. At the junction of these paths, a small gravel circle is created on which a bird bath is placed as a central feature.

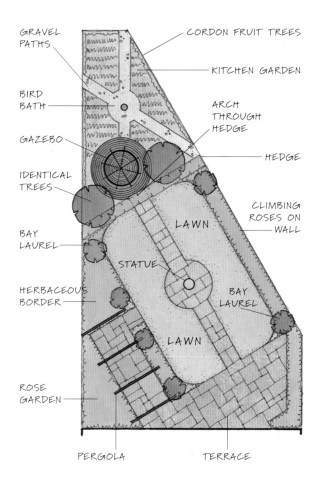

Within the main body of the ornamental garden, planting is in a traditional style, with herbaceous borders around the lawn, a mixture of roses, of course, in the rose garden around the pergola, and climbing roses, honeysuckle and clematis trained up onto the boundary walls and the pergola posts. In the kitchen garden, cordon fruit trees on the walls and the straight rows of salads, herbs and other vegetable crops add their own degree of formality to the design

SUGGESTED PLANTS

Trees
Carpinus betulus 'Fastigiata'
Sorbus 'Joseph Rock'

Shrubs and roses
Camellia 'Donation' (against house wall)
Ceaonothus 'Delight' (against garden wall)
Chaenomeles speciosa 'Nivalis' (against garden wall)
Ilex aquifolium 'Pyramidalis' (formal specimens in herbaceous borders)
Laurus nobilis (as an alternative to *Ilex*)
Lavandula angustifolia 'Munstead'

Rosa 'Buff Beauty'
Rosa 'Geranium'
Rosa glauca
Floribunda roses (mixed varieties in rose garden)
Hybrid tea roses (mixed varieties in rose garden)

Perennials
Artemisia 'Powis Castle'
Aster novi-belgii 'Lady in Blue'
Astilbe 'Bressingham Beauty'
Bergenia cordifolia 'Purpurea'
Crocosmia 'Lucifer'
Delphinium New Century Hybrids
Dianthus 'Mrs Sinkins'
Dicentra spectabilis 'Alba'
Iris 'Frost and Flame'
Lupinus Dwarf Gallery Hybrids
Paeonia lactiflora 'Sarah Bernhardt'
Phlox paniculata 'White Admiral'
Rudbeckia fulgida var. *sullivantii* 'Goldsturm'

Climbers
Clematis alpina
Clematis armandii 'Apple Blossom'
Clematis flammula
Clematis 'Henryi'
Clematis 'Jackmanii Superba'
Lonicera japonica var. *repens*
Lonicera periclymenum 'Serotina'
Lonicera x *tellmanniana*
Rosa 'Albertine'
Rosa 'Golden Showers'
Rosa 'Iceberg'
Rosa 'Maigold'
Rosa 'Pink Perpétué'
Rosa 'Zéphirine Drouhin'

Conifers
Taxus baccata (for the hedge)
Taxus baccata 'Fastigiata Robusta' (for a narrower hedge needing less trimming)

Annuals
Pelargonium (in containers)

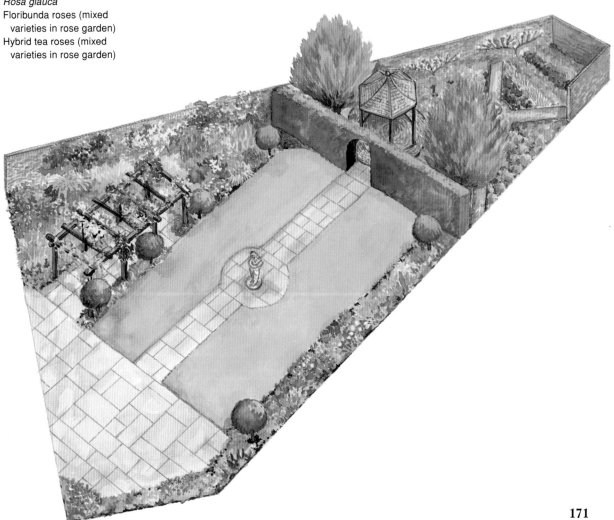

RECTANGULAR PLOT

Normally, any design for an informal garden on a rectangular plot would try to disguise the shape and straight lines. However, the rectangular shape of this particular design has been deliberately emphasized to increase the degree of formality and structured layout. Notice, however, how the most obvious axis of symmetry in the garden, which is from end to end, is ignored in favour of a diagonal one, which adds much greater interest.

This diagonal axis is marked at one end by a square, York stone terrace, which is edged in brick, with a simple raised pool and fountain on the corner by the lawn, as a foreground feature. At the other end of the axis, interest is focused on a white-painted, circular wrought iron gazebo, which is set on a quarter-circle of old red brick paving. These two features are linked by straight brick paths running around the outside of the almost rectangular lawn, and parallel to all four

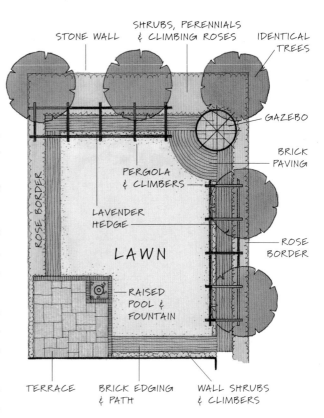

garden boundaries, and in doing so they mirror the rectangular shape of the garden as a whole.

The two paths immediately on either side of the gazebo are straddled by sawn oak pergolas, which are allowed to weather quite naturally without the addition of artificial stain or preservative, and the heavy upright posts are planted with climbing roses, jasmine, clematis and wisteria. On the lawn side of the pergola, a simple lavender hedge links the bases of the oak posts and creates a straight line along the edge of the lawn for easy mowing and maintenance.

Apart from the pergola, planting is entirely confined to a perimeter border, which lies between the brick paths and the natural stone walls that form the garden boundary, and is based on a traditional mix of perennials and roses to soften what could have been a austere design. Behind the pergola and gazebo, five equally spaced trees – all *Sorbus aria* 'Lutescens' – give additional height and structure to the planting and add their own element of formality.

This intricate knot garden looks complicated, but slow-growing box (*Buxus*) needs trimming only once or twice a year to keep it in shape.

SUGGESTED PLANTS

Trees
Sorbus aria 'Lutescens' or
  Malus tschonoskii

Shrubs and roses
Ceanothus dentatus
  (against garden wall)
Cotoneaster horizontalis
  (against garden wall)
Lavandula angustifolia
  'Hidcote'
Prunus lusitanica (as
  backdrop to gazebo)
Pyracantha coccinea
  'Lalandei' (against garden
  wall)
Floribunda roses (mixed
  varieties in rose border)
Hybrid tea roses (mixed
  varieties in rose border)

Perennials
Aster amellus 'King George'
Astrantia major
Campanula lactiflora 'White
  Pouffe'
Coreopsis verticillata
  'Moonbeam'
Delphinium Galahad Group
Helleborus niger
Hemerocallis 'Stella de Oro'
Iris sibirica 'Perry's Blue'
Nepeta x *faassenii*
Phlox paniculata
  'Sandringham'
Schizostylis coccinea 'Mrs
  Hegarty'
Verbascum chaixii
  'Gainsborough'

Climbers
Clematis alpina 'Burford
  White'
Clematis montana var.
  rubens
Clematis orientalis
Clematis 'The President'
Jasminum nudiflorum
  (against garden wall)

Jasminum officinale f. *affine*
Jasminum x *stephanense*
Rosa 'Casino'
Rosa 'Gloire de Dijon'
Rosa 'Handel'
Rosa 'Iceberg'
Rosa 'Maigold'
Rosa 'New Dawn'
Wisteria floribunda
  'Longissima Alba'
Wisteria sinensis 'Rosea'

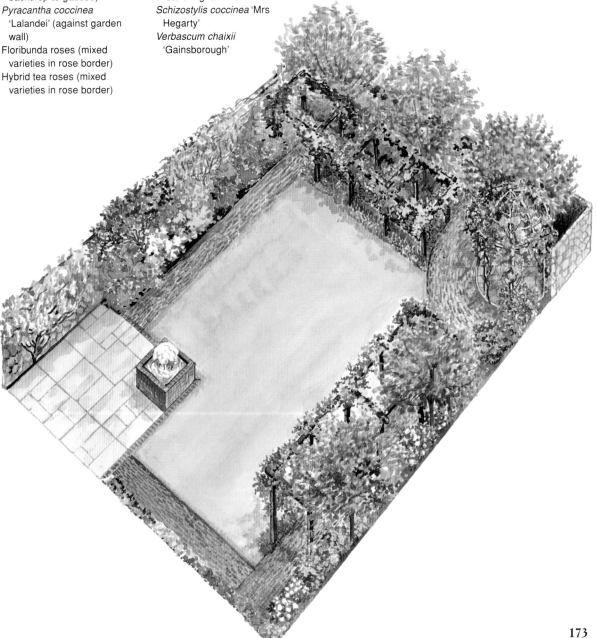

L-SHAPED PLOT

One of the distinct advantages of an L-shaped garden, or indeed of any other garden shape made up of simple rectangles and squares, is the way in which it can be readily divided into a number of distinct and separate spaces, and this arrangement lends itself quite readily to creating both the symmetry and geometric patterns that are a distinguishing feature of most formal gardens. This design divides the garden neatly into three areas, each formal, but distinct, by using neatly trimmed conifer hedging for the boundaries.

At the end of the garden nearest the house, a rectangular terrace of York stone is connected to the rose garden at the other end by a central stone path, which runs beneath a wooden pergola and is flanked by a rectangular lawn on each side. The view down the garden from the terrace is focused through a gap in the hedge separating

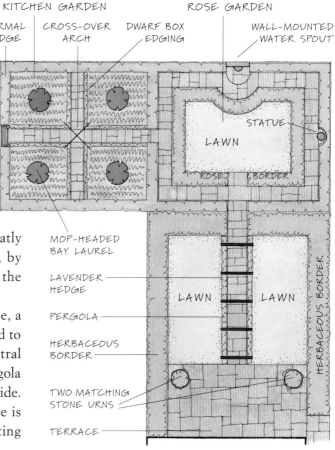

KITCHEN GARDEN — ROSE GARDEN — FORMAL HEDGE — CROSS-OVER ARCH — DWARF BOX EDGING — WALL-MOUNTED WATER SPOUT — BENCH — STATUE — LAWN — ROSE BORDER — MOP-HEADED BAY LAUREL — LAVENDER HEDGE — PERGOLA — HERBACEOUS BORDER — LAWN — LAWN — HERBACEOUS BORDER — TWO MATCHING STONE URNS — TERRACE

The brick and flag paving, although rather crudely laid, brings a strong, formal structure to this potager, planted with variegated strawberries (*Duchesnea indica* 'Harlequin') and box (*Buxus*).

these two areas onto a simple water feature on the wall of the rose garden beyond. The rose garden itself consists of a simple, square lawn, which is bounded on all sides by a narrow border and flagstone path. A wall-mounted lion's head water spout produces a simple but elegant jet of water, which falls into a stone trough below, from where the water is recycled back to the spout.

To the side of this garden, and passing through another hedge, lies the kitchen garden, which is divided into four equal squares by narrow paths, each square featuring a centrally placed mop-headed bay laurel (*Laurus nobilis*). At the junction of the two paths, a simple wrought iron cross-over arch provides ample support for growing sweetpeas or runner beans.

SUGGESTED PLANTS

Trees
Laurus nobilis (mop-headed on clear stems)

Shrubs and roses
Lavandula angustifolia 'Hidcote Pink'
Floribunda roses (mixed varieties in rose border)
Hybrid tea roses (mixed varieties in rose border)

Perennials
Aster novae-angliae 'Harrington's Pink'
Campanula takesimanum
Dianthus 'Doris'
Dicentra 'Luxuriant'
Eryngium planum
Euphorbia amygdaloides 'Purpurea' (syn. *E. a.* 'Rubra')
Helleborus foetidus Wester Flisk Group
Hemerocallis 'Catherine Woodbery'
Heuchera micrantha var. *diversifolia* 'Palace Purple'
Iris pallida 'Variegata'
Lavandula angustifolia 'Munstead'
Linum narbonense
Lupinus 'The Governor'

Paeonia lactiflora 'White Wings'
Phlox maculata 'Omega'
Sedum spectabile 'Iceberg'
Veronica gentianoides

Climbers
Clematis armandii
Clematis tangutica
Jasminum x stephanense
Lonicera periclymenum 'Graham Thomas'
Rosa 'Seagull'
Rosa 'Zéphirine Drouhin'
Vitis coignetiae
Vitis vinifera 'Purpurea'
Wisteria floribunda 'Multijuga'

Conifers
Thuja plicata 'Atrovirens' or *Taxus baccata* (for hedge)

Annuals
Pelargonium (in stone urns on terrace)
Sweetpea (over arch in kitchen garden)

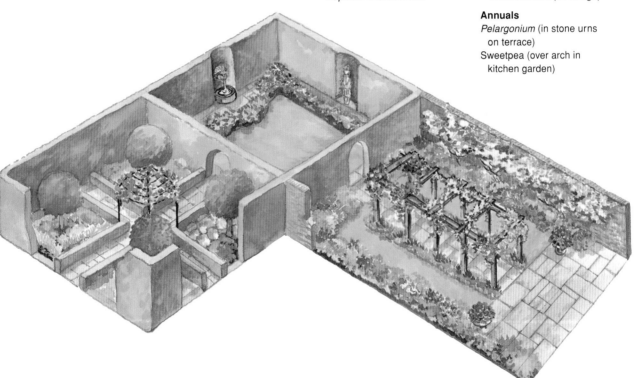

The planting throughout the garden is simple and restrained, using traditional perennials and lavender hedging in the main garden by the terrace, roses in the rose garden, and a mixture of fruit, vegetables and salad crops in the kitchen garden. The formal hedge that separates the three gardens is of the conifer *Thuja plicata* 'Atrovirens', which is faster growing than yew (*Taxus baccata*) and which has neat, dark green, glossy foliage.

WIDE, SHALLOW PLOT

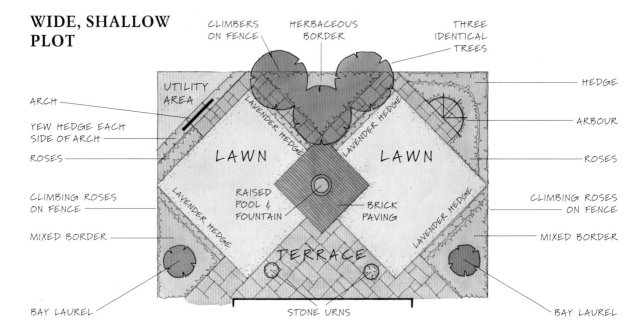

CLIMBERS ON FENCE

HERBACEOUS BORDER

THREE IDENTICAL TREES

UTILITY AREA

ARCH

YEW HEDGE EACH SIDE OF ARCH

ROSES

CLIMBING ROSES ON FENCE

MIXED BORDER

LAVENDER HEDGE

LAWN

RAISED POOL & FOUNTAIN

LAVENDER HEDGE

LAWN

LAVENDER HEDGE

BRICK PAVING

LAVENDER HEDGE

TERRACE

BAY LAUREL

STONE URNS

HEDGE

ARBOUR

ROSES

CLIMBING ROSES ON FENCE

MIXED BORDER

BAY LAUREL

The formality of this design is created by the use of squares and diagonal lines, and by rotating these squares to form a series of diamond and triangular shapes, the shallow, over-wide effect of the plot is well camouflaged. In addition, a degree of symmetry between the two halves of the garden is created, and this focuses attention in several directions and away from the nearest boundary. The generous York stone terrace along the house is broadly triangular in shape, and this arrangement helps to direct views to the two far corners of the garden and also into the centre of the garden, where it joins a square of old brick paving on which is situated a small, raised, circular pool containing a tiny fountain.

To either side of this central brick square are identical, almost square lawns, which effectively cut off the four corners of the rectangular garden into a series of triangles. The two triangles nearest to the house form quite substantial areas of planting at the extreme ends of the terrace. Of the remaining two triangles, the one in the far left-hand corner is hidden from view by a yew hedge, creating an area behind that is suitable for compost heaps and general garden storage. The second triangle, in the far right-hand corner, is used to form a sheltered sitting area on which is a stone bench beneath a semicircular wrought iron arbour, enclosed behind by another yew hedge.

The utility area and arbour are both directly accessible from the two lawns, or indirectly by two York flagstone paths, which lead from the far side of the central square of brick paving.

Dwarf lavender hedging is used to soften some of the straight lawn boundaries. Planting elsewhere in the garden consists of a more traditional mixture of herbaceous perennials and roses, with climbing roses and other flowering climbers, such as clematis, honeysuckle and jasmine, planted against the boundary fences, on the archway leading to the utility area through the yew hedge and over the arbour. A group of three identical trees is planted in the triangular herbaceous border at the far side of the garden immediately behind the brick square to give height, to emphasize the symmetry of the design and, not least, to break up the pronounced line of the long, near boundary at this point.

SUGGESTED PLANTS

Trees
Sorbus aria 'Lutescens'or
  Tilia 'Petiolaris' (for larger
  gardens)

Shrubs and roses
Laurus nobilis (trained into
  narrow cones)
Lavandula x *intermedia*
  'Grappenhall'
Hybrid tea roses (mixed
  varieties in rose beds)
Floribunda roses (mixed
  varieties in rose beds)

Perennials
Aster amellus
  'Veilchenkönigin' ('Violet
  Queen')
Bergenia 'Wintermärchen'
Campanula persicifolia var.
  alba
Coreopsis verticillata
  'Zagreb'
Crocosmia x
  crocosmiiflora 'Solfaterre'
Delphinium Black Knight
  Group
Dianthus 'Haytor White'
Euphorbia dulcis
  'Chamaeleon'
Helleborus argutifolius
Hemerocallis 'Sammy
  Russell'
Iris 'Green Spot'
Paeonia lactiflora 'Bowl of
  Beauty'
Phlox paniculata 'Prospero'
Sedum spectabile 'Brilliant'
Sidalcea 'Rose Queen'
Solidago 'Queenie' (syn. *S.*
  'Golden Thumb')
Veronica spicata 'Rotfuchs'
  ('Red Fox')

Climbers
Clematis armandii
Clematis cirrhosa Freckles
Clematis 'Gipsy Queen'
Clematis 'Hagley Hybrid'
Clematis orientalis 'Bill
  MacKenzie'
Hedera colchica 'Sulphur
  Heart'
Hedera hibernica
Jasminum officinale 'Fiona
  Sunrise'
Jasminum polyanthum
Lonicera japonica
  'Aureoreticulata'
Lonicera periclymenum
  'Serotina'
Rosa 'Albertine'
Rosa 'Golden Showers'
Rosa 'Madame Grégoire
  Staechelin'
Rosa 'Meg'
Rosa 'Rambling Rector'

Conifers
Taxus baccata (for hedge)
Taxus baccata 'Fastigiata
  Robusta' (for narrower
  hedge with less trimming)

Annuals
Red *Pelargonium*
  (in urns on terrace)

LONG, NARROW PLOT

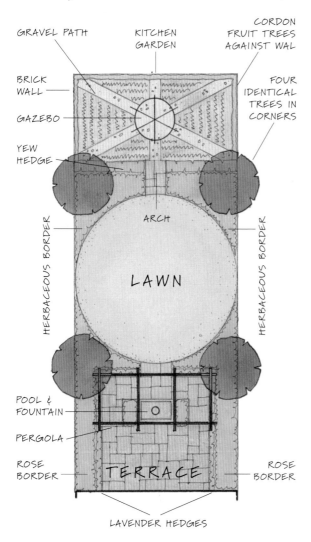

GRAVEL PATH

KITCHEN GARDEN

CORDON FRUIT TREES AGAINST WAL

BRICK WALL

GAZEBO

YEW HEDGE

FOUR IDENTICAL TREES IN CORNERS

HERBACEOUS BORDER

ARCH

LAWN

HERBACEOUS BORDER

POOL & FOUNTAIN

PERGOLA

ROSE BORDER

TERRACE

ROSE BORDER

LAVENDER HEDGES

A rectangular York stone terrace by the house is almost completely enclosed by a lavender hedge and a timber and brick pergola running across the garden at the far end of the terrace. Beneath this pergola, a small rectangular pool with a central fountain forms a strong focal point along the main axis of the garden and helps to increase the feeling of separation at this point in the garden.

Beyond the pergola, a perfectly circular lawn extends across the full width of the garden between the old red brick boundary walls. A yew (*Taxus*) hedge just beyond the lawn acts not only as a backdrop but also separates the lawn from the kitchen garden that lies beyond. Within the yew hedge, an arch is cut to create an entrance to the kitchen garden, and the arch itself acts as a focal point when it is viewed from further up the garden.

The rectangular kitchen garden, which is nicely sheltered by the boundary walls and yew hedge, is divided into triangular planting areas around a central axis by narrow gravel paths from each corner. The paths meet in the centre beneath a circular, wrought iron gazebo, which can just be glimpsed from the rest of the garden through the arch in the yew hedge.

The symmetry of this garden, created by the use of a long central axis, forms identically shaped planting areas on each side of it. These beds and borders are planted so that the left- and right-hand sides of the garden are mirror images of each other. Perennials and roses form the bulk of the planting, with four hollies, shaped and trimmed to form uniform cones, placed symmetrically in the four corner beds around the lawn, accentuating the strong formality of the design and adding valuable height. To complete the effect, a hedge of old English lavender (*Lavandula angustifolia*) is planted around the terrace.

The use of circular and rectangular shapes, which are organized symmetrically about a central axis running from end to end, makes the layout in this garden formal and organized. However, although the garden is divided into three distinct areas to overcome the tunnel-like effect caused by the long, narrow shape, the way in which this is organized still leaves a large amount of uninterrupted space, particularly for the lawn and terrace, and this makes the garden both practical to use and attractive to look at.

SUGGESTED PLANTS

Trees

Ilex aquifolium 'Pyramidalis' (trimmed to maintain tall, conical shape)

Shrubs and roses

Camellia 'Lady Vansittart' (against house wall, each side of door)
Lavandula angustifolia
Floribunda roses (mixed varieties in rose borders)
Hybrid tea roses (mixed varieties in rose borders)

Perennials

Achillea 'Moonshine'
Aconitum 'Ivorine'
Anchusa azurea 'Loddon Royalist'
Anthemis punctata ssp. *cupaniana*
Aster novi-belgii 'Little Pink Beauty'

Astilbe 'Sprite'
Astrantia major ssp. *involucrata* 'Shaggy'
Bergenia 'Sunningdale'
Campanula persicifolia 'Telham Beauty'
Delphinium Pacific Hybrids
Euphorbia griffithii 'Fireglow'
Helleborus foetidus
Hemerocallis 'Burning Daylight'
Iris sibirica 'Flight of Butterflies'
Pulmonaria rubra 'Redstart'
Sidalcea 'Mrs T. Alderson'
Solidago 'Cloth of Gold'

Climbers

Clematis montana 'Elizabeth'
Jasminum x *stephanense*
Lonicera periclymenum 'Graham Thomas'
Rosa 'Albertine'
Rosa 'Golden Showers'
Rosa 'Iceberg'
Rosa 'Zéphirine Drouhin'
Vitis coignetiae
Wisteria x *formosa* 'Issai'

Conifers

Taxus baccata or *Thuja plicata* 'Atrovirens' (for hedge)

Annuals

Pelargonium (in containers on terrace)
Sweetpeas (on gazebo in kitchen garden)

Aquatics

Iris pseudoacorus 'Variegata' (edge of pool)

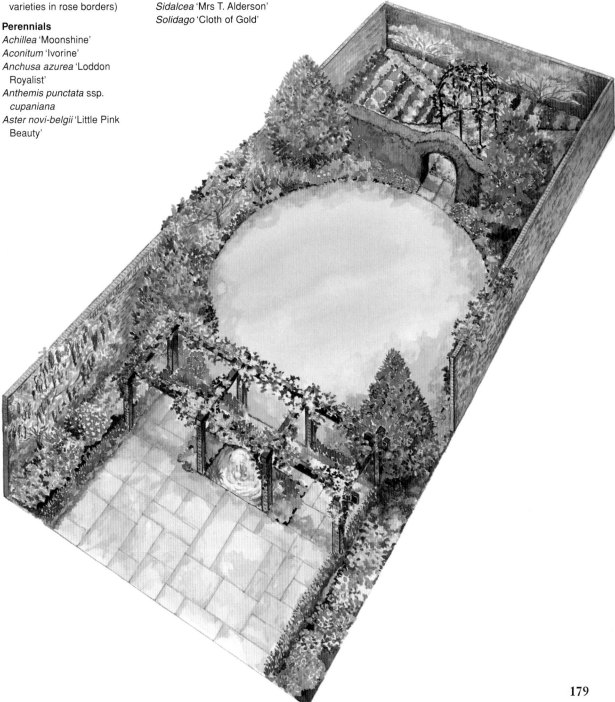

Plant lover's gardens

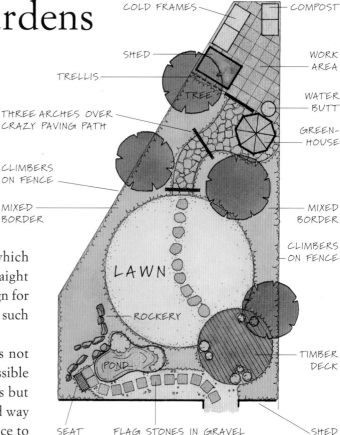

COLD FRAMES — COMPOST

SHED

TRELLIS

THREE ARCHES OVER
CRAZY PAVING PATH

CLIMBERS
ON FENCE

MIXED
BORDER

WORK
AREA

WATER
BUTT

GREEN-
HOUSE

TREE

LAWN

ROCKERY

POND

SEAT   FLAG STONES IN GRAVEL

MIXED
BORDER

CLIMBERS
ON FENCE

TIMBER
DECK

SHED

TRIANGULAR PLOT

The informal nature of this garden, in which there is an almost complete absence of straight lines and right angles, makes it an ideal design for use in an awkward or unusually shaped plot, such as this one.

The underlying purpose of the design is not only to provide as much opportunity as possible for growing a wide range of different plants but also to be able to do so in a well-structured way that will give an attractive overall appearance to the garden.

This basic structure is principally determined by the simple, yet striking combination of a circular lawn and a smaller, overlapping, circular, timber-decked sitting area. The benefit of this arrangement is that it creates a generous space immediately in front of the sitting room windows for an informal pond, which makes a prominent and delightful foreground feature. Soil from excavating the pond is gently backed up behind it to form a shallow rock bank planted with alpines. There is enough space left between the pond and the house for a gravel path, which leads to a small seat overlooking the water's edge and across the lawn towards an ornamental greenhouse.

From the deck, a simple stepping-stone path leads across the lawn to join a meandering path

of crazy paving, which passes beneath three rustic arches. This path swings round to the small greenhouse, which is partially tucked away behind an area of mixed planting.

Beyond the greenhouse, the narrowest point of the triangular plot is separated by a trellis screen and the last of the three arches. It is used as a general outdoor work area. This area is paved for convenience with plain slabs, and there is room for a tool or potting shed, compost bins, cold frames and a water butt.

The carefully planned, modest yet adequate areas of hard landscaping and lawn, leave plenty of room and opportunity for a wide variety of plants to be grown, ranging from trees, shrubs and perennials to climbers, alpines, bog plants and aquatics.

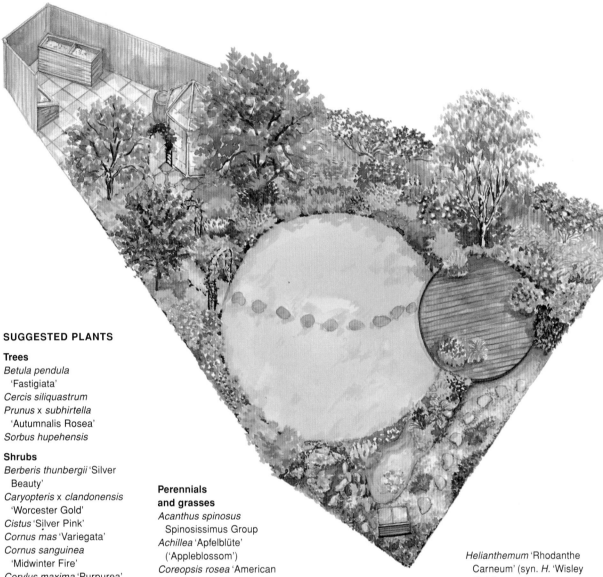

SUGGESTED PLANTS

Trees
Betula pendula 'Fastigiata'
Cercis siliquastrum
Prunus x *subhirtella* 'Autumnalis Rosea'
Sorbus hupehensis

Shrubs
Berberis thunbergii 'Silver Beauty'
Caryopteris x *clandonensis* 'Worcester Gold'
Cistus 'Silver Pink'
Cornus mas 'Variegata'
Cornus sanguinea 'Midwinter Fire'
Corylus maxima 'Purpurea'
Forsythia x *intermedia* 'Lynwood'
Ilex crenata 'Golden Gem'
Mahonia x *media* 'Winter Sun'
Osmanthus heterophyllus 'Gulftide'
Philadelphus coronarius 'Aureus'
Pittosporum tenuifolium
Potentilla fruticosa 'Red Ace'
Ribes sanguineum 'Brocklebankii'
Spiraea betulifolia var. *aemiliana*
Viburnum x *juddii*
Viburnum plicatum 'Pink Beauty'

Perennials and grasses
Acanthus spinosus Spinosissimus Group
Achillea 'Apfelblüte' ('Appleblossom')
Coreopsis rosea 'American Dream'
Hemerocallis 'Buzz Bomb'
Iris unguicularis
Knautia macedonica
Macleaya cordata
Pleioblastus auricomus
Scabiosa 'Butterfly Blue'
Stipa gigantea
Verbascum 'Helen Johnson'
Veronica spicata 'Heidekind'
Vinca minor 'La Grave'

Climbers
Actinidia kolomikta
Akebia quinata
Clematis flammula
Hedera helix 'Parsley Crested' (syn. *H. h.* 'Cristata')
Lonicera sempervirens
Trachelospermum jasminoides 'Variegatum'
Vitis vinifera 'Purpurea

Conifers, heathers and alpines
Artemisia schmidtiana 'Nana'
Aubrieta 'Doctor Mules'
Calluna vulgaris 'Robert Chapman'
Dianthus 'Pike's Pink'
Erica arborea 'Estrella Gold'
Erica carnea 'Vivellii'
Helianthemum 'Rhodanthe Carneum' (syn. *H.* 'Wisley Pink')
Juniperus communis 'Compressa'
Picea pungens 'Globosa'
Pinus mugo 'Mops'
Thuja orientalis 'Aurea Nana

Aquatics, marginals and bog plants
Astilbe x *arendsii* 'Snowdrift'
Ceratophyllum demersum
Hosta 'Krossa Regal'
Iris laevigata 'Alba'
Lobelia cardinalis
Nymphaea 'Odorata Sulphurea'
Potamogeton crispus
Primula denticulata
Rodgersia pinnata 'Superba'

RECTANGULAR PLOT

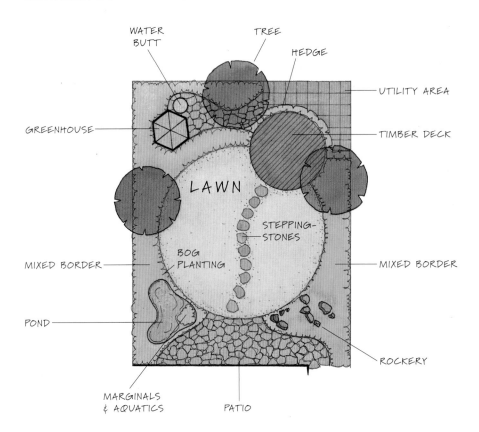

WATER BUTT

TREE

HEDGE

GREENHOUSE

UTILITY AREA

TIMBER DECK

LAWN

STEPPING-STONES

MIXED BORDER

BOG PLANTING

MIXED BORDER

POND

ROCKERY

MARGINALS & AQUATICS

PATIO

SUGGESTED PLANTS

Trees
Gleditsia triacanthos 'Sunburst'
Laburnum x *watereri* 'Vossii'
Malus x *robusta* 'Red Siberian'

Shrubs, perennials and grasses
Acanthus mollis Latifolius Group
Acer palmatum 'Bloodgood'
Aquilegia vulgaris 'Nora Barlow'
Aronia arbutifolia
Aster amellus 'Brilliant'
Aster thomsonii 'Nanus'
Berberis x *lologensis* 'Apricot Queen'
Berberis thunbergii 'Atropurpurea Nana'
Brunnera macrophylla 'Langtrees'
Carex comans Bronze Form
Ceratostigma plumbaginoides
Cornus kousa var. *chinensis*
Crocosmia x *crocosmiflora* 'Emily McKenzie'
Dryopteris erythrosora
Epimedium x *rubrum*
Eryngium variifolium
Euphorbia palustris
Fargesia murieliae 'Simba'
Fargesia nitida
Fuchsia magellanica 'Versicolor'
Geranium macrorrhizum 'Album'
Geranium sanguineum 'Album'
Hakonechloa macra 'Alboaurea'
Hebe armstrongii
Helleborus niger
Hydrangea quercifolia 'Snow Flake'
Hydrangea serrata 'Bluebird'
Ilex aquifolium 'Ferox Argentea'
Iris foetidissima var. *citrinus*
Iris pallida 'Variegata'
Kniphofia 'Ada'
Laurus nobilis 'Aurea'
Lavandula stoechas
Lonicera x *purpusii*
Lysimachia ciliata 'Firecracker'
Miscanthus sinensis 'Morning Light'

The use of a circular theme is an excellent way of disguising the shape of virtually any garden, but especially so if it is a square or, as here, a rectangle. In this example, the lawn has been made quite generous, and an additional patio or sitting area is suggested, so that although plants form the main structure of the garden around the dominant circular theme, it is also practical and usable.

An informally curved crazy paving patio in front of the house leads directly onto the circular lawn for easy access, and a stepping-stone path crosses the lawn to reach a circular timber deck just in front of the diagonally opposite corner. The deck is raised by several inches to increase its dramatic effect, and its strong, uniform shape is further emphasized by the curved yew hedge

Ophiopogon planiscapus
  'Nigrescens'
Paeonia mlokosewitschii
Persicaria tenuicaulis
Phlox carolina 'Bill Baker'
Phlox maculata 'Alpha'
Phormium tenax Purpureum
  Group
Photinia davidiana 'Palette'
Rudbeckia fulgida var.
  deamii
Salix 'Boydii'
Salix caprea var. pendula
Salvia nemorosa
  'Ostfriesland' ('East
  Friesland')
Schizostylis coccinea 'Major'
Stachys byzantina 'Primrose
  Heron'
Tradescantia x andersoniana
  'Isis'
Viburnum plicatum
  'Watanabe'
Viola 'Clementina'
Weigela 'Florida Variegata'
Yucca filamentosa
  'Bright Edge'

Climbers
Clematis cirrhosa var.
  balearica
Clematis florida 'Sieboldii'
Hedera helix 'Buttercup'
Jasminum officinale 'Fiona
  Sunrise'
Lonicera x brownii
  'Fuchsioides'
Passiflora caerulea
Solanum crispum
  'Glasnevin'
Trachelospermum asiaticum
Vitis vinifera 'Apiifolia'

**Conifers, heathers
and alpines**
Arabis ferdinandi-coburgi
Calluna vulgaris 'Silver
  Queen'
Campanula carpatica
Dianthus 'Garland'
Erica carnea 'Springwood
  White'
Erica x darleyensis 'Ada
  S. Collings'
Erica vagans 'Saint Keverne'
Helianthemum 'Wisley
  White'
Iberis sempervirens
  'Weisser Zwerg' ('Little
  Gem')

Phlox subulata 'Oakington
  Blue Eyes'
Picea glauca var. albertiana
  'Laurin'
Taxus baccata 'Standishii'
Tsuga canadensis 'Cole's
  Prostrate'

**Aquatics, marginals
and bog plants**
Astilbe 'Deutschland'
Astilboides tabularis (syn.
  Rodgersia tabularis)
Caltha palustris var. alba
Glyceria aquatica
  'Marginata'
Hosta undulata var.
  albomarginata (syn. H.
  'Thomas Hogg')
Hottonia palustris
Houttuynia cordata 'Flore
  Pleno'
Iris ensata (syn. I.
  kaempferi)
Ligularia 'The Rocket'
Primula Candelabra Hybrids

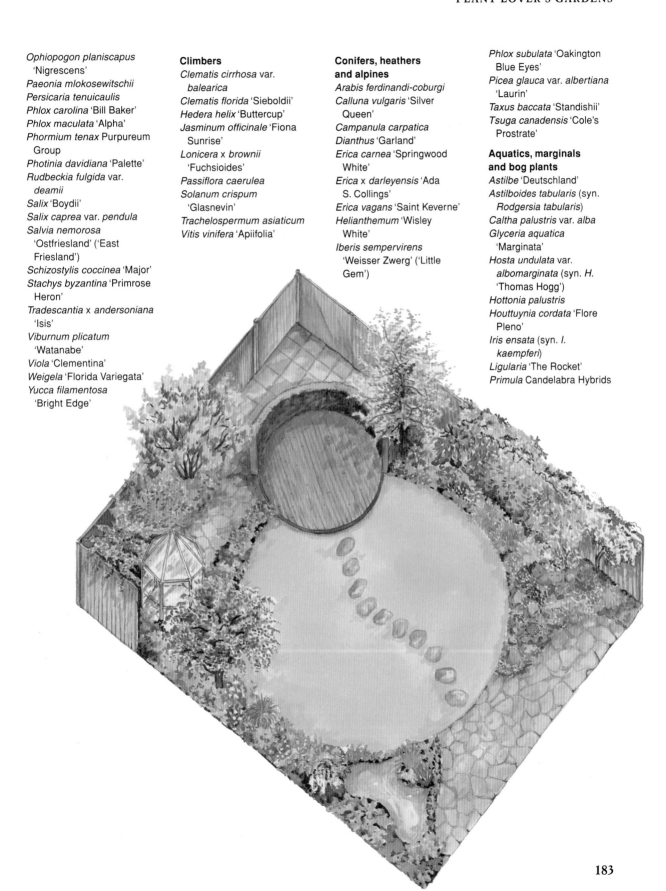

Left: A plant lover is more likely to want wide borders than a lawn or patio in which to grow the widest possible range of plants for year-round interest. The poppy *Papaver commutatum* is a striking contrast to *Genista lydia* and *Viola* 'Mauve Radiance'.

Right: A natural pond, such as this one, backed by *Clematis* 'Gipsy Queen', offers opportunities for marginal and bog planting as well as purely aquatic plants.

immediately behind it. The careful positioning of the deck and hedge allows sufficient space in the corner behind for a small garden store or general utility area, which is hidden from sight and is reached through a narrow gap between the left-hand end of the hedge and the shrub border against the far boundary fence.

From the deck, a random stone path leads to a small, ornamental cedarwood greenhouse in the opposite corner, which is partly obscured from view by the mixed border of shrubs and perennials in front of it. The two spaces created on either side of the junction of the patio and lawn make ideal locations for an informal pond on one side and a rockery on the other. The pond will benefit from being in shade for part of the day, while the rockery has the advantage of being in a much sunnier position.

Apart from the yew hedge, planting is contained almost entirely in two perimeter borders, which vary in depth. A general mixture of shrubs, perennials, alpines and climbers has been chosen to provide as much year-round interest as possible, with just three slow-growing, modestly sized trees planted to provide a degree of height without causing excessive shade or dryness at their roots, which would be to the detriment of the smaller plants. The layout of the borders would make it straightforward to install a simple irrigation system as an added option.

L-SHAPED PLOT

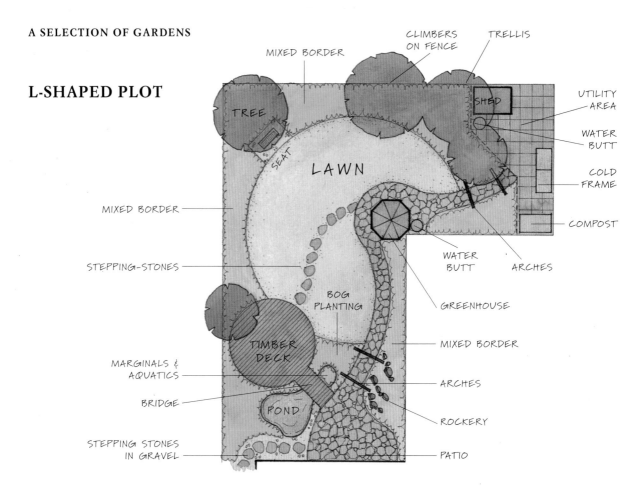

The configuration of this garden lends itself perfectly to the use of dramatic, sweeping curves and circles, which are not only effective in creating an informal effect but also in disguising the rigid, angular boundary fences or walls.

The patio by the house is connected to a circular timber deck by a wooden bridge, which spans an informally shaped pond. An area of gravel and stones between the pond and the house allows access for window cleaning and maintenance, as well as leaving sufficient space to place a small bench seat if required, and on the far side of the pond, beyond the bridge, is a bog garden.

From the patio, a narrow path in the same stone leads beneath two rustic arches before it curves around an ornamental greenhouse, which is placed right on the corner as a feature or focal point. The path then continues into the foot of the L-shape, which is hidden from general view, where it passes beneath two more arches before

leading into a paved garden storage and utility area, which is tucked away behind a screen of free-standing trellis panels.

In the diagonally opposite corner from the octagonal greenhouse is a small area of gravel paving set into the perimeter border and edged with timber boards to keep the gravel and soil separate. This provides a cool sitting area for hot days, in the shade of the tree in the corner.

The almost circular lawn provides a strong theme, linking the various garden features together, and its shape is also effective in creating some generous planting areas and giving variety to the border shapes. Because of the way in which the garden is planned, these areas vary in their characteristics, ranging from shady and dry to moist and sunny, and this allows a wide and interesting range of plants to be grown, including deciduous trees, shrubs, perennials, grasses, climbers, alpines and, of course, aquatics.

SUGGESTED PLANTS

Trees

Acer negundo
  'Aureovariegatum'
Davidia involucrata
Malus floribunda
Prunus serrula var. *tibetica*
Tilia 'Petiolaris'

Shrubs

Amelanchier canadensis
Buddleja davidii 'Pink
  Beauty'
Carpenteria californica
Elaeagnus x *ebbingei*
  'Limelight'
Fuchsia magellanica
  'Alba'
Hydrangea paniculata
  'Tardiva'
Ligustrum 'Vicaryi'
Magnolia 'Susan'
Mahonia x *media*
  'Charity'
Nandina domestica
  'Richmond'

Osmanthus heterophyllus
  'Goshiki'
Photinia x *fraseri* 'Robusta'
Physocarpus opulifolius
  'Dart's Gold'
Pittosporum 'Garnettii'

Climbers

Campsis x *tagliabuana*
  'Madame Galen'

Clematis cirrhosa var.
  balearica
Clematis tangutica
Hedera helix 'Angularis
  Aurea'
Humulus lupulus 'Aureus'
Hydrangea anomala ssp.
  petiolaris
Rubus henryi var.
  bambusarum
Vitis coignetiae

Conifers, heathers and alpines

Calluna vulgaris 'H.E. Beale'
Campanula carpatica
  'Chewton Joy'
Chamaecyparis obtusa
  'Nana Gracilis'
Erica carnea 'King George'
Erica tetralix 'Alba Mollis'
Erica vagans 'Mrs D.F.
  Maxwell'
Geranium cinereum 'Apple
  Blossom'
Iberis commutata
Juniperus chinensis
  'Kaizuka'
Picea glauca 'Echiniformis'
Pinus mugo 'Ophir'

Aquatics, marginals and bog plants

Astilbe x *arendsii* 'Fanal'
Caltha palustris var.
  palustris 'Plena'
Hosta sieboldiana var.
  elegans
Iris laevigata 'Variegata'
Ligularia dentata
  'Desdemona'
Nymphaea 'Marliacea
  Rosea'
Potamogeton crispus

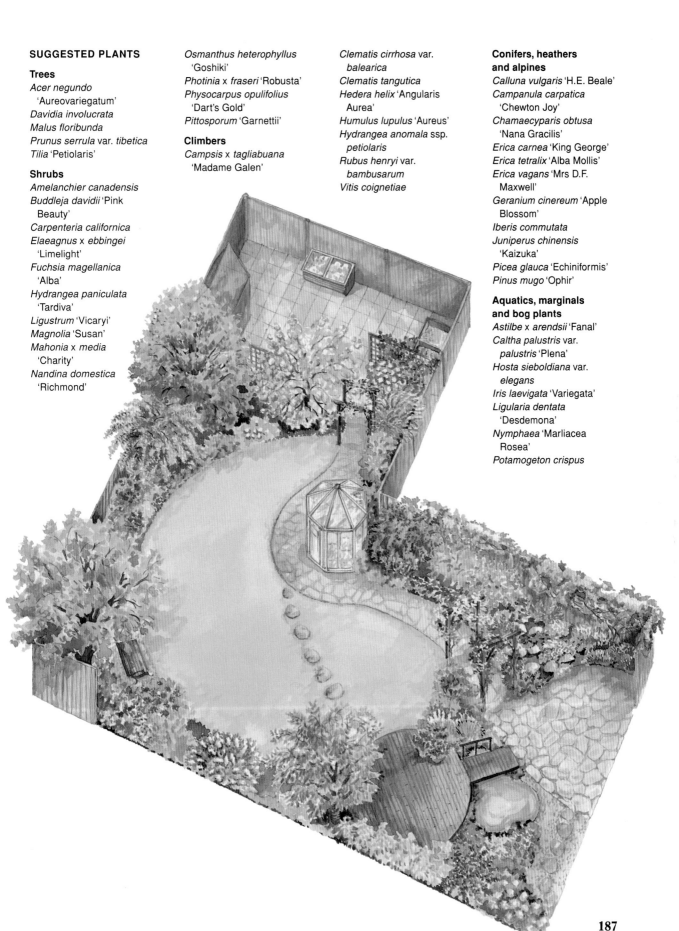

WIDE, SHALLOW PLOT

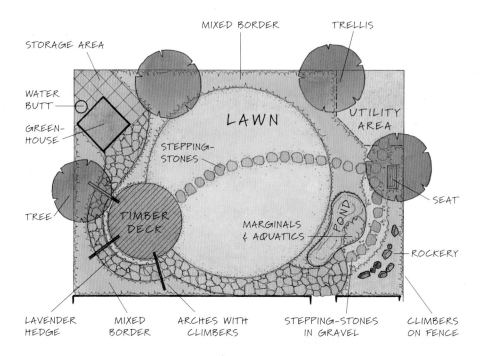

STORAGE AREA

MIXED BORDER

TRELLIS

WATER
BUTT

GREEN-
HOUSE

LAWN

UTILITY
AREA

STEPPING-
STONES

SEAT

TREE

TIMBER
DECK

MARGINALS
& AQUATICS

POND

ROCKERY

LAVENDER
HEDGE

MIXED
BORDER

ARCHES WITH
CLIMBERS

STEPPING-STONES
IN GRAVEL

CLIMBERS
ON FENCE

A circular lawn is the dominant feature of this particular design, and it is complemented by the smaller circle of a timber deck. These combine with the curving paths and borders to create a garden that gives no indication of the actual shape or size of the plot.

The slightly raised circular timber deck sitting area is set in one corner of the garden near the house, overlapping the lawn. The view from the deck focuses on a small bench seat set among an area of gravel paving on the opposite side of the lawn, and a stepping-stone path provides both a visual and a practical link across the lawn between these two sitting areas.

In the corner on the opposite side of the garden from the deck, an informal pond makes a striking feature. The best quality soil from the pond excavation has been placed behind it to form a gently sloping rockery, which catches plenty of sun, and this is separated from the pond by a stepping-stone path that is laid among gravel,

leading to the bench seat. Beyond the seat, the corner of the garden is used as a utility area, and this is screened from the rest of the garden by an angled trellis fence.

The rockery and pond are joined to the timber deck by a crazy paving path. which separates the lawn from the house. This path swings around behind the deck, beneath three arches, and continues into the far left-hand corner, where it meets an area of flag paving on which is placed a square, ornamental greenhouse, with space for a small storage area behind.

There are plenty of opportunities to grow a wide range of plants in this garden, with a mixture of trees, shrubs and perennials in the perimeter borders, climbers planted on both of the extensive boundary fences, the house and garage walls, and the trellis screen; and more specialized areas of planting, such as the bog garden around the pond and alpines in the sunny rockery just behind this.

SUGGESTED PLANTS

Trees
Acer negundo 'Kelly's Gold'
Betula pendula 'Purpurea'
Liquidambar styraciflua
  'Worplesdon'

Shrubs
Berberis thunbergii
  'Harlequin'
Buddleja lindleyana
Buxus sempervirens
  'Elegantissima'
Diervilla x *splendens*
Garrya elliptica 'James
  Roof' (against house wall)
Hamamelis x *intermedia*
  'Diane'
Hibiscus syriacus 'Hamabo'
Hydrangea 'Preziosa'
Lavandula angustifolia
  'Nana Alba' (for low hedge
  around deck)
Ligustrum japonicum
Magnolia x *soulangeana*
  'Lennei'

Photinia x *fraseri* 'Rubens'
Prunus incisa 'Kojo-no-mai'
Rhododendron
  yakushimanum
Ulmus x *hollandica*
  'Jacqueline Hillier'

Perennials and grasses
Artemisia 'Powis Castle'
Eryngium x *tripartitum*
Euphorbia polychroma
Foeniculum vulgare 'Giant
  Bronze'
Helleborus argutifolius
Heuchera 'Rachel'
Iris 'Black Swan'
Leucanthemum x *superbum*
  'Snowcap'
Milium effusum 'Aureum'
Persicaria affinis 'Donald
  Lowndes'
Phormium tenax
Sasa veitchii

Climbers
Akebia quinata
Berberidopsis corallina
Celastrus orbiculatus
  Hermaphrodite Group
Jasminum officinale
  'Argenteovariegatum'
Parthenocissus henryana

Conifers, heathers and alpines
Cephalaria alpina (syn.
  Scabiosa alpina)
Erica arborea
Erica erigena 'Irish Salmon'
Geranium cinereum
  'Ballerina'

Juniperus communis
  'Schneverdingen
  Goldmachandel' ('Golden
  Showers')
Phlox subulata 'Emerald
  Cushion Blue'
Picea glauca var. *albertiana*
  'Alberta Globe'
Saponaria 'Bressingham'

Aquatics, marginals and bog plants
Filipendula ulmaria
  'Variegata'
Hosta crispula
Houttuynia cordata
Hydrocharis morsus-ranae
Iris pseudacorus 'Variegata'
Ranunculus aquatilis
Rheum 'Ace of Hearts'
Rodgersia pinnata 'Elegans'

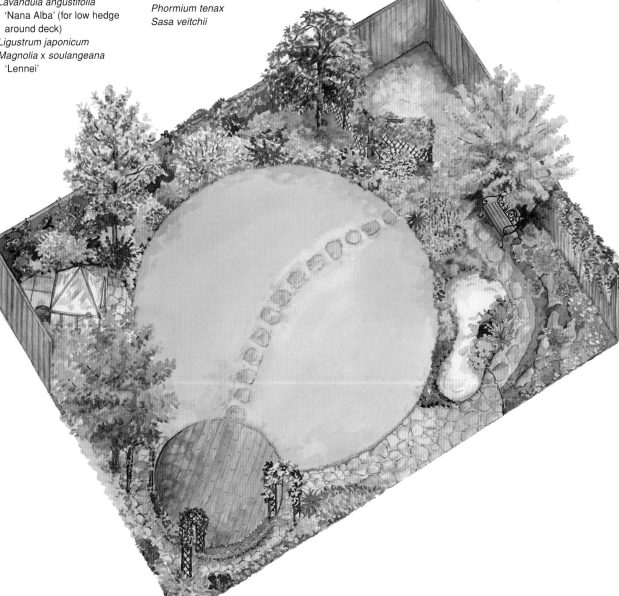

LONG, NARROW PLOT

A simple combination of circles and long, sweeping curves is used to transform what could have been an ordinary looking garden into a striking display of plants and other garden features. This use of informal shapes and lines is also an effective way of disguising the long, narrow corridor effect of the garden, without having to sub-divide or partition it into completely separate areas, which, in this example, would interrupt the dramatic flow of the curves.

The main patio is laid with stone crazy paving, and its curving shape gradually transforms it into a narrow path, which swings around the side of an informal pond that makes a striking feature in the foreground of the garden. This path then sweeps back across the garden behind the pond and patio, enclosing a sunny border, which is ideal for a rockery or scree garden. A succession of arches across the path provides continuing vertical interest, with the last arch forming an entrance onto the circular lawn.

The lawn runs right across the width of the garden, to make it as large and dramatic as possible. It is partially overlapped by the smaller circle of a timber deck, which is enclosed behind by dense planting and provides an alternative, secluded sitting area to the stone patio. A narrow, stepping-stone path through the planting provides just enough room to reach the deck from the path behind.

Diagonally opposite the deck, on the far side of the lawn, a circular ornamental greenhouse provides a focal point and continues the geometric theme of the design. It is connected to the crazy paving path with stepping-stones across the lawn. The space immediately around this greenhouse is paved with stone in the same style as the patio, and a small space is left behind in the corner for a water butt or for general storage.

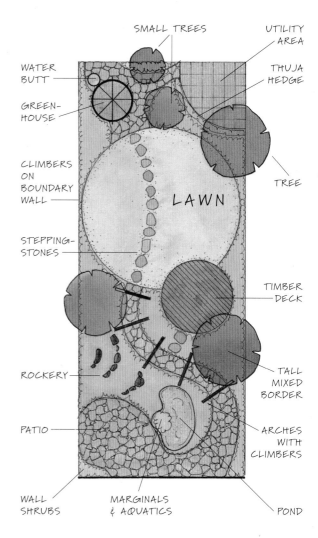

In the opposite corner from the greenhouse, a dense hedge of thuja is planted to form a quarter-circle, and the space left behind this is paved with square flags to create a utility area for a compost bin.

Even within such a relatively limited space, there is still plenty of scope to grow a wide range of plants to suit the different conditions found here, such as sun, shade, dryness and damp. There are opportunities to grow trees, shrubs, perennials, grasses, alpines in the rockery, climbers on boundary fences and the arches, and, of course, aquatic and marginal plants in and around the pond.

SUGGESTED PLANTS

Trees
Acer griseum
Crataegus x *lavalleei*
Prunus sargentii

Shrubs
Arbutus unedo
Azalea 'Gibraltar'
Buddleja alternifolia
Choisya ternata 'Sundance'
Cornus alba 'Kesselringii'
Fremontodendron
  californicum (against
  house wall)
Hydrangea serrata 'Diadem'
Ligustrum lucidum
  'Excelsum Superbum'
Parrotia persica
Phygelius x *rectus* 'African
  Queen'
Pittosporum tenuifolium
  'Irene Paterson'
Rubus thibetanus
  'Silver Fern'
Spiraea japonica
  'Anthony Waterer'
Viburnum opulus
  'Roseum'
Viburnum tinus
  'Purpureum'

Perennials and grasses
Aconitum carmichaelii
  'Arendsii'
Echinacea purpurea '
  White Lustre'
Epimedium pinnatum ssp.
  colchicum
Geranium phaeum
Hemerocallis 'Stafford'
Iris 'Berkeley Gold'
Leymus arenarius
Miscanthus sinensis var.
  purpurascens
Phyllostachys aurea
Scabiosa caucasica 'Clive
  Greaves'
Veronica gentianoides
  'Variegata'
Viola 'Belmont Blue'
Yucca filamentosa
  'Variegata'

Climbers
Campsis radicans f. *flava*
Clematis x *jouiniana*
  'Praecox'
Hedera colchica 'Sulphur
  Heart'
Jasminum officinale 'Aureum'
Lonicera etrusca
Rubus henryi
Solanum jasminoides 'Album'

Conifers, heathers and alpines
Chamaecyparis lawsoniana
  'Gimbornii'
Erica erigena 'Golden Lady'
Erica tetralix 'Hookstone Pink'
Juniperus squamata 'Blue
  Star'
Linum narbonense
Persicaria vacciniifolia
Pinus mugo 'Humpy'
Sedum spurium 'Purpur-
  teppich' ('Purple Carpet')
Thuja plicata 'Atrovirens'
  (hedge)
Tsuga canadensis 'Jeddeloh'
Veronica prostrata

Aquatics, marginals and bog plants
Astilbe x *arendsii* 'Irrlicht'
Filipendula ulmaria
Hosta fortunei var. *albopicta*
Iris chrysographes
Lobelia 'Queen Victoria'
Myriophyllum aquaticum
  (syn. *M proserpinacoides*)
Primula elatior
Stratiotes aloides

191

Family gardens

TRIANGULAR PLOT

Designs for triangular plots can sometimes result in gardens where the available space is not used to its best effect. This design has been carefully thought through to ensure that every piece of ground is used for a particular purpose, and in doing this it incorporates a surprising number of features to suit family use. The basic design is simple and straightforward, the combination of circle, curves, straight lines and angles proving to be effective on this odd-shaped plot.

At the far end of the plot, the narrowest part of the triangle is taken up by a kitchen garden, which is separated and hidden from view from the rest of the garden by a mixed shrub border.

The generous, broadly rectangular patio is slightly angled for greater interest, and directs attention across the centrally placed circular lawn to a narrow, curving, bark-covered path, which provides access into the kitchen garden beyond, passing as it does so beneath three simple arches,

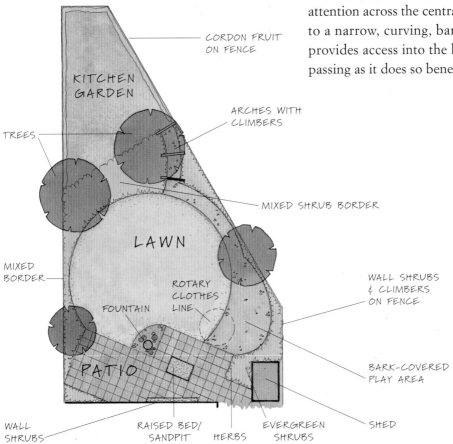

CORDON FRUIT ON FENCE

KITCHEN GARDEN

ARCHES WITH CLIMBERS

TREES

MIXED SHRUB BORDER

LAWN

MIXED BORDER

ROTARY CLOTHES LINE

WALL SHRUBS & CLIMBERS ON FENCE

FOUNTAIN

BARK-COVERED PLAY AREA

PATIO

WALL SHRUBS

RAISED BED/ SANDPIT

HERBS

EVERGREEN SHRUBS

SHED

SUGGESTED PLANTS

Trees
Malus 'John Downie'
Prunus 'Pandora'
Prunus cerasifera 'Nigra'
  (syn. *P.* 'Pissardii Nigra')
Sorbus 'Joseph Rock'

Shrubs
Arbutus unedo
Buddleja davidii 'Nanho
  Blue'
Ceanothus 'Delight' (against
  house wall)
Choisya ternata 'Sundance'
Cornus alba 'Spaethii'
Corylus maxima 'Purpurea'
Diervilla x *splendens*
Elaeagnus x *ebbingei*
  'Limelight'
Escallonia 'Apple Blossom'
Euonymus fortunei 'Emerald
  Gaiety'
Hebe 'Marjorie'
Hydrangea macrophylla
  'Forever Pink'
Lavandula angustifolia
  'Munstead'
Osmanthus x *burkwoodii*
  (against shed)
Pittosporum tenuifolium
Prunus laurocerasus 'Otto
  Luyken'
Viburnum x *bodnantense*
  'Dawn'
Weigela florida 'Foliis
  Purpureis'

Perennials
and grasses
Achillea
  'Moonshine'
Artemisia
  'Powis Castle'
Aster novi-belgii
  'Lady in Blue'
Coreopsis verticillata
  'Grandiflora'
Epimedium x *versicolor*
  'Sulphureum'
Festuca glauca 'Blauglut'
  ('Blue Glow')
Geranium ibericum
Hemerocallis 'Cherry
  Cheeks'
Iris sibirica 'Tropic Night'
Liriope muscari
Primula Polyanthus
Salvia x *superba*

Solidago 'Cloth of Gold'
Tradescantia x *andersoniana*
  'Purple Dome'
Vinca minor
  'Argenteovariegata

Climbers
Clematis 'Jackmanii Superba'
Clematis montana 'Alba'
Hedera colchica 'Sulphur
  Heart'
Hydrangea anomala ssp.
  petiolaris
Jasminum nudiflorum
Jasminum officinale
Lonicera japonica 'Halliana'
Lonicera periclymenum
  'Belgica'
Parthenocissus henryana

Conifers and heathers
Chamaecyparis lawsoniana
  'Little Spire'
Erica x *darleyensis*
  'Silberschmelze' ('Molten
  Silver')
Erica vagans 'Lyonesse'
Juniperus x *pfitzeriana* 'Gold
  Sovereign'
Thuja orientalis 'Aurea
  Nana'

all of which are planted with climbers. This path then leads back to the house, swinging around the right-hand side of the lawn and expanding just before it reaches the patio into a larger, roughly semicircular shape, which can be used either as a small, children's play area, that can be easily supervised from the house and elsewhere in the garden, or as an additional area for sitting out, particularly early in the day when the patio may be in shadow from the house. A raised bed is placed on the patio, just off centre, to break up what would otherwise be a large and possibly uninteresting area of paving. It can be used either for planting alpines or winter heathers or, while the children are young, as a sandpit.

The sandpit is ideally positioned in full view of the house and next to the large lawn, but it is screened by the narrow bed so that it is not visible from the main sitting area.

A rotary clothes line is conveniently placed at the junction of the patio and play area to catch the sun, but not cause an obstruction. On the far right-hand side of the garden there is space for a small shed, which is conveniently placed for easy access. Evergreen shrubs screen this from view, and the small bed between the shed and the edge of the paving makes an ideal herb garden.

Between the lawn and the patio, a quarter-circle of gravel conceals an underground sump, which provides water to a small fountain, creating an attractive, yet safe water feature.

The relatively narrow beds and borders are planted with a mixture of easy-care and reliable trees, shrubs and perennials for year-round interest, with a selection of climbers trained on wires and trellis, which are attached to the boundary fences and the house walls.

RECTANGULAR PLOT

A small family garden strikes a good balance between the space for recreation on the lawn and patio and the plant interest in the borders and containers.

This is a simple, but nevertheless effective design for a typically rectangular garden that not only gives a feeling of space but at the same time takes into account all the various practical needs of a young family.

The patio, which runs across the full width of the plot, provides a generous paved area. It is effectively divided into two halves by a centrally

placed raised bed, which might initially be used as a sandpit, for later conversion into a herb garden or pond. On the left-hand side of the patio is a utility area of paving, which accommodates a shed and bin store, while to the right of the raised bed the larger area of paving is ideal for garden recreation and outdoor entertaining in the summer.

A small rectangular kitchen garden occupies the far right-hand corner of the garden, and this arrangement leaves room for a curved, roughly oval lawn, which extends into the opposite corner from the kitchen garden to maximize the available space and also to focus attention from the patio to a specimen tree at the other end of the lawn.

The patio and kitchen garden are joined together by an area covered in chipped bark, which is separated from the lawn to the left-hand side by a low, evergreen hedge. This barked area not only acts as a path, but is sufficiently large to be used as a small play area for children.

On the corner of the patio is a rotary clothes line, and at the junction of the patio and play area a reproduction millstone is set on a bed of gravel and cobbles, with a concealed tank and submersible pump set in the ground below, to make a striking water feature that everyone will enjoy looking at.

Planting is confined to a main border around most of the lawn, and a narrower border, which runs along the right-hand boundary fence. The choice of plants is deliberately restricted to include only those shrubs, perennials and climbers that are not only easy to grow and look after but that will also give some interest all year round. In addition, they are safe to grow where there are small children present.

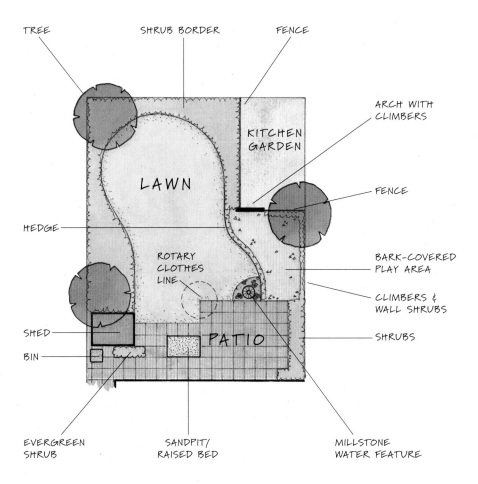

TREE

SHRUB BORDER

FENCE

ARCH WITH
CLIMBERS

KITCHEN
GARDEN

LAWN

FENCE

HEDGE

ROTARY
CLOTHES
LINE

BARK-COVERED
PLAY AREA

CLIMBERS &
WALL SHRUBS

SHED

BIN

PATIO

SHRUBS

EVERGREEN
SHRUB

SANDPIT/
RAISED BED

MILLSTONE
WATER FEATURE

SUGGESTED PLANTS

Trees
Malus domestica
  'Bramley's Seedling'
Prunus 'Pink Perfection'
Sorbus aria Lutescens

Shrubs
Abelia x *grandiflora*
Buddleja 'Lochinch'
Ceanothus impressus
  (against shed)
Choisya ternata
Cornus alba 'Sibirica'
Cotinus coggygria
  Rubrifolius Group
Deutzia x *elegantissima*
  'Rosealind'
Elaeagnus x *ebbingei*
Escallonia 'Donard Seedling'
Euonymus fortunei 'Emerald
  'n' Gold' (for hedge to play
  area)
Hebe subalpina
Hydrangea serrata 'Bluebird'
Photinia x *fraseri* 'Red Robin'
Salix integra 'Hakura-nishiki'
Skimmia japonica 'Rubella'
Spiraea japonica 'Little
  Princess'
Syringa meyeri 'Palibin'
Viburnum tinus 'Eve Price'
Weigela 'Florida Variegata'

Perennials and grasses
Aster amellus 'King George'
Geranium x *cantabrigiense*
  'Cambridge'
Hemerocallis dumortieri
Iris sibirica 'Perry's Blue'
Molinia caerulea ssp.
  caerulea 'Variegata'
Nepeta x *faassenii*
Phlox paniculata 'White
  Admiral'
Pleioblastus auricomus
Sedum spectabile 'Brilliant'
Tellima grandiflora Rubra
  Group
Vinca minor 'Atropurpurea'
Viola riviniana Purpurea
  Group

Climbers
Clematis montana 'Elizabeth'
Clematis orientalis 'Bill
  MacKenzie'
Clematis 'The President'
Hedera canariensis 'Gloire
  de Marengo'
  (syn. *H. h.* 'Variegata')
Jasminum officinale f. *affine*
Lonicera periclymenum
  'Serotina'
Parthenocissus tricuspidata
  'Veitchii'
Vitis vinifera 'Purpurea'
Wisteria floribunda 'Alba'

Conifers and heathers
Calluna vulgaris 'Sir John
  Charrington'
Chamaecyparis thyoides
  'Rubicon'
Erica carnea 'Springwood
  Pink'
Erica x *darleyensis*
  'Silberschmelze' ('Molten
  Silver')
Erica vagans 'Mrs D.F.
  Maxwell'
Juniperus virginiana 'Blue
  Cloud'
Thuja occidentalis 'Smaragd'

CORNER PLOT

Although it may require a little more thought, a corner plot can often provide a garden that is just as satisfying and interesting as an equivalent and more conventional rectangular one. In this example the carefully positioned patio at the corner of the house provides the ideal opportunity to divide the garden into ornamental and utility areas, to suit all the members of the family.

The striking contrast between the nearly square patio, set at an angle to the house, and the informal, almost figure-of-eight lawn is effective at disguising what might have been the dominant right angles and straight lines of the boundaries. At the same time, this arrangement focuses attention into the far corners of the garden rather than the nearest point of the fence. The provision of a millstone water feature on the corner of the patio also creates an additional focal point, but this time in the foreground.

On the left-hand side of the patio, a simple arch, covered with climbers, creates an entrance onto the lawn and also frames a view of a specimen tree in the corner of the garden beyond. At the other end of the patio, the entrance path from the road is deliberately dog-legged so that a space is created for the inclusion of a rotary clothes line, and an area covered in chipped bark that makes an ideal spot for children's play. A hedge of *Thuja plicata* 'Atrovirens' provides an element of security for this play area as well as screening the utility area of the garden from the more ornamental section.

The larger part of the utility area is taken up by a kitchen garden, where there is space for a shed and greenhouse. Extra screening is afforded by a trellis fence running along the path on the opposite side to the thuja hedge, and the entrance to

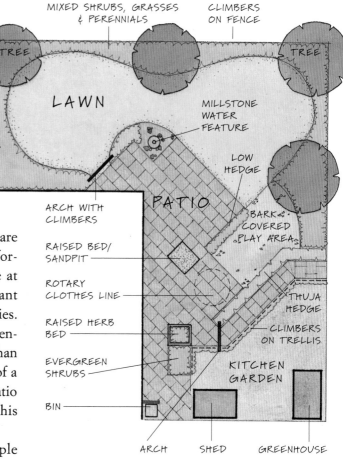

the patio area is marked by an arch over the path. Two raised beds break up what is a potentially large area of paving, one for use as a herb garden and the other as a sandpit, at least while the children are small, but for later conversion into a pool or other type of water feature.

The extra space afforded by this layout means that additional taller shrubs can be planted, together with perennials, around the boundaries for greater screening and privacy. A low hedge of *Potentilla fruticosa* separates the patio from the play area, and climbers on the trellis fence provide extra shelter and screening for the kitchen garden without taking up too much valuable ground space.

198

SUGGESTED PLANTS

Trees

Alnus incana 'Laciniata'
Betula utilis var.
 jacquemontii
Malus tschonoskii
Prunus 'Taihaku'

Shrubs

Acer negundo 'Flamingo'
Arbutus unedo
Buddleja x *weyeriana*
 'Sungold'
Ceanothus x *veitchianus*
Ceratostigma willmottianum
Choisya ternata
Cornus mas 'Aurea'
Cornus stolonifera
 'Flaviramea'
Deutzia x *elegantissima*
Elaeagnus pungens
 'Maculata'

Forsythia x *intermedia*
 'Spectabilis'
Hypericum 'Hidcote'
Kerria japonica 'Pleniflora'
Photinia davidiana 'Palette'
Potentilla fruticosa
 'Abbotswood'
Ribes sanguineum
 'Pulborough Scarlet'
Salix hastata 'Wehrhahnii'
Sorbus koehneana
Viburnum farreri

Perennials and grasses

Allium schoenoprasum
 'Forescate'
Anemone hupehensis var.
 japonica 'Bressingham
 Glow'
Carex morrowii 'Variegata'
Crocosmia 'Lucifer'
Erigeron 'Schwarzes Meer'
 ('Black Sea')
Geranium himalayense
 'Plenum'

Helenium 'Coppelia'
Heuchera micrantha var.
 diversifolia 'Palace Purple'
Iris pseudacorus 'Variegata'
Lamium maculatum 'Pink
 Pewter'
Leucanthemum superbum
 'Wirral Supreme'
Miscanthus sacchariflorus
Prunella grandiflora 'Pink
 Loveliness'
Pseudosasa japonica
Pulmonaria officinalis
 'Sissinghurst White'
Stachys byzantina 'Primrose
 Heron'

Climbers

Actinidia kolomikta
Clematis 'Jackmanii'
Clematis 'Ville de Lyon'
Jasminum nudiflorum 'Aureum'
Lonicera henryi
Lonicera x *tellmanniana*
Schizophragma hydrangeoides

Conifers and heathers

Calluna vulgaris 'Gold Haze'
Cedrus deodara 'Golden
 Horizon'
Erica carnea 'Pink Spangles'
Erica x *darleyensis* 'Furzey'
Erica erigena 'W.T. Rackliff'
Erica vagans 'Mrs D.F.
 Maxwell'
Juniperus x *pfitzeriana* 'Gold
 Coast'
Thuja plicata 'Atrovirens'

WIDE, SHALLOW PLOT

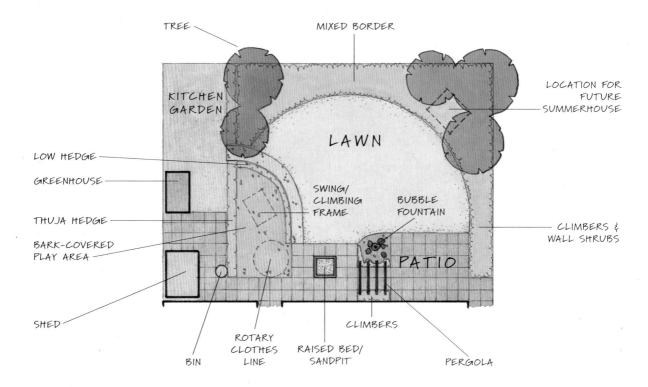

TREE

MIXED BORDER

KITCHEN GARDEN

LOCATION FOR FUTURE SUMMERHOUSE

LAWN

LOW HEDGE

GREENHOUSE

SWING/ CLIMBING FRAME

BUBBLE FOUNTAIN

THUJA HEDGE

CLIMBERS & WALL SHRUBS

BARK-COVERED PLAY AREA

PATIO

SHED

CLIMBERS

BIN

ROTARY CLOTHES LINE

RAISED BED/ SANDPIT

PERGOLA

In this strikingly simple and well-organized layout, the strength of the lawn's dramatic curve is very eye-catching. When it is combined with the extra depth of the shrub planting areas that this creates against the boundary, especially in the far corners, it effectively hides the boundary fence and the overall rectangular shape of the garden.

The extra width of the plot allows for a kitchen garden and a paved utility area to be placed along the left-hand boundary immediately behind the garage, and these are screened from the rest of the garden by a hedge of thuja. Access to both these areas can be either directly from the patio by way of a gate or indirectly by means of a curved gravel path, which separates the lawn from a bark-covered space that is suitable for a children's play area but that also leaves room for a rotary clothes line.

Although the patio runs almost the full width of the house, it is effectively divided into two separate areas by a bubble fountain water feature, set among rocks and stones, and a wooden pergola, which provides the link between these two areas of paving. The left-hand section of the patio is more utilitarian and could be used to extend the available play area.

Small shrubs, grasses and perennials provide the main foreground plant interest around the bubble fountain, and climbers are planted on the pergola for additional height, and to emphasize the division. However, the bulk of planting is in the generous perimeter border, which, because of its shape, allows room for taller shrubs and plants at the back, particularly the two corners, which, together with the smaller shrubs, perennials and ground-cover plants towards the front, completely hides the odd proportions of this plot.

SUGGESTED PLANTS

Trees

Acer negundo 'Flamingo'
Malus 'Red Glow'
Prunus padus 'Watereri'
Robinia pseudoacacia 'Frisia'
Sorbus hupehensis

Shrubs

Buddleja davidii 'Harlequin'
Caryopteris x *clandonensis*
  'Heavenly Blue'
Cornus sanguinea 'Midwinter
  Fire'
Corylus maxima 'Purpurea'
Elaeagnus x *ebbingei*
Kerria japonica 'Variegata'
Kolkwitzia amabilis 'Pink
  Cloud'
Laurus nobilis
Mahonia aquifolium 'Apollo'
Photinia x *fraseri* 'Robusta'
Pittosporum tenuifolium
  'Warnham Gold'
Potentilla fruticosa 'Princess'
  (for hedge around front of
  play area)
Rhododendron
  'Cunningham's Blush'
Viburnum farreri
Viburnum tinus 'Gwenllian'
Weigela 'Bristol Ruby'

Perennials and grasses

Anemone x *hybrida*
  'Honorine Jobert'
  (syn. *A.* x *h.* 'Alba')
Aster novi-belgii
  'Schneekissen' ('Snow
  Cushion')
Campanula persicifolia var.
  alba
Carex comans Bronze Form
Dianthus 'Doris'
Epimedium x *rubrum*
Geranium ibericum
Hemerocallis 'George
  Cunningham'
Iris unguicularis
Milium effusum 'Aureum'
Phlox paniculata 'White
  Admiral'
Phormium tenax
Rudbeckia fulgida var. deamii
Salvia x *sylvestris* 'Mainacht'
  ('May Night')
Sasa veitchii
Vinca minor 'Alba Variegata'

Climbers

Clematis macropetala
  'Markham's Pink'
Clematis montana
  'Elizabeth'
Hedera helix 'Oro di
  Bogliasco' ('Goldheart')
Hedera hibernica
Lonicera henryi
Lonicera japonica
  'Aureoreticulata'
Parthenocissus tricuspidata
  'Veitchii'
Vitis coignetiae

Conifers and heathers

Erica arborea 'Albert's Gold'
Erica x *darleyensis* 'Ada
  S. Collings'
Erica vagans 'Saint Keverne'
Juniperus horizontalis
  'Emerald Spreader'
Juniperus squamata 'Blue
  Star'
Pinus mugo var. *pumilio*
Thuja plicata 'Atrovirens' (for
  hedge to kitchen garden)
  or *T. occidentalis* 'Smaragd'
  (if smaller hedge to kitchen
  garden required)

LONG, NARROW PLOT

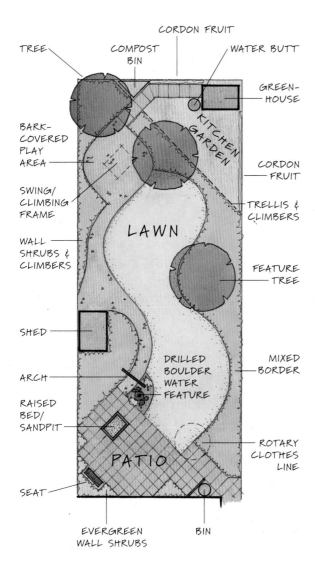

TREE

CORDON FRUIT

COMPOST BIN

WATER BUTT

GREEN-HOUSE

BARK-COVERED PLAY AREA

KITCHEN GARDEN

CORDON FRUIT

SWING/ CLIMBING FRAME

TRELLIS & CLIMBERS

WALL SHRUBS & CLIMBERS

LAWN

FEATURE TREE

SHED

DRILLED BOULDER WATER FEATURE

MIXED BORDER

ARCH

RAISED BED/ SANDPIT

PATIO

ROTARY CLOTHES LINE

SEAT

EVERGREEN WALL SHRUBS

BIN

The strength of this attractive, sinuous design lies in the way that the deliberately chosen angles of the triangular kitchen garden and the diagonally opposite patio, are combined with the sweeping curves of the borders, lawn and path to provide constantly changing focal points as you move from one end of the garden to the other and back again.

The nearly rectangular patio is connected to the path at the other side of the house by a dog-leg extension of the same paving. On one side of this is a rotary clothes line and a concealed bin store made from wooden laths. In the corner immediately behind the patio, a small bench seat is set on a gravel base to provide a permanent, sheltered sitting area, and just off the centre of the patio is a raised bed, which can initially be used as a sandpit and later on could be converted into, say, a raised area for growing herbs or alpine scree.

A winding, bark-covered path leads from the left-hand corner of the patio down to a larger area covered in the same material to form a play area, where there is room for a swing or slide. Beyond this it connects with the kitchen garden, which is reached through a gateway in a trellis fence that is covered in climbers, forming the boundary. Within the kitchen garden, there is enough space for a small greenhouse, water butt and a compost heap, while the boundary fence itself makes an ideal location for growing cordon fruit trees.

At the junction of the bark path, patio and lawn, a striking feature is created by water from an underground sump being pumped up through the centre of a drilled boulder, and this combines with a simple arch to create interest in the foreground. Just beyond this, a small shed is positioned well up the garden, which leaves plenty of room for planting shrubs and taller perennials around it to screen it from the patio and house.

The informal layout of this design provides plenty of opportunity for planting a range of easy-care and long-lived trees, shrubs and perennials, which can be chosen to give some interest all year round as well as completely disguising the rather rigid, straight boundaries of this long and narrow plot.

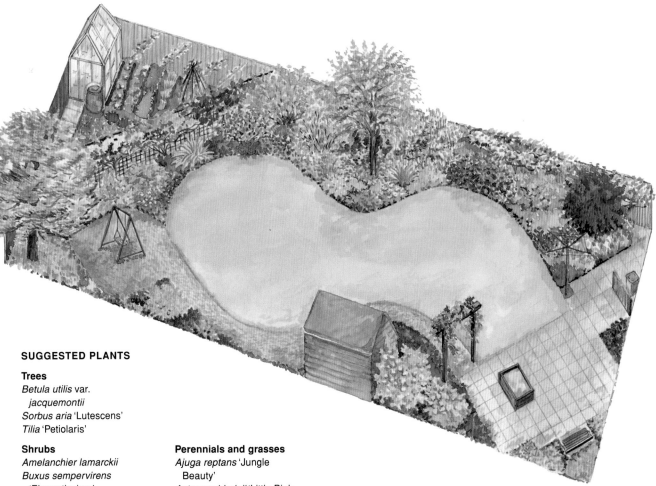

SUGGESTED PLANTS

Trees
Betula utilis var.
 jacquemontii
Sorbus aria 'Lutescens'
Tilia 'Petiolaris'

Shrubs
Amelanchier lamarckii
Buxus sempervirens
 'Elegantissima'
Ceanothus 'Concha'
Cornus alba 'Kesselringii'
Deutzia x *kalmiiflora*
Euonymus fortunei
 'Sheridan Gold'
Fatsia japonica
Garrya elliptica 'James
 Roof' (against end of
 shed)
Hebe 'Bowles Hybrid'
Hibiscus syriacus 'Oiseau
 Blue' ('Blue Bird')
Hydrangea paniculata
 'Grandiflora'
Hypericum forrestii
Philadelphus coronarius
 'Aureus'
Prunus x *cistena* 'Crimson
 Dwarf'
Sambucus nigra 'Guincho
 Purple'
Syringa pubescens ssp.
 microphylla 'Superba'
Viburnum opulus 'Roseum'
Viburnum rhytidophyllum

Perennials and grasses
Ajuga reptans 'Jungle
 Beauty'
Aster novi-belgii 'Little Pink
 Beauty'
Bergenia cordifolia
 'Purpurea'
Crocosmia x *crocosmiiflora*
Epimedium x *cantabrigiense*
Geranium 'Johnson's Blue'
Geum rivale 'Album'
Hemerocallis fulva
Heuchera 'Rachel'
Leucanthemum x *superbum*
 'Snowcap'
Oenothera fruticosa
 'Fyrverkeri' ('Fireworks')
Osteospermum ecklonis
Persicaria amplexicaulis
 'Inverleith'
Phormium 'Yellow Wave'
Plantago major 'Rubrifolia'
Pulmonaria saccharata
 Argentea Group
Rudbeckia 'Goldquelle'
Symphytum 'Hidcote Pink'
Vinca minor
 'Argenteovariegata'
Waldsteinia ternata

Climbers
Actinidia deliciosa
Celastrus orbiculatus
 Hermaphrodite Group
Clematis armandii 'Apple
 Blossom'
Hydrangea anomala ssp.
 petiolaris
Jasminum officinale f. *affine*
Lonicera x *brownii*
 'Fuchsioides'
Lonicera periclymenum
 'Graham Thomas'
Parthenocissus henryana
Vitis vinifera 'Purpurea'

Conifers and heathers
Calluna vulgaris 'Silver
 Queen'
Chamaecyparis lawsoniana
 'Minima Aurea'
Chamaecyparis pisifera
 'Filifera Aurea'
Erica arborea 'Estrella Gold'
Erica x *darleyensis* 'Darley
 Dale'
Erica vagans 'Valerie
 Proudley'
Juniperus horizontalis 'Blue
 Chip'
Microbiota decussata

Index

Acknowledgements

Garden Picture Library/Jerry Pavia 14(t)/**Sunniva Harte** 23/ **John Glover** 36–7/**Steven Wooster** 40–1/**John Miller** 49(t)/ **Brigitte Thomas** 49(b), 59/**Ron Sutherland** 56/**Juliette Wade** 79/**J.S. Sira** 92/**Roger Hyam** 103/**Mayer/Le Scanff** 158/**Jon Bouchier** 195

Jerry Harpur 4–5 (Simon Fraser, Middx), 13 (Arabella Lennox-Boyd, London), 15 (Nick & Pam Coote, Oxon), 19(b) (Lisette Pleasance, London), 20 (Dr Ind, London), 45 (Fudlers Hall, Essex), 51 (Michael Balston, Wilts), 55 (Jean Goldberry, London), 62(t) (John Plummer, London), 71 (Berry's Garden Centre, London), 73 (Dr & Mrs Parris, Essex), 81 (Home Farm, Oxon), 85 (Helen Yemm, East Sussex), 89 (Michael Balstow, Wilts), 97 (Coton Manor, Northants), 108 and 111 (Julie Toll, Herts), 115 (Simon Fraser, Middx), 133 and 147 (Judith Sharpe, London), 138 (Andrew Weaving, London), 144 (Daly & Charman, Surrey), 194 (Ryl Newell, Sussex)

Anne Hyde 1, 6–7, 8–9, 27, 42(b), 96, 101, 127, 131, 141, 152, 168, 172, 174
Andrew Lawson 31, 35, 78, 120, 123 (Bosvigo House, Cornwall), 149/50 (Eastgrove Cottage)
Clive Nichols 2–3 (The Anchorage), 10 (Sue Berger), 14(b) (Ivy Cottage, Dorset), 19(t) (Sue Guerney), 22 (R. & J. Passmore), 29 (Jill Billington), 42(t) (Sticky Wicket, Dorset), 54 (Lucy Gent), 62(b) (Lower Hall, Shrops), 64, 69 (Christopher Masson), 84 (Olivia Clark), 116 (The Anchorage), 121 (Mrs Preston), 142 (Paula Rainey Crofts), 184 (Southview Nurseries, Hants)
Hugh Palmer 162 (Fovant Hut)
Derek St Romaine 185
Juliette Wade 112–3

040-966-01